BRITAIN IN THE TWENTIETH CE

People in Change

JOSH BROOMAN

with MALCOLM CHANDLER

General Editor: Josh Brooman

Contents

People at Work   3
The changing world of work   5
Focus study: Women in work, 1910–21   26

People and Politics   45
Voters, parties and politics   47
Focus study: The impact of the Depression   67

A Caring People   87
Changing care and welfare   89
Focus study: Creating the Welfare State   110

A Changing Nation   129
National identities   131
Focus study: Conflict and co-operation in Northern Ireland   148

Communication and Culture   171
A changing world of communications   173
Coursework assignments: Changing culture and communications   191

Index   208

LONGMAN

Longman Group Limited

Longman House, Burnt Mill, Harlow, Essex

CM20 2JE, England and Associated Companies throughout the world

The publishers' policy is to use paper manufactured from sustainable forests.

First published 1994
Second impression 1994

ISBN 0 582 22665 1

Set in Concorde and Tekton

Printed in Great Britain

by Butler and Tanner Ltd, Frome and London

Design and Production by Hart Mcleod

Illustrations by Stephen Hawes, Sheila Betts

Cover photograph *London's Fairs* by William Roberts. Courtesy London Transport Museum.

BRITAIN IN THE TWENTIETH CENTURY

People at Work

JOSH BROOMAN

General Editor: Josh Brooman

Contents

The changing world of work

1 'It was a struggle'   6
2 The advance of machinery   10
3 Gains and losses   13
4 The experience of work   17
5 Death of the old industries   21
   Review: The changing world of work   25

Focus study · Women in work, 1910–21

1 Women at work before the First World War   27
2 Women workers in the First World War   31
3 Women in uniform   34
4 From 'heroines' to 'scroungers': women in 1918   37
5 Women's work in the 1920s   39
   Review: Women in work 1910–1921   43

Longman Group UK Limited
Longman House, Burnt Mill, Harlow, Essex
CM20 2JE, England and Associated Companies throughout the World.

© Josh Brooman 1994.

First published 1994

ISBN 0582 245958

Set in Concorde and Tekton

Printed in Great Britain
by Butler and Tanner Ltd, Frome and London

The Publishers' policy is to use paper manufactured from sustainable forests.

Design and production by Hart McLeod

Cover photograph *Ruby Loftus screwing a breech-ring* by Dame Laura Knight. © Imperial War Museum.

Acknowledgements

The written sources in this book are taken from many different kinds of published material. Some were originally written in old-fashioned or unusual language. This has not been altered in any way. In most cases, unusual or difficult words are explained in the margin. In many of the sources words have been left out. A cut in the middle of a sentence is shown like this ...; and at the end of a sentence like this ....

We are grateful to the following for permission to reproduce photographs. The numbers refer to page numbers.

Barnaby's Picture Library, 40; © BBC 1991, 44; Bodleian Library, Oxford, 11; Bristol Museums & Art Gallery, 7; E.T. Archive, 31 left; Mary Evans Picture Library, 29, 30; *Farmers Weekly*, 10 below, 12; Ford Motor Company, 19; From the collections of Henry Ford Museum & Greenfield Village. Rockwell Calenche (0-5237-A(T)), 18; Glasgow University Archives, 33; Hulton-Deutsch Collection, 9, 15, 23, 38; Illustrated London News Picture Library, 41; Imperial War Museum, London, 31 right, 35, 36(neg. Q.2676); Magnum Photos/Richard Kalvar, 20; Oldham Local Interest Museum, 22; Rural History Centre, University of Reading, 10 above; from George Sims: *Living London*, Vol. 2 1903, 26; The Ethel Thomas Avonmouth Collection, 14, 16; Ulster Museum, Belfast, 5.

The changing world of work

Workers stream out of the Harland and Wolff shipbuilding yard in Belfast in 1911. Behind them is the ship they are building, the *Titanic*, the largest ship in the world at that time. Think about how this scene differs from a street today when workers are coming out of work.

Most people spend a large part of their lives working to make money. The average person in paid work today works from the age of sixteen to 60 or 65, and spends 44 hours a week doing so. When we add on the hours it takes to get to and from work, nearly half our waking hours are taken up with paid work.

As well as working for money, everybody has to work inside the home – cooking, cleaning, ironing, mending and doing all the things needed to maintain a household. Domestic work can take up even more time than paid work outside the home.

Since people spend so much of their time working, the work they do has important effects on their personal and social lives. It decides how much money they have to spend. That in turn decides what kind of home they live in and the kind of lifestyle they lead. It often affects what other people think about them and what they think about themselves. For some, work is interesting, satisfying and profitable. For others it can be hard, boring and poorly paid. Whichever it is, work is never a trivial thing in a person's life.

The first part of this book looks at work and at how it has changed in the twentieth century. It examines the reasons for those changes and describes some of the consequences. We begin by looking at people's work in the early years of the century, from 1900 to the 1920s.

1 'It was a struggle'

A little over 16 million people had paid jobs in 1900. Source 1 shows the ten most common kinds of work that they did. Of 12.5 million people not in paid work, nearly 10 million were women who worked at home.

Source 1

British Labour Statistics, Historical Abstract, Department of Employment and Productivity, 1972.

The ten largest paid occupations in 1901

Domestic service (e.g. maids, cooks, butlers)	2,344,000
Metal manufacture (e.g. steel making, shipbuilding)	1,569,000
Transport (e.g. railway workers, bus drivers)	1,436,000
Agriculture (e.g. farmers, shepherds, foresters)	1,406,000
Textiles (e.g. cotton spinners, weavers)	1,352,000
Building (e.g. bricklayers, carpenters, plumbers)	1,216,000
Clothing (e.g. dress-makers, hatters, shoemakers)	1,215,000
Mining (e.g. coalminers, slate quarriers)	937,000
Food, drink and tobacco (e.g. bakers, brewers)	917,000
Commerce (e.g. shopkeepers, typists)	673,000

There are many sources of evidence about these people's work. The most interesting sources are often the memories that they left in interviews, diaries, and autobiographies. We soon discover from such sources that work early in this century was very different from work today.

Working conditions in the early twentieth century

Source 2 is part of an interview. A retired coalminer is talking to a writer, Judith Cook. He is ill in bed with a lung disease, pneumoconiosis, and is breathing with the aid of an oxygen mask.

Source 2

Harry Horton, a retired coalminer, talking in 1982 to Judith Cook, in Close to the Earth, Living Social History of the British Isles.

I started work at fourteen. My first job was to work under the conveyor belt, which shook the coal into different-sized pieces and the dust just rained down on me, six days a week, all day. I was told then that coal-dust didn't hurt you. It was even good for you, they said. Look at me now!

This statement shows two important differences between work then and now. One is that people worked longer hours in the early years of the century. Until 1919 a 55-hour, six-day working week was common. Then many industries came down to a 48-hour week. Today it is 41 hours. Another difference is that people started work younger. Before 1918 most people started work at twelve. This rose to fourteen after the First World War, fifteen after the Second World War and reached sixteen only in 1973. And people did not retire from work at 60 or 65, as many do today. They worked for as long as their health lasted.

Many jobs were physically demanding. Source 3 shows one of the toughest: coalmining. Source 4 describes another. It is taken from an interview for a radio programme in which a London dock worker recalled a particularly hard day's work.

Source 3

This photograph was taken in Easton colliery in Bristol in 1910. It shows a miner pulling coal on a tugger out of a narrow seam. Look at the chain around his waist and at the candle strapped to his head.

Source 4

From *A Gentle, Easy-Flowing River*, a BBC Radio documentary made by Alasdair Clayre in 1965.

One of the hardest day's work in my life was going to a wharf called Lawrence's Mill which dealt only in rice. Rice is in two hundredweight bags and we used to have to load a 100 ton of that, on our own, one man. I did 75 ton on the first day ... and when I went home – I was in diggings then – I was a young man about 24 then – the landlady cried when she saw me shoulders. That's the truth, they was all raw red.

You can tell from Sources 2, 3 and 4 that some employers did little to protect the health and safety of their workers. Workers as well as employers took it for granted that accidents would happen. Source 5 tells what happened to a worker in a chemical-making plant in Widnes in about 1900.

Source 5

From *People of the Abyss*, an investigation by American journalist Jack London into the lives of poor people in the East End of London, 1902.

£25 in 1900 was worth about £900 in 1994 prices.

I had to cross the yard. It was ten o'clock at night, and there was no light about. While crossing the yard I felt something take hold of my leg and screw it off. I became unconscious .... On the following Sunday night I came to my senses, and found myself in the hospital. I asked the nurse what was to do with my legs, and she told me both legs were off.

There was a stationary crank in the yard, let into the ground; the hole was eighteen inches long, fifteen inches deep, and fifteen inches wide. The crank revolved in the hole three revolutions a minute. There was no fence or covering over the hole. Since my accident they have stopped it altogether and have covered up the hole .... They gave me £25*. They didn't reckon that as compensation; they said it was only for charity's sake.

In every occupation workers had less job security than they do today. Some were employed on a month's notice, some on a week's notice and some even by the hour. Workers therefore lived in fear of the foremen who had the right to hire and fire them. As a former railway worker at the railway works in Swindon recalled:

Source 6

Jeremy Seabrook,
The Leisure Society, 1988.

The foremen were tyrants – you had to bribe them with vegetables from your allotment or eggs from your own fowls. If a new foreman or chief clerk was appointed, people would even change their religion to be seen with him at chapel or church.

Then, as now, people worked to make money. In the 1900s the average wage for manual workers in industry was around £1.75 for a week of 50-54 hours work. In 1990 the average weekly wage of manual workers in major industries was £231.85 for an average week of 42.9 hours. To make sense of these figures, we have to adjust them for inflation, because money has steadily lost value since 1900. In 1900 £1 would buy the same amount of goods as about £35 in 1990. We must therefore multiply the 1900 worker's wage by 35 to find its value in 1990. Try doing this with the figures in Source 7.

Source 7

Adapted from a report of an enquiry into earnings and hours by the Board of Trade, 1906–7, and from *Employment Gazette*, May 1991.

Average weekly wages for manual workers in industry in 1906 and 1990

	1906			1990		
	Men	Women	Hours	Men	Women	Hours
Cotton workers	£1.47	93p	55.5	£187.9l	£143.94	43.1
Shoe makers	£1.43	65p	53.5	£204.53	£142.36	39.5
Shipbuilders	£1.79	73p	52.9	£243.05	£166.47	42.1
Bakers	£1.45	63p	55.9	£228.30	£154.26	43.9
Leather tanners	£1.45	65p	55.4	£197.02	£142.03	43.1
Iron and steel makers	£1.95	–	54.4	£276.78	–	40
Building workers	£1.65	–	–	£239.46	£138.94	44.9
Printers	£1.84	61p	51.6	£323.34	£202.55	4l

Nearly 10 million people did not receive wages for their work. They were women who worked at home, raising children, cooking, shopping, cleaning and mending. A Lancashire housewife described her working week in an interview in 1904:

Source 8

M.L. Davies, *The Women's Co-operative Guild*, 1904.

mangled After washing, water was wrung out of clothes by squeezing them between two rollers in a machine called a mangle.

scullery A room for washing dishes and preparing food.

On Monday I clear up all the rooms after Sunday, brush and put away all the Sunday clothes, and then separate and put to soak all soiled clothes for washing. On Tuesday the washing is done, the clothes folded and mangled*. After the washing, the scullery* receives a thorough cleaning for the week. Wednesday is the day for starching and ironing, and stocking darning, as well as the usual week's mending. On Thursday I bake the bread and clean the bedrooms. On Friday I clean the parlour, lobby and staircase, as well as the living room. Saturday morning is left for all outside cleaning – windows and stonework – besides putting all the clean linen on the beds. I finish work on Saturday about 2 p.m., the rest of the day being free.

Source 9

This photograph taken in 1910 shows a woman giving her children tea in the kitchen, which was also the family's living room. The father was probably a skilled worker, perhaps a clerk.

Questions

1 What do Sources 2 and 3 tell us about working conditions in coalmines in the early years of the century?

2 Look at Source 4.
   a There are twenty hundredweight in one ton. How many sacks did the docker take off the ship in one day?
   b One hundredweight is about 51 kg. Give yourself an idea of the weight of the sacks by lifting a friend who weighs around 50 kg.

3 Read Source 5.
   a In what ways was this a dangerous workplace?
   b Suggest why the employer gave the man charity but not compensation.

4 Look at Source 7. Multiply the 1906 figures for men and women by 35 to show roughly what they were worth in 1990 prices. Now compare them to the figures in the right-hand column. What does this tell you about average wages in 1900?

5 Look at Sources 8 and 9. What similarities and differences are there between household work today and household work in the 1900s?

6 'It was a struggle.' (retired docker commenting on his working life). Use the sources and information in this section to explain why work for many people in the early part of the century could be described as 'a struggle'.

2 'The advance of machinery'

In the twentieth century people's work has been transformed by machinery. Work which once was done by hand is now often done by machines. Cars are assembled by robot arms. Crops are gathered from fields by giant combine harvesters.

Some of the reasons for the increased use of machinery are obvious. One mechanical digger can do the work of twenty men with spades. One crane can unload a ship faster than 100 dockers. One computer-controlled robot arm can assemble a car more accurately than human hands.

Are speed and efficiency the only reasons why machines have taken over so much work, or are there other forces in action? This section looks at how one of the main kinds of work in 1900 – farming – has been transformed by machinery. As you read it, look for reasons other than speed and efficiency. You should be able to find two.

Why has farming changed so much?

Look at Source 1 and then at Source 2. The same work is being done in both photographs, but it is obvious that technology has transformed the way it is done. What brought about such a great change? Why do farmers not still make hay in the old-fashioned way?

Source 1

Haymaking in Somerset in 1900. The hay harvest involved almost the whole village. After a team of men mowed the grass with scythes it was turned to dry in the sun. The women then raked it into haycocks to keep it from the damp ground. Then it was loaded into carts and built into haystacks at the edge of the field.

Source 2

Haymaking in the 1990s. Using a tractor fitted with mowers front and back, one person can do the work done by a whole village in 1900.

Most farms in the first quarter of this century were small and run on very traditional lines. In Source 3, Edith Bredon describes the farm which she and her husband took over in the Midlands in the 1920s.

Source 3

Edith Bredon, aged 93, talking to Judith Cook in *Close to the Earth, Living Social History of the British Isles*, 1984.

When we first started there was hardly any machinery .... All the ploughing was done with horses. Things were so very different. We had only a medium-sized farm, but we had to employ a ploughman, a waggoner, a couple of labourers and a girl in the house.

Now farming is all specialised, but it was proper mixed farming in those days. You grew crops of all kinds, but you also kept cows, pigs, sheep, hens, ducks, geese, even guinea-fowl – a real mixed farm. All the milking was done by hand, naturally ....

Many horses were needed to pull machinery, so farms had to grow fodder to feed them with. This affected the way farms were organised and run. In Source 4 a retired farm worker describes what farms were like in his native Sussex during the 1920s.

Source 4

Mr L.F.M. Clarke, *Change on the Sussex Downs*, 1991.

Most farms consisted of a series of small fields bounded by hedges or streams in the river valleys .... The fields would be crop rotated to produce hay. Clover would be sown, the first crop often thrashed for seed, and the second crop dried and harvested for fodder. Sheep would be grazed on the third crop, which would then be ploughed in to prepare for the winter wheat.

Farms like those in Source 4 needed lots of workers to run them. Paying so many workers meant that food grown on such farms cost more to produce than food grown in some foreign countries. Farmers in America and Australia, for example, used modern machines and modern methods to grow crops on land they had bought cheaply. They could therefore sell their produce cheaply. As a result, Britain imported much of its food, especially wheat, from abroad. British farmers could not easily compete with this cheap foreign food, and many went out of business (Source 5).

Many farmers were saved from ruin by war. In both world wars, the dangers of sailing food-carrying ships through seas patrolled by German submarines meant that more food had to be grown in Britain. In the Second World War, the government encouraged British farmers to grow more food in a 'Dig for Victory' campaign. Extra workers were provided by the Women's Land Army and by refugees and prisoners of war. By 1945 Britain was producing 80 per cent of its own food.

When the war ended, however, refugees and prisoners of war returned to their own countries and the Women's Land Army was disbanded. There was now a shortage of farm workers. Farmers had to find new ways of producing the same amount of food. One way was to use more machinery, especially tractors. In Source 6 Mr Clarke, who described mixed farms in Source 4, explains how this changed farms in Sussex.

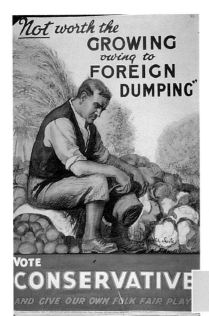

Source 5

A 1931 election poster. It shows a British farmer who couldn't sell his produce because foreign farmers were selling theirs at lower prices.

Source 6

Mr Clarke, *Change on the Sussex Downs*, 1991.

coppices Woods made up of small trees.

The wartime advance of machinery meant that the single ploughshare of the horse was superseded by the three to five ploughshares of the tractor-drawn machine .... The north scarp of the Downs could now be ploughed and large machines pulled up and burned the coppices*. Sheep were no longer kept and the shepherd disappeared .... The fields became larger by removing hedges, trees and fences. A farm which had twenty fields in the Thirties had only four or five in the Seventies. The farm staff dwindled to the tractor driver.

... A walk on the Downs 40 years ago was a pleasant experience, like walking over a lawn. Now ... the whole of the hillside and every valley is corn – a vast desert of brownish yellow in the autumn sun.

As farmers used more and more machines they specialised in what they grew. Otherwise, expensive machinery would spend much of the year unused. They grew only one or two crops and after the harvest immediately prepared the land for another autumn-sown crop.

Specialisation reduced the need for crop sequences like that described in Source 4. If a farmer had no horses there was no need to make hay to feed them in the winter. If there was no need to make hay there was no need to rotate the fields for seed and grazing. With no need to rotate crops there was little point in keeping the hedges that divided the fields. Between 1946 and 1974 farmers ripped out around a quarter of all the hedgerows in Britain and made their fields bigger.

Larger fields allowed farmers to use more and bigger machinery, such as combine harvesters which cut and threshed grain in a single operation. By the 1990s, combine harvesters were very sophisticated machines. Look at Source 7. The aerial on the roof of this combine harvester receives signals from four satellites orbiting the Earth. The signals fix the combine's position in the field. At the same time a monitor inside the combine measures the amount of wheat it is gathering. An on-board computer plots the position and the amount on a graph to make a map to show the most and least fertile parts of the field. The farmer uses this information the following year to decide which parts of the field need to be fertilised before sowing.

Source 7

A combine harvester gathering a harvest of wheat in 1992.

Questions

1
  a What different kinds of farmwork are described in Sources 3 and 4?
  b Suggest why such farms consisted of a series of small fields.
  c If tractors instead of horses had been used to pull machinery, which activity in Source 4 would have been unnecessary? Why would small fields have also been unnecessary?

2
  a How does the farmwork shown in Sources 2, 6 and 7 differ from the farmwork described in Sources 1, 3 and 4?
  b What part did new machinery play in bringing about those changes?
  c How did the Second World War help to change farmwork?
  d If there had been no war, might farmers have started using new machines for some other reason? Explain your answer.

3 Read Source 6.
  a How does Mr Clarke imply that the changes he described were bad?
  b How might a farmer reply to Mr Clarke's criticism?

3 Gains and losses

It is not just farming that has been changed by the use of technology in the twentieth century. Digging machines cut coal in mines where men used only picks and shovels 50 years ago. The dangerous work of fuelling steel furnaces or handling chemicals is done by remote control. Wordprocessors and fax machines have replaced pens and messenger boys in offices. Washing machines, central heating and vacuum cleaners have made domestic work easier than ever before.

The transformation of work by technology has brought many benefits. Machines have made work safer, cleaner and physically easier for millions of people. Have all the changes been for the better? In the next two sections of the book we will look at the ways in which technology transformed two kinds of work. As you read about them, think about whether the workers have had to pay a price for the changes.

Dock work: change for the better?

Britain is an island, so much of our trade has to be done by sea. Many of Britain's greatest cities grew up around its ports: London and Southampton, Edinburgh and Glasgow, Belfast and Liverpool, Cardiff and Bristol. For hundreds of years that trade was handled in the ports by dock workers who loaded and unloaded cargoes from the holds of ships.

In the first half of this century most cargoes were transported in sacks, boxes, barrels and packets. These were loaded and unloaded by hand, as three dockers remembered in a radio programme in 1965:

Source 1

Alasdair Clayre, *A Gentle Easy-Flowing River*, BBC radio documentary, 1965.

puncheon A large barrel containing 70 to 120 gallons of liquid.

We carry wheat, flour, timber, cork. We load marble. You got to be an expert in loading marble. Another day you will be loading puncheons* of rum or brandy; another day you would be loading butter ....

We had some queer cargo in our time. One of the filthiest cargo we ever loaded was camel bones from Egypt, raw, with the flesh running off them and loaded with maggots ....

Cement, cement, it's terrible. Years ago it used to come over in jute bags. If you had three or four days work at that, after that, you'd a job really to touch your bootlaces. I know, I have experienced it. The tips of your fingers were red raw.

Source 2

A banana boat being unloaded, 'one man, one stem', at Avonmouth docks near Bristol in July 1910.

Until 1967 all work in the docks was casual labour. This meant that the dockers did not have permanent, full-time jobs. The dock owners hired men by the half day or the hour as and when a ship needed to be loaded or unloaded. Men turned up at the dock gates early in the morning and a foreman called as many of them as were needed for the day. In this world of casual labour, the foreman who chose men for work was all-powerful. Dockers not only had to struggle to catch his eye during the morning call, they also often had to keep him sweet, as Source 3 shows.

Source 3

Stephen Hill, *The Dockers*, 1976, a sociological study of dockers in London.

tanner   A silver sixpenny (6d) coin. A 'tanner' in 1950 was worth about 50 pence in 1994 prices.

When I first started down the hold you had to buy your job off one of the shipworkers. Every night he used to go to the local and get his beer money off the barman – we all had to chip in a tanner* and the barman kept a list of who'd paid. Any time you refused, you'd be on the stones next call looking for a job.

The dockers who did chip in their tanners were the foreman's 'blue-eyed boys' – the ones whom he favoured and who were most likely to get work. However, whether they were blue-eyed boys or not, dockers had more to worry about than catching the foreman's eye. Bad weather and low tides could keep ships out of port, for example. As you can see in Source 4, trade between countries could dry up when times were hard, reducing cargoes and shipping movements.

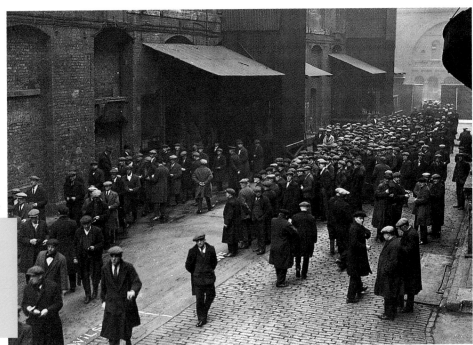

Source 4

This photograph was taken outside a dockyard in London in 1931, at the height of the Great Depression. On the left, dockers who have been chosen to work are being given their tallies, or tickets.

Except on the busiest days, there were men who did not get chosen for work, and competition for jobs was fierce, as Sources 5 and 6 show. In Source 5 one man talks about dock work at the turn of the century.

Source 5

Walter Greenwood, *How the Other Man Lives*, 1938.

tally A brass token or a ticket given out by the foreman entitling a man to work for one day.

There was no dole then, and if a docker was lucky enough to get a week's wages it only amounted to 27 shillings (£1.35). Most of them had wives and families and a home. To keep that a fellow would fight tooth and nail to get his hand on a tally.

Source 6

A fight between two dockers waiting for work in 1949.

The casual labour system was scrapped in 1967. Dockers became regular employees of the port authorities. However, by this time the way in which ports were run was also changing. Ship owners were always trying to cut the time it took to load and unload their ships; a ship in port does not earn money and can cost thousands of pounds each day in port charges and crew and maintenance costs. One way to reduce this idle time was to put cargo into larger loads which could be moved entirely by overhead cranes, as Source 7 shows.

Source 7

Like Source 2, this photograph, taken in 1976, shows bananas being unloaded from a ship in Avonmouth docks near Bristol.

Even larger loads could be stored in lorry-sized containers. In Source 8 a dock manager described the new system of moving cargo in containers.

Source 8

From *The Dockers' Tragedy* (1970), the autobiography of Colonel R.B. Oram, a dock manager working for the Port of London Authority.

struck   Loaded or unloaded.

During the summer of 1967 I watched on one of the new berths, built at Tilbury docks for the new container ships ... an operation that left me speechless .... From one of the new sheds emerged a 30-ton capacity forklift truck, driven by a young driver. Sliding its forks under a full container it reversed into the shed and placed its load ready for shipment. This very ordinary young man ... moved four containers during the five minutes that I stood there. I realised that I was watching something that none of my predecessors over the six generations during which men like me had worked in the docks had ever seen. One man had 'struck'* about a 100 tons of exports in a few minutes .... Package by package this would have provided work for twelve men for twelve hours.

The more cargo that was moved in containers, the less work there was for old-fashioned dockers. As 'containerisation' became common, new ports were built to handle them, leaving older docks to close down. Source 9 reflects this development.

Source 9

Employment Gazette, 1990.

Numbers of registered dock workers 1947–1987

1947	74,000
1955	58,000
1967	57,000
1977	29,168
1987	10,455
1989	9,400

Questions

1. Look at Sources 2 and 7.
   a What changes have taken place between the taking of the two photographs?
   b Suggest what caused these changes.

2. What do Sources 1–6 tell you about dock workers':
   a conditions of work
   b conditions of employment
   c pay
   in the first half of this century? Quote from the sources to illustrate your answers.

3. a How could you use Source 8 to suggest that 'containerisation' improved dock work in the 1960s?
   b How could you use Source 9 to disagree with that view?

4 The experience of work

For some people work is interesting and rewarding. For some it is dull and pointless. They do it only because they need to earn money.

The quality of people's experience of work depends on many things. The conditions in which they work, the amount of money they earn, and who they work with, are just a few of them. You can probably think of more.

Research into how people experience their work suggests that the following three conditions are the most important:

1 the range of tasks involved. The more varied the job, the more a worker is likely to enjoy it.
2 the amount of responsibility the worker has. Workers who can decide for themselves how to do their work are usually happier than workers who must follow strict instructions.
3 the amount of control over workers. Workers' feelings about their jobs are affected by the way managers or supervisors control their work.

For example, a worker on an assembly line making televisions has a single task to perform, which is repeated many times each day and is inspected frequently by supervisors. In contrast, a farmer must perform many tasks in a day, each needing skill and experience, and nobody checks whether the work has been done properly. So, even if the weather is bad or the task unpleasant, the farmer is likely to have a better experience of work than the television assembler.

The quality of work experienced by an assembly line worker has become more common in the twentieth century. In many industries, work has become less varied, workers have less responsibility for their work and they are more controlled. We can see how this has happened by looking at the development of one of the new industries of the twentieth century.

Car assembly lines

Source 1

United States artist Norman Rockwell painted this picture in 1953 for the 50th anniversary of the Ford Motor Company. It shows Henry Ford, watched by his wife, building his first car at home in their garage in 1897.

At the start of the century cars were made by small firms of skilled workers. Mechanical engineers built the engine and chassis, and carriage makers built on a body to the customer's specification.

Cars built in this way took a long time to make. The longer they took to make, the more expensive they were because of the wages paid to the workers. In the United States, a businessman called Frederick Taylor devised a way of reducing the time that workers took to make things. 'Taylorism', as his method was known, involved breaking down jobs into stages, each as small as possible, and each done by a different worker. 'Time and motion' studies showed exactly how long it should take a worker to perform a task.

The American car-maker Henry Ford used Taylor's methods to increase his output of cars. He did so by making them on an assembly line. Instead of workers moving around a car, doing a variety of skilled tasks to it, workers stayed in one place while the cars moved past them. Ford described the system in his autobiography in Source 2.

Source 2

Henry Ford, *My Life and Work*, 1923.

In the chassis assembly are 45 separate operations or stations. The first men fasten four mud-guard brackets to the chassis frame; the motor arrives in the tenth operation and so on .... The man who places a part does not fasten it. The man who puts in a bolt does not put on the nut, the man who puts on the nut does not tighten it. On operation number 34 the budding motor gets its gasoline; it has previously received lubrication; on operation number 44 the radiator is filled with water and on operation number 45 the car arrives out into John R. Street.

Source 3

This photograph was taken on the magneto assembly line in the Ford automobile factory in 1913. As a magneto moved slowly along the line, each man added a part to it until it was complete.

By using an assembly line, Henry Ford was able to make large numbers of cars quickly. The time it took to make a chassis fell from twelve and a half man-hours to 93 minutes. Mass production on an assembly line required fewer workers, and that cut the cost of paying wages. This in turn reduced the selling price of the car, encouraging more and more people to buy cars. Between 1909 and 1928 15 million people bought the Model T, Henry Ford's most popular car.

Car makers in other countries followed Ford's example, hoping to make profits like his. In Britain William Morris, who had a car factory at Cowley near Oxford, introduced an assembly line after the First World War. By 1926 the factory was producing about 1,300 cars per week. Before the war it had been making that number in a year. When a mechanical assembly line was introduced in 1934, output rose to 2,000 per week.

After the Second World War, assembly lines became faster and more operations were subdivided. In other words, workers' tasks became simpler, but had to be done faster. A car worker in Coventry described the effect of this in a letter to a local newspaper (Source 4).

Source 4

Coventry Evening Telegraph, 26 September 1973.

Everything on the track seemed to be a rush. Men would be running everywhere in an attempt to get a few cars ahead so that, when the bell went for the end of tea break, you would have a few minutes to yourself. There just seemed no end to it. The assembly track would start running dead on 8.00 p.m. when I arrived for the night shift and it would not stop until exactly 10.30 when we would have a ten-minute tea break. By then the men, cramped together, fighting to get a few cars ahead on the track would be shouting and screaming at each other.

A worker in the Ford car factory at Dagenham told a researcher:

Source 5

H. Beynon, *Working for Ford*, 1973.

It's the most boring job in the world. It's the same thing over and over again. There's no change in it, it wears you out. It makes you awful tired. It slows your thinking down. There's no need to think .... You just carry on. You just endure it for the money. That's what we're paid for – to endure the boredom of it .... Ford class you more as a machine than men. They're on top of you all the time. They expect you to work every minute of the day.

Managers and supervisors can affect how workers feel by the way they control their work. Source 6 describes what happened when a supervisor in the Chrysler car works told a group of workers to do their job in exactly the way their written instructions said it should be done. Until then, they had decided for themselves how to organise the work.

Source 6

Red Notes: *A Battle for Power – the Motor Industry Crisis in Britain*, 1975–76.

On the door-hanging section last year, the Superintendent instructed the men ... to do fourteen two-door cars, fourteen Estates, and 21 four-door saloon cars ... but management couldn't get the cars into correct rotation. The result was chaos, as the workers did just what they had been told to. Two-door cars were coming down the line with doors for four-door cars – seven inches too short .... Estate car doors were being smashed into position on whatever car turned up next! The Superintendent begged the men to return to their own patterns of working, but the men insisted on working strictly to their instructions for the rest of the shift. The result was that management allowed us to work our own work patterns. They left it to us.

Source 7

The computer-controlled robot arm is welding the body of a car on an assembly line at a Nissan plant.

In the 1980s most car companies introduced a new form of technology to their assembly lines (Source 7). Computer-controlled robot arms could be programmed to duplicate the movements of many of the workers on assembly lines. Unlike the workers, however, robot arms could work without tiring for as long as was required.

Questions

1 Look at Source 1. How was the work of making this car very skilled?

2 Compare Sources 1 and 3.
   a How had car-making changed by the time Source 3 was photographed?
   b Was there anything skilled about the work in Source 3?

3 Compare the assembly line in Source 7 with the one in Source 3. Which do you think Henry Ford would have admired most if he could have lived to see them both? Explain your answer.

4 Look at the three factors which affect the experience of work on page 17. Using the sources and information in this section, explain how each has changed for car assembly workers in the twentieth century.

5 Death of the old industries

The biggest changes in work have been in Britain's old heavy industries: coal, iron and steel, shipbuilding and textiles. All four industries declined rapidly after the First World War. As pits and factories closed down, miners, foundrymen, shipwrights, spinners and weavers were forced into new occupations or onto the dole.

The death of the old industries had many causes. One was competition from other countries like the United States and Japan. They had modern steel plants, textile factories and shipyards that could produce goods more cheaply than their British rivals. Another was the shrinking of markets. As petrol-driven cars and lorries became common, for example, less coal was needed to run steam engines on the railways.

The industry that declined fastest was the cotton industry, based in Lancashire. This section investigates the decline of 'King Cotton' and shows how it affected the people who were thrown out of work.

Why did the cotton industry decline so quickly?

At the start of this century cotton was 'king' of the industries in Lancashire. Around 600,000 men and women worked in cotton mills, more than any other kind of manufacturing. The cotton that they spun and wove was Britain's most valuable export, bringing in 25 per cent of all its overseas earnings. They produced so much cotton that Britain had two thirds of the world's cotton trade. Sources 1 and 2 give us an idea of the work that some of them did. Source 1 shows spinners at work while Source 2, written by a former spinner, describes his job as a 'doffer'. He started work when he was twelve.

Source 1

These spinners in a Lancashire mill, around 1910, were 'doffing' – changing the bobbins of cotton thread on the spinning machine behind them. They were barefoot because spinning mills were kept very hot and humid to make the cotton easier to handle. Their overalls were stained with oil that sprayed from the machines.

Source 2

Jack Hilton, a former cotton worker, in Jack Common's book *Seven Shifts*, a collection of accounts of work published in 1938.

Being in a mill was like being in a prison, and it had the further disadvantage that one was slowly being melted away. In my two years my weight remained stationary, although I grew a couple of inches. Most of us lads seemed to develop speed, but we lacked weight and strength. The work made us ... human whippets. We would run about with a doffing box on our shoulders .... One day was like another. It was throb, throb, throb, spin, spin, spin, cotton passing from bobbins to bobbins, piecing the broken ends up, taking away the full bobbins, putting the empty bobbins.

Cotton had made Britain into the world's first and leading industrial nation in the nineteenth century. In the first quarter of the twentieth century it was still Britain's most important manufacturing industry. To the cotton masters who ran the mills it seemed that no other country would ever be able to match Britain's output. Source 3 explains one mill owner's confidence.

Source 3

B. Bowker, *Lancashire Under the Hammer*, 1928.

In the first place, we've got the only climate in the world where cotton piece goods in any quantity can ever be produced. In the second place, no foreign Johnnies can ever be bred that can spin and weave like Lancashire lasses and lads. In the third place there are more spindles in Oldham than in all the world put together. Last of all, if they had the climate and the men and the spindles – which they can never have – foreigners could never find the brains Lancashire cotton men have for the job. We've been making all the world's cotton cloth that matters for more years than I can tell, and we always shall.

Nine tenths of Lancashire's cotton output was sold overseas. Lancashire mills sent umbrella cloth to Japan, turbans to India, and sheets to Africa. However, the First World War damaged this trade. From 1914–1918 Britain could not sell its cotton goods abroad. Their usual customers bought from new suppliers, especially Japanese companies whose mills were newer and more modern than Lancashire's mills. Japanese workers also received lower wages. Japan could therefore sell its cotton more cheaply. When the war ended, many of Lancashire's usual customers continued to buy from Japan.

Some mill owners tried to compete with their foreign rivals by modernising their machinery and increasing their output. In 1926 a textile worker described how this affected her and her fellow weavers (Source 4).

Source 4

Margaret A. Pollock (Ed), *Working Days. Being the Personal Records of Sixteen Working Men and Women written by themselves*, 1926.

One looks with wonder at the automatic looms of today which stop just at the right moment and dispose of the empty shuttle, pick up a full one and re-start as though possessed of magic power. One is inclined to think 'what a boon to the worker', but this is not the case, because a weaver of ordinary looms tends two but an automatic weaver tends four with very little difference in wages. This is one of many cases where invention exploits the worker.

Source 5

Gandhi visiting Darwen, a mill town in Lancashire, on 26 September 1931. He is wearing the traditional Indian cotton wrap, the *dhoti*.

However, even mills like the one described in Source 4 were soon outclassed by foreign mills. Lancashire workers might now tend four

machines where before they operated two. In the United States and Japan one worker might run 40 automatic looms at once.

Foreign competition wasn't the only problem facing the Lancashire mills in the 1920s. Business could also be suddenly harmed by economic developments over which mill owners had no control. In 1929 the world went into a deep economic depression. Trade between nations broke down and many banks went out of business. Thousands of cotton workers were thrown out of work.

Cotton workers also faced an additional threat to their jobs during the Great Depression. For many years Britain had sold more cloth to India, its largest colony, than to any other country. In the 1920s, however, Indian nationalists mounted a series of protests against British rule in India. Led by Mohandas Gandhi, their aim was to force the British to give them the right to govern themselves. They refused to pay British taxes, or to co-operate with the British authorities. Above all they refused to buy British goods, especially cotton goods. This boycott further reduced the market for Lancashire cotton. By 1930 one in four millworkers was out of work.

As Source 5 shows, Gandhi visited Lancashire in 1931. He was in Britain for talks about Indian self-government. When told about the hardship that the Indian boycott was causing in Lancashire, he said:

Source 6

Speech by Gandhi on 26 September 1931, quoted in D.G. Tenduklar, *Mahatma. Life of Mohandas Karamchand Gandhi*, 1952.

You have nearly 3 million unemployed, but we have nearly 300 million unemployed for half the year. Your average unemployment dole is 70 shillings (£3.50). Our average income is seven shillings and sixpence ($37\frac{1}{2}$p) a month . Even in your misery you are comparatively happy. I do not grudge that happiness. I wish well to you all, but do not think of prospering on the tomb of the poor millions of India .... You should cherish no hope of reviving the old Lancashire trade. Do not attribute your misery to India. Think of the world forces that are powerfully working against you.

Questions

1 Read Sources 2 and 4 again.
   a Both workers in these sources were complaining about their work. What was it they disliked?
   b Why might Jack Hilton in Source 2 have considered the work in Source 4 an improvement on the work he was doing?
   c Do you think the worker in Source 4 would have considered her work an improvement on Jack Hilton's work in Source 2? Explain your answer.

2 In 1931 a quarter of all Lancashire millworkers were unemployed.
   a Why might Gandhi have been blamed for this?
   b In Source 5 how do the millworkers seem to be getting on with Gandhi? Why is this surprising?
   c How does Source 6 help to explain the millworkers' behaviour?

3 In Source 6 Gandhi said to the mill workers 'Think of the world forces that are powerfully working against you'.
   a Using the sources and other information in this section, find three 'world forces' that you think were working against the millworkers.
   b In each case, explain how it worked against them.

Review: The changing world of work

1 Investigation

This book has so far shown how several kinds of work have changed during the twentieth century, and has examined the different reasons for those changes. You can extend your knowledge and understanding of the topic by making your own investigation into another kind of work. You will get the best results if you choose one that you already know something about. For example:

Work in the home
a Make a list of all the work that needs to be done to keep your home running: for example, cleaning, washing clothes, cooking, mending. For each task, make a note of any machinery used, e.g. vacuum cleaner for cleaning floors.
b Find out from older people how these jobs were done when they were your age, and whether any different kinds of machine were used.
c Find out from books in your library (e.g. an encyclopaedia) how these jobs were done much earlier in the twentieth century.
d Make a wall display, or prepare a tape, or write an essay, explaining (i) how domestic work has changed, (ii) how far new technology has been the cause of those changes, (iii) assessing whether these changes have been for the better.

Other investigations to consider are: work done by a parent or relative that you can ask them about; work which is very important in your locality; work which you may have done part-time, e.g. shop work or a paper round.

2 Essay question

Write an answer to one of these GCSE examination questions:

a 'New technology completely changed and improved people's work in the twentieth century.' Do you agree? Illustrate your answer with examples from at least one of the following: factory work; agricultural work, domestic work.

b Three reasons why Britain's old industries declined in the twentieth century were (i) the disruption of trade by two world wars, (ii) competition from foreign businesses, (iii) slowness to introduce new technology. Which do you think was most important?

Focus study · Women in work, 1910–1921

Cities in the 1900s were dirty places, with smoking coal fires and horse-drawn vehicles polluting both the air and the streets. Keeping clean was difficult and time-consuming. Having a clean front door step was a mark of respectability, and washing them was a regular household chore. Better-off households, both working class and middle class, paid step-girls like these to do it for them.

So far in this unit you have found out about changes in people's work over a long time-span. This focus study looks in depth at changes over a much shorter period. It shows how the work that many women did changed dramatically during the First World War of 1914–1918. When you have finished reading this study you should be able to understand and explain three things:

- What was women's work like before the First World War?
- How did the war change the work that women did?
- Did these changes improve women's lives and opportunities?

As you read, think about the women in the photograph above, four 'step-girls' at work in London in the early 1900s. Although we do not know who they were, we can use the evidence in this focus study to try to imagine what women like them felt about their work and about the changes which they experienced.

1   Women at work before the First World War

In 1910 nearly 4.8 million women worked in paid jobs. Around 10 million more worked in the home, looking after their families and running the household. Many did both.

We can find out about the paid work that women did by looking at the census of 1911. This was the ten-yearly count of the population when everybody had to give the government information about themselves. The census showed exactly how many people worked and what their jobs were as Source 1 shows.

Source 1

Adapted from *Census of England and Wales*, 1911. Volume 10: *Occupations and Industries*, 1914, and *British Labour Statistics, Historical Abstract*,

Occupations of persons, (males and females), aged ten years and upwards... 1911.

	Thousands	
	Males	Females
Public administration (e.g. civil servants, post office workers)	271	50
Defence of the country (e.g. army, navy)	221	–
Professional occupations (e.g. lawyers, doctors, teachers)	413	383
Domestic service (e.g. servants, cooks, cleaners)	456	2127
Commercial occupations (e.g. clerks, typists)	739	157
Transport (e.g. train drivers, bus conductors, dockers)	1571	38
Agriculture (e.g. farmers, foresters, gardeners)	1436	60
Mines and quarries (e.g. coalminers, slate quarriers)	1202	8
Metals and machines (e.g. steel-workers, shipbuilders, clock-makers)	1795	128
Building (e.g. bricklayers, carpenters, plumbers)	1140	5
Wood, furniture, fittings, decoration (e.g. upholsterers, painters)	287	35
Brick, cement, pottery, glass (e.g. stone masons, china workers)	145	42
Chemicals, oil, grease etc. (e.g. dye makers, salt makers, chemists)	155	46
Skins, leather, hair and feathers (e.g. saddlers, furriers)	90	32
Paper, prints, books, stationery (e.g. book binders)	253	144
Textiles (e.g. cotton weavers, wool spinners, lace-makers)	639	870
Dress (e.g. hat, shoe, wig, glove, umbrella, corset-makers)	432	825
Food, tobacco, drink, lodging (e.g. bakers, brewers, publicans)	806	308
Gas, water, electricity supply and sanitary service	86	0.1
General and undefined workers (e.g. shop assistants, factory hands)	741	98
Without occupations (e.g. retired, students, housewives)	2515	11432

The figures in Source 1 are totals for the whole country. As you can see in Source 2 there were parts of the country where the picture looked very different.

Source 2

Mr Alfred Sears, former dock worker in Sheerness (Kent), interviewed by a sociologist, R.E. Pahl, in his book *Divisions of Labour*, 1984.

In Sheerness very few women worked before the First World War. They stayed at home and almost every other house in these streets would have 'Bed and Breakfast' in the window in the summer time. Earn a little extra money that way. Oh yes, that's quite right. Women didn't go out to work then and it wasn't the thing for women anywhere really. Up in the North they did in the mills, and in London they would go working, but in a place like Sheerness it was frowned on for a woman to work if she was a married woman. Single women would be in the shops, but a married woman – her place was in the home.

As Source 2 suggests, most women in paid work were unmarried – 55 per cent of single women worked compared with 14 per cent of married women. Some of them had interesting and well-paid jobs – teachers, for example – but most did not. A government enquiry in the 1890s found that the most unpleasant jobs in each trade were usually done by women. It also showed that women always got lower wages than men who did similar work.

Why was women's work often worse than men's work?

To understand why women often had unpleasant, badly paid jobs we must begin in the home. Most women did a great deal of work running their homes: raising children, cooking, shopping, cleaning, mending. Many families, however, could not live on a man's earnings alone. Over half a million married women went out to work to supplement the family income. This doubled a woman's work, as Source 3 shows. It is an account of a typical day's work by a woman worker in a London jam factory.

Source 3

From an essay by Anna Martin, *The Married Working Woman. A Study*, 1910. Anna Martin was a campaigner for women's rights. She wrote down this woman's words at a social club for working women in London. The woman had been asked 'how do you manage about housework if you are out all day?'

I rise at 4.45 a.m., sweep the place a bit and get my husband his breakfast. He must be off before six. Then I wake and wash the children, give them each a slice of bread and butter and the remains of the tea, and leave out the oats and sugar for Harry to prepare for the rest later on. (Harry is 10 years old.) Then I open up the beds and take the baby to Mrs T. My own work begins at 7 a.m. At 8.30 a.m. the firm sends us round a mug of tea and I eat the bread and butter I have brought with me. I used to go home in the dinner hour, but my feet are now so bad that I get a halfpenny cup of coffee in a shop and eat the rest of what I have brought. At 4.30 I have another cup of tea and get home a little before 7 p.m. I do the hearth up, get my husband his supper and make the beds. Then I get out the mending and am usually in bed by 11 p.m.

Many working-class women combined household work with paid work by doing 'outwork' in their own homes. Most outwork consisted of assembling articles for manufacturers. They made matchboxes, toothbrushes, paper bags, peaks for soldiers' caps, safety pins, slippers, coffin tassels, straw hats, and hundreds of other small items. Such work involved long hours and was very badly paid. It was therefore known as sweated labour.

Source 4 helps us to understand what sweated labour was like. It comes from the catalogue of an exhibition held in London in 1906 to show the conditions of sweated labour. In the exhibition hall 45 workers, mostly women, did sweated work in stalls for the public to watch. Notices like this explained what was going on in each stall.

You can work out from Source 1 that over 2 million women worked as domestic servants. Although this was the largest occupation for women, it was not at all popular. We can understand why this was so, by reading the accounts of women who worked as servants. In Source 5 one of them, a girl called Rose, recalled being 13 in 1905.

Source 4

This picture of matchbox makers comes from *Sweated Industries*, the handbook of the *Daily News* Sweated Industries Exhibition, held in London in May 1906.

Stall II.		Worker No. 3.
Description of Work	... ...	**Matchbox Making.**
Rates paid...	...	2d. gross.
Worker's outlay for sundries ...	...	Has to find paste, hemp (for tying up), and firing to dry wet boxes.
Time lost in fetching and returning work	...	About 2 hours a day.
Average working day	...	12 hours.
Average earnings...	...	Not 5/- a week. Highest is 8/2 for full week, including Sundays.
Regular or intermittent work ...	...	Occasionally works Sunday and Monday. Otherwise the average is five days a week.
Retail price of article	...	The matches retail at from 2d. per dozen boxes.
Worker's Rent	...	2/6 per week.
No. of Rooms	...	One small room (7 persons).

Process.—See Stall.

Remarks.—This worker has five children—the eldest of whom is 11.   She also has to support her husband, who is consumptive, and who has been unable to work for 6 years.   They have been compelled to take parish relief intermittently since 1901, in times of sickness, &c.   The eldest girl (11), after morning school, makes a gross of outside cases before going back to afternoon lessons at 2 p.m., and again works from 4.30 to 5.30 p.m., fitting up the boxes.

Source 5

From Elizabeth Roberts, *A Woman's Place. An Oral History of Working Class Women* 1890–1940, 1984. The author based her book on interviews, like this one, which she recorded in the 1980s with 160 men and women born in Lancashire in the 1890s and 1900s.

Christmas day come and I was a bit homesick, you know, and we had our Christmas day's dinner, I washed up and all that, and she said, 'Has tha finished now?' I said 'Yes madam', so she said, 'Well if thou get all that paper there, you'll see a lot of paper there and there's a big needle and a ball of string, if you go down to the paddock (that was the toilet), sit there and take the scissors and cut some paper and thread it for the lavatory.' And I sat there on Christmas Day and I think I cried a bucketful of tears. Christmas afternoon and I was sat ... cutting bits of paper ..., threading them and tying knots in them and tying them on these hoops, till about half past four when I went in for m'tea.

Another young woman explained why she disliked domestic service in a letter she wrote in 1906. (The original spelling has not been altered.)

Source 6

From Edward Cadbury, M. Cécile Matheson, George Shann, *Women's Work and Wages*, 1906. This was a survey of social and industrial conditions for women in Birmingham, based on interviews with over 6,000 women and on letters, like this one, written by some of them.

Why I Pefare Working in a Factory Than going To Service. – When I was about fourteen years of age I went to service for about eighteen months and I did not like it at all because you was on from morning to night and you never did know when you was done and you never did get your meals in peace for you are up and down all the time, you only get half a day a week ... and you never get very large wages in service. You never know when you are going to get a good place That What I Think About Service.

Source 7

Cleaning silver was a common job for domestic servants because silver tableware was widely used at that time. This advertisement suggests that Glosso metal polish will make the servant's work easier.

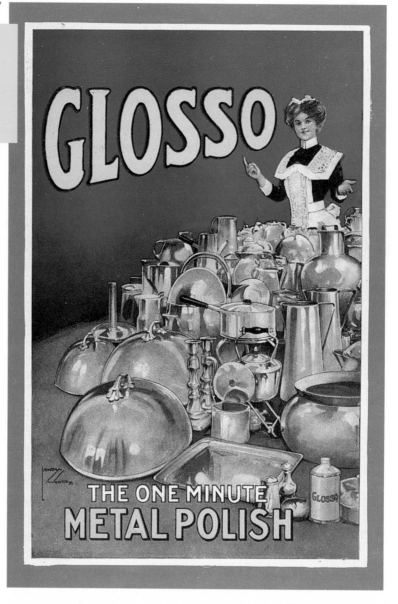

Questions

1 Look at Source 1. What were the four most common occupations of women in 1911?

2 Look at Source 4.
a Why were some kinds of work called 'sweated labour'?
b Why could the work in Source 4 be described as sweated labour?
c How do the 'Remarks' in Source 4 help us understand why the woman in the picture was willing to do sweated work?

3 a In what ways was household work (Source 8 on page 8) similar to domestic service (Sources 5 and 6)?
b The woman on page 4 was not complaining about her work; the women in Sources 5 and 6 were. What was the difference that might explain their different attitudes?

4 Use Sources 3–7 to describe ways in which work for many women was hard and unpleasant.

2   Women workers in the First World War

In August 1914 Britain went to war with Germany. The immediate effect on women workers was to put many out of their jobs. For example, women fish gutters were put out of work when trawlers stopped fishing in waters patrolled by German warships. For a while in September 1914 nearly half of all women workers were unemployed.

This soon changed. As the army grew in size women found work making equipment for soldiers, such as uniforms, boots and medical dressings. During 1915 many women also took over the work of husbands, brothers or fathers who had joined the army. They became bank clerks, tram conductors, window cleaners, and so on.

As the war went on, the army generals demanded more and more men to fight. They also demanded more munitions, especially shells. The only way to give them more men and more munitions was for women to make munitions in place of male workers who joined the army. The government made an agreement with the trade unions that, for as long as the war lasted, semi-skilled or unskilled women could do industrial jobs normally done by skilled men. This was known as 'dilution'.

The result of dilution was a sharp rise in the number of women in work, from 4.83 million before the war to 6.19 million in 1916. When conscription – that is compulsory military service for men aged eighteen to 41 – was introduced in 1916, the number rose still further. By 1917 one in three working women was replacing a male worker in industry.

Did war work help women?

From 1915–1918 the government produced propaganda to encourage women to do war work. Posters like Source 1 portrayed women workers as brave, patriotic and important. A government newspaper, *Dilution Bulletin*, described how women could earn good wages in good conditions, live in hostels for low rents, and enjoy organised entertainments. Pictures like Source 2 reinforced such images.

Source 1

A poster issued by the British Government in 1916, to encourage women to work in munitions factories.

Source 2

This painting by E.F. Skinner, *For King and Country* shows women working in a munitions factory making shells.

But was war work really like that? Source 3 gives a very different picture.

Source 3

Barbara Drake, *Women in the Engineering Trades*, 1917, a report prepared by two socialist groups in 1917, the Fabian Women's Group and the Fabian Research Department, for use by trade unionists.

The strain of work is severe everywhere. The absence of fourteen to sixteen hours from home on a twelve-hour shift; the crowded journey in the train or tram to and from the factory ...; the high cost of living in crowded munition areas, and bed paid at 10s or 12s a week and shared with another woman sleeping 'Box and Cox'; the fares amounting to 1s a day; the early start with or without a hot breakfast or breakfast at all ..; the inadequate sanitary, cloakroom, 'rest-room' accommodation; the defective heating or lighting arrangements; the exposure to weather in half-finished or open sheds; the draughts and wet floors in the aircraft sheds and shipyards.

Munitions work wasn't only hard, it was also dangerous, as Source 4 shows. It is taken from the autobiography of a well-known socialist and campaigner for women's rights, Sylvia Pankhurst.

Source 4

E. Sylvia Pankhurst, *The Home Front. A Mirror to Life in England During the First World War*, 1932.

In July (1916) I was approached by women working at a London aircraft works. They were painting aircraft wings with dope varnish at a wage of 15s. a week, for which they had to work from 8 a.m. to 6.30 p.m. They were frequently expected to work on till 8 p.m. and were paid only bare time rates for this overtime .... It was common, they told me, for six or more of the 30 women dope painters to be lying ill on the stones outside the workshop, for half an hour, or three-quarters, before being able to return to their toil....

Handling explosive chemicals such as TNT (Trinitrotoluene) discoloured the skin, as one worker recalled:

Source 5

Caroline Rennles, from an interview tape-recorded in 1975 by the Imperial War Museum, London.

We had bright yellow faces, because we had no masks ...and our front hair was all bright ginger. They used to call us canaries .... Sometimes the train would be packed. The porter would say, 'Go on, girl, hop in there' and they used to open the first class carriages. And there'd be all the officers sitting in there and some of them used to look at us as if we were insects. Others used to mutter, 'well, they're doing their bit'.

As Caroline Rennles hinted in Source 5, some men disliked women working in munitions, even though their work was essential for the war effort. Another woman who faced male dislike was a skilled engineer called Dorothy Poole, who wrote an account of her war work shortly after the end of the war. By her own account, she disliked socialists and trade unionists and had made her views clear at work.

Source 6

Dorothy Poole, typescript written in 1919 and now kept in the Imperial War Museum, women's collection,

Over and over again the foreman gave me wrong or incomplete directions and altered them in such a way as to give me hours more work .... I had no tools that I needed, and it was only on Saturdays that I could get to a shop. It was out of the question to borrow anything from the men. Two shop stewards informed me on the first day that they had no objection (!) to my working there provided I received the full men's rate of pay (1/3 an hour). But after this none of the men spoke to me for a long time, and would give me no help as to where to find things. My drawer was nailed up by the men, and oil was poured over everything in it through a crack another night .

Source 7

A photograph of munitions workers. The board in the window behind them says 'When the boys come back we are not going to keep you any longer – girls'.

Despite the danger and discomfort, 400,000 domestic servants left their jobs to do munitions work. What were the attractions? One woman explained why she did so in a letter which she wrote in 1976:

Source 8

Mrs H.A. Felstead, letter to the Imperial War Museum, 27 January 1976.

I was in domestic service and 'hated every minute of it' when war broke out, earning £2 a month working from 6.00 a.m. to 9 p.m. So when the need came for women 'war workers' my chance came to 'out'. I started on hand cutting shell fuses .... We worked twelve hours a day apart from the journey morning and night .... As for wages I thought I was very well off earning £5 a week.

The recommended minimum wage for munitions workers was £1 a week, nearly twice the wages of pre-war female workers in industry. Many had to work overtime, so wages of £2 to £3 a week were common. Some, like Mrs Felstead could earn as much as £5. Women's purchasing power therefore increased dramatically as Source 9 shows.

Source 9

Elsie McIntyre, interview tape-recorded in 1976 by the Imperial War Museum.

I started getting clothes, silk stockings and a white fox fur, but it was imitation because it kept coming off onto my clothes. I remember buying a piano because they were in fashion but I never learned it .... and necklaces were starting to come in then, long beads.

A Birmingham factory owner who employed women wrote in 1917:

Source 10

A.W. Kirkaldy, *Industry and Finance*, 1917.

Typical cases which have come under my personal observation show that women prefer factory life. They like the freedom, the spirit of independence fostered by their new-found earning power, the social life. The children, they say, are better off than before, better fed, housed and clothed.

But it wasn't only money that attracted women into munitions work. One Liverpool woman interviewed many years after the war explained her feelings in Source 11.

Source 11

P. Thompson and T. Vigne, *Family Life and Work Experience before 1918*, project interviews at the University of Essex.

I started there in July 1915 – there 'til 1917 – 'til I was having me second baby. I stayed until I was nearly four weeks off me time. Oh, the girls was lovely. You know, we all knew one another and they were all married women – we all understood – oh, and they all went mad when I said – I'll have to be leaving soon and when I told 'em why – ooh, oh, Katy, why didn't you watch out. Well, I said I couldn't help these things. You know we were all like – ah, awful happy.

Questions

1 a Look at Source 2 and think about the title of the painting. Suggest what the artist wanted people to think about women war workers.
   b Now look at Source 7. How might this photograph make people think in a different way about women war workers?
   c If you had to choose only one of these pictures to put in a book about women's war work, which do you think would illustrate it best? Why?

2 Sources 3 and 4 say that women's war work was dangerous, badly paid and unpleasant. Both sources were written by socialists, whose aim was to improve the rights and conditions of all workers. Does this affect their reliability or usefulness in any way?

3 Read Source 8.
   a How much did Mrs Felstead earn each week, and how many hours did she work each day, before the war?
   b What were her earnings and working hours during the war?
   c How does this help to explain why she became a munitions worker?

4 Study Sources 7–11.
   a Using these sources as evidence, describe briefly what women felt about working in munitions factories.
   b Does the description that you have given using these sources differ from the impression created by Sources 3–6? How?

3   Women in uniform

Industrial work wasn't the only new kind of work that women took up during the war. Many thousands joined women's sections of the army, navy and air force. Over 100,000 women worked as nurses caring for injured soldiers. Still more worked on farms, producing desperately needed food.

Attitudes towards women in uniform

There is a great deal of evidence that working in the uniformed services increased women's self-confidence and self-esteem. There is also evidence that many men disliked the women's services. Why did men and women have such different attitudes towards women in uniform?

Let us begin by looking at why women chose to go into uniform. Source 2 comes from a tape-recording made by a woman who joined the Land Army, a labour force set up in 1917 to replace male farmworkers who had joined the army.

Source 1

This wartime advertisement for soap shows VAD (Volunteer Aid Detachment) nurses caring for wounded soldiers. (There were no synthetic detergents at the time of the First World War, and soap was used not only for personal washing but for cleaning floors and washing clothes and dishes.)

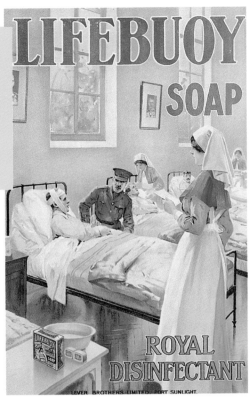

Source 2

Patricia Vernon, sound recording in the Imperial War Museum.

Well, when I was fourteen my mother put me into service. Er, well, I was disastrous from the start, because there was a flight of stairs up to the hall – every time I went up I tripped on the same step so, of course, carrying a tray of crockery up to the nursery which was three floors up, I invariably slipped on here and crash bang wallop the crockery went all over the place.... I lasted three weeks. So I thought to myself, well I'm not going into service again. I happened to look out and see this advert for land girls – join the Land Army and you're working for Britain – so I just put on my hat and coat and rushed out .... I went in and said 'I want to join the Land Army' and they said 'How old are you?' I said 'Oh I'm eighteen' – had enough sense for that.

Work in the uniformed services was hard and often unpleasant. Vera Brittain, an upper-class woman who became a VAD (Volunteer Aid Detachment) nurse in 1915, described her first month's work in Source 3:

Source 3

Vera Brittain, *Testament of Youth. An Autobiographical Study of the Years 1900–1925*, 1933.

We went on duty at 7.30 a.m., and came off at 8 p.m .... For this work we received the magnificent sum of £20 a year, plus a tiny uniform allowance and the cost of our laundry.

We all acquired puffy hands, chapped faces, chilblains and swollen ankles, but we seldom actually went sick, somehow managing to remain on duty with colds, bilious attacks, neuralgia, septic fingers .... Every task, from the dressing of a dangerous wound to the scrubbing of a bed mackintosh, had for us in those early days a sacred glamour .... Our one fear was to be found wanting in the smallest respect; no conceivable fate seemed more humiliating than that of being returned to Devonshire House as 'unsuitable' after a month's training.

Source 4

These two nurses, Mairi Chisholm and Elsie Knocker, became famous for treating wounded soldiers in a First Aid Post just behind the front line in Belgium for three and a half years.

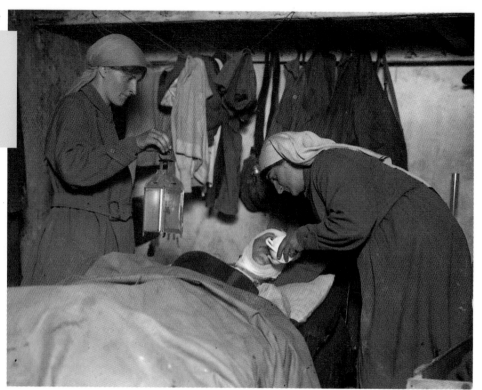

Many other VAD nurses looked back on their experiences with similar feelings:

Source 5

A letter to Mrs C.S. Peel, quoted in her book, *How We Lived Then, 1914–1918. A Sketch of Social and Domestic Life in England During the War*, 1929.

Looking back on my time as a V.A.D. in hospital, I think it was the happiest time I ever spent, for it was all so worthwhile. The men who suffered did so because of their wonderful heroism, not just because they had ... pneumonia or because they had been run over in the street. And no matter how tired one was, what horrible things one had to do, it was worthwhile to work until one could work no longer ... helping to make things a little better.

Despite the willingness of women to work hard in difficult conditions, many men did not like women in uniform joining them in the workplace. This was especially true of farmers. When Land Girls did start work on farms they were often given a hard time. One of them, Mary Lees, describes in Source 6 what happened when she arrived for her first day of work. The farmer, 'Old Tapp', was waiting for her in the yard with a sack and a pair of shears.

Source 6

Mary Lees, sound recording in the Imperial War Museum, London.

He handed me the sack and shears. 'Now' he said 'go up the road, first gate on the left down over, under the hedge', he said 'you'll find an old ewe. Her's been dead three weeks. I want the wool'.... So I took them and I went down. And, of course, the old sheep, I didn't need the shears. The body was bright blue. So I pulled off all the wool.... And I went back. And he was still standing there. I said, 'Oh, Mr Tapp, I didn't need the shears because, you see, the wool really came out quite easily.' .... And do you know, he looked at me. 'Gor', he said 'you done it?' He said 'I were testing you. Will you shake hands?'

Questions

1 Study Sources 3, 4 and 5.
   a How do these sources suggest that nursing during the war could be hard and unpleasant?
   b What did the nurses in Sources 3 and 5 feel about what they were doing?

2 Look at Source 1.
   a What impression does the advertisement create of the nurses?
   b How does this impression differ from that created by Source 4?
   c Suggest why the artist portrayed nurses in this setting rather than in a setting like that in Source 4.
   d How might an advertisement like Source 1 have affected the way men thought about women in uniform during the war?

3 a Suggest why Old Tapp (Source 6) gave Mary Lees this job to do on the first day on the farm.
   b If Mary had not come back with the wool, what do you think would have happened?

4 From 'heroines' to 'scroungers': women in 1918

The First World War ended on 11 November 1918. Four million British servicemen got ready to return to their homes and jobs.

Women had been allowed to take over skilled industrial jobs normally done by men for as long as the war lasted. Now that the war was over, they were expected to give up their jobs to returning servicemen. Even in factories that had not existed before the war, many women were pressurised into handing in their notice. Within months of the end of the war, hundreds of thousands of women were out of work.

Many of these women did not want to go back into traditional 'women's work' when they lost their jobs. Domestic service was especially unpopular. One unemployed munitions worker said when she went to an employment exchange looking for work: 'I feel so pleased the war's over that I'll take any old job that comes along'. However, when she was offered work as a domestic servant she added: 'Anything but that'.

Many women stayed on the dole rather than go into domestic service. These women faced fierce criticism. Newspapers mounted a campaign against them, calling them idlers and parasites. Women who only months before had been called 'heroines' and 'gallant girls' were now called 'scroungers' and 'pin-money girls'. The government reduced unemployment benefit to force them back into work.

Why did so many women leave their jobs after the war?

Why did so many women give their jobs to men when they did not want to return to 'women's work'? To understand that, we have to try to understand the pressure on women to return to traditional female work. Source 1 shows one of the ways in which men put such pressure on them.

Source 1

An Appeal to Women who are Employed in Occupations which Normally were held by Men, Live Wire, October 1920.

I ask you, young lady, who are now able to wear expensive hats and gloves and shoes and stockings to just stop and think for a minute – think of the hundreds of acres adorned with small wooden crosses; think of the agonies some of the bodies under those crosses endured ...; think of the cripples you see around you wherever you go ...; and then, having considered all this, don't you think that cotton stockings will do instead of silk ones, and your last year's hat will suffice for this year? I am sure the thought of denying yourself these luxuries in giving up your job for one of these men who has done so much for you, will be more than enough reward.

As this magazine article in Source 1 states, there were disabled ex-servicemen looking for work in every city. Source 2 shows just a few of them.

Source 2

Disabled, out-of-work civil servants protesting in Whitehall in 1921. The man at the front's placard says that 'men and women of independent means' (people who have no financial need to work) have government jobs while men like him have no work, no money, no food.

Most women gave in to such pressures. Source 3 is an interview recorded in the 1980s, in which a woman called Mrs Peters explained why she gave up work.

Source 3

Elizabeth Roberts, *A Woman's Place*, 1984.

You worked at Lune Mills, didn't you, in the war? ... And you lost your job afterwards?
    After the men came back .... Yes.
Did you accept that, or did it bother you at the time?
    No. Well I knew I was engaged to be married and ... you see in those days as soon as you were going to be married you left a job. You knew you were going to be a housekeeper and be at home all the time .... That's the only thing we girls had to look forward to ... getting married and sort of being on our own, and getting our bottom drawer together and various things like that. Yes, that was the ambition of girls then.

By no means all women gave up work easily. In Source 4 a former munitions worker recalled protesting outside Parliament in November 1918.

Source 4

Caroline Rennles, interview recorded in 1975 by the Imperial War Museum.

Thousands of us – it must have been two or three thousand – walked over the bridge, protesting that we'd been thrown out. We went right up to the door of the Houses of Parliament and before you could say 'Jack Robinson' there were hundreds of policemen on horseback dispersing us .... We ran down the Embankment, everywhere, from those policemen. But that was the beginning of our dole. Lloyd George gave us that. We was all thrown out, as much as to say 'well, that's it – it's finished.

Source 5 is a letter to a newspaper written by a woman under pressure to give up her job. In it, she pointed out that no men had come forward to claim her job:

Source 5

Letter to the *Hull Daily Mail*, 30 April 1919.

I myself am working in a man's place, but still, if I give it up, my employer will start another girl in my place .... If our men come back, I, like others, am willing to give it up for them, as it is only fair that they should have it back again. I have been employed in this place for four years, and then have to be insulted in the street, whilst on my way to work – 'When are you going to throw your – job in, and let your men come back?'

Questions

1. Use Sources 1–3 to describe why many women felt they had to give up their jobs after the war had ended.

2. How does the writer of Source 1 suggest that a woman's role at work was not very important?

3. Sources 2 and 4 are both about demonstrations near the Houses of Parliament. Which do you think was likely to attract most support from the general public? Explain your answer.

4. In Source 5 the woman was under strong pressure to give up her job. Why did she not do so?

5 Women's work in the 1920s

In the 1920s many people thought that the war had brought about a revolution in women's lives. Financially they were better off. Women's average wages rose from eleven shillings (55 pence) a week in 1914 to 25 shillings (£1.25) in 1919. Socially they were more free. During the war women had got used to doing things that were frowned upon before, such as smoking, going out alone, and wearing shorter skirts. Politically their position improved, for in 1918 married women over 30 gained the right to vote. At work, a new law in 1919 stopped discrimination against married women holding jobs. Such changes led many people in the 1920s to talk about 'the New Woman' (Source 1).

Source 1

'New women' smoking and drinking in a restaurant in 1920.

The 'New Woman'?

Source 2

Adapted from *British Labour Statistics, Historical Abstract 1886–1968*, Department of Employment and Productivity, 1971.

Had the war really changed women's job opportunities? How new was the 'new woman' of the 1920s? We can start finding answers to these question by going back to the census. The census figures for 1921 reveal what women workers were doing two years after the end of the war.

Occupations of women in 1921

Public administration (e.g. civil servants, post office workers)	81
Defence of the country (e.g. army, navy, air force)	–
Professional occupations (e.g. lawyers, doctors, teachers)	441
Domestic service (e.g. servants, cooks, cleaners)	1845
Commercial occupations (e.g. clerks, typists)	587
Transport (e.g. engine drivers, bus conductors, dock workers)	72
Agriculture (e.g. farmers, foresters, gardeners)	90
Mines and quarries (e.g. coalminers, slate quarriers)	9
Metals and machines (e.g. steel workers, shipbuilders, clock-makers)	175
Building (e.g. bricklayers, carpenters, plumbers)	5
Wood, furniture, fittings, decoration (e.g. upholsterers, painters)	31
Brick, cement, pottery, glass (e.g. stone masons, china workers)	45
Chemicals, oil, grease, etc. (e.g. dye makers, salt makers, chemists)	35
Skins, leather, hair and feathers (e.g. saddlers, furriers)	33
Paper, prints, books, stationery (e.g. book binders)	121
Textiles (e.g. cotton weavers, wool spinners, lace-makers)	701
Dress (e.g. hat-, shoe, wig-, glove-, umbrella-, corset-makers)	602
Food, tobacco, drink, lodging (e.g. bakers, brewers, publicans)	123
Gas, water, electricity supply and sanitary service	0.1
General and undefined workers (e.g. shop assistants, factory hands)	688
Without occupations (e.g. retired people, housewives)	11983

Source 3 shows how the trend was reversed. Within five years of the war's end, according to the Ministry of Labour:

Source 3

Ministry of Labour Gazette, September 1924.

...the reversal of the process of substitution which was so striking a feature of wartime industry is now practically complete. Women have returned to women's industries, and very few of them are to be found even in those sections of men's trades for which wartime ... experience showed them to be peculiarly well-fitted.

The return of women to 'women's industries' is reflected in the advertisement below:

Source 4

This advertisement for cotton fabrics appeared in *The Illustrated London News* in 1919. Britannia, the symbol of Great Britain, is giving up the helmet, armour and sword she has worn during the war. In their place she is taking a distaff, a stick for holding wool or cotton in spinning.

1 Britannia is giving up her armour for a distaff. What does this suggest she will do instead of war work?

2 How are Britannia and the other women portrayed. Suggest what the artist wanted us to think about them.

If working-class women found that their opportunities were disappearing, some middle-class women certainly had reason to think that theirs were improving. In 1919 a State Register of Nurses was set up, and nursing was recognised for the first time as a full profession. Also in 1919 an act of parliament, the Sex Disqualification (Removal) Act, said that being female or being married could not stop a person from getting a job in the government, in the law or any other profession. This meant that women could now enter the highest ranking jobs in the Civil Service, the Law and local government.

In practice, however, this Act changed little. Although it said that being married was not a bar to getting any job, it did not say that a woman could not be dismissed from a job when she got married. Many employers therefore carried on in the same way as before.

One reason why women were still discriminated against in this way was that people's attitudes towards women's work had not changed. Many women as well as men continued to think that 'a woman's place is in the home'. Then, as now, it was difficult not to be influenced by what everyone else seemed to think, and there were so many ways in which people could be influenced. One way was through the press. Think, for example, how the advertisement on page 41 suggested certain things about women workers.

Some advertisements were more obvious than that. Source 5 is taken from an advertisement which appeared in a woman's magazine in 1919.

Source 5

Advertisement for 'Oatine' face cream in *Everywoman's* magazine, 8 February 1919.

Now the war is won, many women and girls are leaving work, their war job finished. They are naturally desirous of regaining their good complexions and soft white hands freely sacrificed to the National need. Oatine is invaluable for this purpose.

The 1920s and 1930s saw a great increase in the number of women's magazines appearing each week. Readership soared. Most had the same kind of format, with articles showing women how to make themselves more physically attractive, how to look after their homes, and how to make their families more happy. They are therefore a very useful source of evidence about attitudes to women in the Twenties and Thirties. Sources 6 and 7 give an idea of the way such magazines viewed women working outside the home. Source 6 comes from the very first issue of *Woman's Own*.

Source 6

Woman's Own, 15 October 1932.

How Do You Do?

We introduce ourselves and our new weekly for the modern young wife who loves her home.

Woman's Own will be a paper with a purpose – a paper thoroughly alive to the altered conditions of the present day. The home paper that makes any girl worth her salt want to be the best housewife ever – and then some.

This first issue of *Woman's Own* contained articles on 'The right sort of frocks', knitting, embroidery, housework, and the life of the Prince of Wales. This format changed little over the following years. Source 7, from the magazine's letters page in 1938, gives the flavour of its outlook.

Source 7

Woman's Own, 1938.

I'm afraid I'm old fashioned enough to want a whol... main interest in life will be her home, her children and... to listen to my troubles, to be ready and willing to soot... I don't want to come back (from work) tired, and fi... comfort her. In fact, I want a wife whose first and only... then, our home .... Later on, there ought to be childre... will not be at all keen to have them .... So let me do the earning. Let her stick to the whole-time job of being my wife.

Questions

1. Compare the figures in Source 2 with the figures in Source 1 on page 27.
   a Which occupations show a large increase in the number of women employed (double or more than double the 1911 figures)?
   b Which occupations show some increase in women's employment?
   c Which occupations show little or no increase in women's employment?
   d In general, what do the figures suggest about women's employment in 1921 as compared to 1911?

2. a What do Sources 4–7 suggest about people's attitudes towards women and work in the 1920s and 1930s?
   b Do these sources support the view that there was such a thing as 'The New Woman' in the Twenties and Thirties? Explain your answer.

Review: Women in work, 1910–1921

The years 1910–1921 have been viewed as an important period in women's history, when women entered new kinds of work and gained fresh opportunities. One of the women who worked in a munitions factory during the war gave her opinion in Source 1.

Source 1

Elsie Farlow, interview recorded in 1976 in the Imperial War Museum, London.

It (the war) allowed women to stand on their own feet. It was the turning point for women.

Some historians have also seen this period as a turning point for women:

Source 2

A.J.P. Taylor, *English History 1914–1945*, 1965.

It was a decisive moment in women's emancipation. Women became more independent and more enterprising. The woman worker in munitions paid for her round of drinks at the public house. Practical needs revolutionised fashion. Never again did skirts sweep the ground. The petticoat disappeared .... Women's hats became neater.

This period of history is often portrayed in films as a time when women became more independent. The BBC TV series *House of Elliott*, for example, tells the story of how two young, modern women set up and run a fashionable clothing business in the early Twenties:

Source 3

Evangeline Elliott from the BBC TV series *The House of Elliott*. Evangeline, together with her sister Beatrice, successfully establishes a London fashion house in the 1920s.

Recently, however, historians have put a different interpretation on this period in women's history.

Source 4

Gail Braybon, *Women Workers in the First World War*, published in 1981.

There are many familiar features of women's work in the 1920s. They were low-paid, confined to few trades, encouraged to leave work on marriage, and excluded by unions or employers from trades classed as skilled; even when their work was quite complex it was not seen as being skilled.

Questions

1 Sources 1–4 are interpretations of the history of women in work in the 1910s and 1920s. For each interpretation, choose at least one source from this unit that can be used to support it. Then choose one source for each that disagrees with it.

2 The historian quoted in Source 2 was male. The historian quoted in Source 4 is female. How might this affect the way they made their interpretations?

3 Which interpretation do you find most convincing: Source 2 or Source 4? Why? Illustrate your answer with information you have read in this book.

4 Suggest why Elsie Farlow (Source 1) had such a different view to that of Gail Braybon (Source 4).

5 Look at Source 3. What issues must film-makers consider when trying to make a historical drama like this as accurate as possible?

BRITAIN IN THE TWENTIETH CENTURY

People and Politics

JOSH BROOMAN

General Editor: Josh Brooman

Contents

Voters, parties and politics

1 Patterns of power	48
2 Party politics	52
3 Votes for women!	56
4 British women get the vote	60
5 Women and politics	63
Review: Voters, parties and politics	66

Focus study · The impact of the Depression

1 How were British people affected by the Depression?	68
2 Depths of depression	70
3 Politicians and the Slump 1929–32	73
4 Politics and the unemployed	76
5 Depression and dictatorship	79
6 Overcoming the Depression 1933–39	83
Review: Slump	85

Longman Group UK Limited
Longman House, Burnt Mill, Harlow, Essex
CM20 2JE, England and Associated Companies throughout the World.

© Josh Brooman 1994

First published 1994

ISBN 0582 245966

Set in Concorde and Tekton

Printed in Great Britain
by Butler and Tanner Ltd, Frome and London

The Publishers' policy is to use paper manufactured from sustainable forests.

Design and production by Hart McLeod

Illustrations by Stephen Hawes

Cover photograph *The new member* by the Honourable John Collier. © Fine Arts Photographs.

Acknowledgements

The written sources in this book are taken from many different kinds of published material. Some were originally written in old-fashioned or unusual language. This has not been altered, but in most cases, unusual or difficult words are explained in the margin. In many of the sources words have been left out. A cut in the middle of a sentence is shown like this ...; and at the end of a sentence like this ....

We are grateful to the following for permission to reproduce photographs. Number refer to page numbers.

© Bildarchiv Preussischer Kulturbesitz, Berlin, 1994 (Photo: Hans, Hubmann), 83; cartoon by Strube from the *Daily Express*, 1936, courtesy the *Daily Express*, 84; Mary Evans Picture Library, 57, 61; from Walter Hannington: *The Problem of the Distressed Areas*, Gollancz, 1937, 69; Hulton-Deutsch Collection, 47, 63, 67, 72, 74, 77, 82; Illustrated London News Picture Library, 70; Library of Congress, 58; MARS, 79; National Museum of Labour History, Manchester, 54; from E. Sylvia Pankhurst: *The Suffragette,* 1911, 60; Popperfoto, 80; Reflections of a Bygone Age, Nottingham, 52; Süddeutscher Verlag Bilderdienst, 75.

Voters, parties and politics

Voters in London during the 1951 General Election watch the results coming in on a wall display near Trafalgar Square. Very few people had television at that time and this was one of the few ways in which the public could find out the results as they came in.

Britain is a democracy. This means that we all have certain rights which cannot be taken away from us, and that everyone over eighteen has a say in how the country is governed.

Voting is probably the most important feature of a democracy. Voting allows people to show how they want to be governed. In Britain, a general election is held at least every five years to allow voters to show which party they want to govern the country. Local elections allow them to show who they want to run their local councils. Occasionally, a national referendum is held to find out what voters think on a particularly important issue.

In theory, election time isn't the only time when people have a say in the government. The people who are elected are supposed to represent everybody's views in between each election. Members of Parliament put forward people's views in the House of Commons. Local councillors are meant to work in the interests of everyone in a locality. In such ways, everyone has a small share in the running of the country. In theory, everyone shares power.

We have not always had this power. At the start of this century, fewer than a third of all adults could vote in general elections. The other two thirds were not properly represented in Parliament. This book shows how some of those people fought to be represented, and brought about a transformation of power in this country.

1 Patterns of power

Source 1

A postcard of 1900 illustrates the words of '*Land of Hope and Glory*' with Britannia, the Union Jack, the British lion, and the Royal Navy.

British people a hundred years ago tended to think their country was not only more powerful but also more free and more democratic than any other country. 'England is the mother of parliaments', was a common saying in the late nineteenth century. 'Land of Hope and Glory, Mother of the Free' (Source 1) was a much-liked song of the 1900s.

Was it true? Was Britain better governed than other countries? Were its people really more free? Let us look more closely at who had power in Britain in the early years of this century, and then compare Britain with some other important countries of the time.

Britain: Mother of the Free?

Britain in 1900 was governed in much the same way as it is governed today. Laws are made by Parliament, which has two chambers: the House of Lords and the House of Commons. A bill, or draft law, must be discussed and approved by both houses. It is then submitted to the Queen for royal assent, before it becomes law as an Act of Parliament.

Most of the ideas for new laws are put forward by the government, which is headed by the Prime Minister and a team of ministers called the Cabinet. A huge body of officials, the Civil Service, helps the government to draw up laws and to put them into effect.

Source 2

How Britain was governed in 1900.

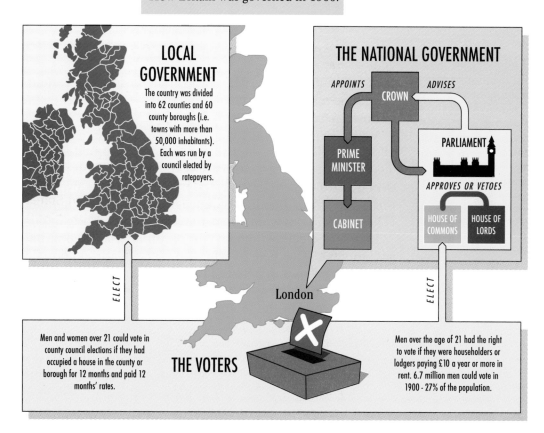

LOCAL GOVERNMENT

The country was divided into 62 counties and 60 county boroughs (i.e. towns with more than 50,000 inhabitants). Each was run by a council elected by ratepayers.

THE NATIONAL GOVERNMENT

APPOINTS   CROWN   ADVISES

PRIME MINISTER

PARLIAMENT

APPROVES OR VETOES

CABINET

HOUSE OF COMMONS   HOUSE OF LORDS

London

ELECT

ELECT

THE VOTERS

Men and women over 21 could vote in county council elections if they had occupied a house in the county or borough for 12 months and paid 12 months' rates.

Men over the age of 21 had the right to vote if they were householders or lodgers paying £10 a year or more in rent. 6.7 million men could vote in 1900 - 27% of the population.

The government has great power, but it does not last. At least once every five years, the people of the country can vote in a general election to show who they want as their Member of Parliament (MP). Most candidates in the election belong to one of the main political parties – Conservative, Labour or Liberal Democrat. The party which gets most MPs in the House of Commons forms the government. The leader of the winning party becomes Prime Minister and chooses a number of the party's MPs to be ministers.

Today, 95 per cent of adults in Britain have the right to vote. In 1900 it was 30 per cent. The only people who could vote were men who held certain voting qualifications, such as owning property or being the head of a household. Women, and men who did not have voting qualifications, were not allowed to vote.

Russia: an autocracy

Compared to some other countries in 1900, British people had a big share of political power. In Russia, the world's largest country at that time, all power was held by its ruler, Tsar Nicholas II.

Nicholas was an autocrat. This meant that he did not have to share his power with any other person or group of people. He could make laws, increase taxes, do exactly as he liked, without consulting anyone. There were no elections and no parliament to limit his power, and he could sack any minister or adviser who disagreed with him.

The United States of America: a democratic republic

At the opposite extreme, people in some countries could claim to share more fully in power than the British. This was especially true of countries which were republics – that is, countries whose head of state is an elected president.

In 1900 the oldest republic in the world was the United States. The job of running it was done by two kinds of government – the national, or federal government in Washington, and the local governments of each of the 48 states.

The federal government was similar to that of Britain. Then, as now, the parliament, called Congress, consisted of two Houses which made the country's laws. The President, like the British Prime Minister, led a cabinet of ministers, called Secretaries, who ran the country. In addition to the Federal government each state had its own Governor to run state affairs, and its own assembly to make state laws.

Unlike the British system, every part of the United States' government was elected. While the British Queen inherited her crown, the American President came to power in an election. Both Houses of Congress were elected, whereas in Britain members of the House of Lords held their positions because they were heads of noble families or bishops of the Church of England. In American elections all men over the age of 21 had the right to vote. In four of the 48 states women also had the right to vote.

The Weimar Republic: a new model of democracy

The British and American systems of government changed little in the twentieth century. That of Russia was transformed in a revolution in 1917, when Tsar Nicholas II was overthrown and Russia became a republic. This triggered off similar revolutions in Europe. In 1918 the German Emperor was overthrown and replaced by a republican government. Known as the

Source 3

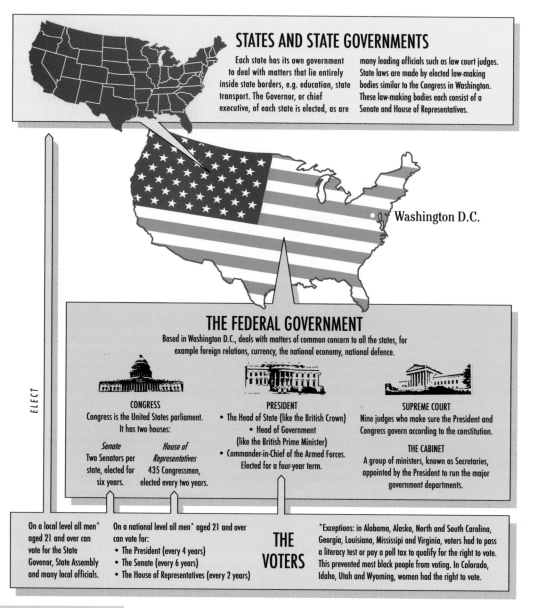

STATES AND STATE GOVERNMENTS

Each state has its own government to deal with matters that lie entirely inside state borders, e.g. education, state transport. The Governor, or chief executive, of each state is elected, as are many leading officials such as law court judges. State laws are made by elected law-making bodies similar to the Congress in Washington. These law-making bodies each consist of a Senate and House of Representatives.

Washington D.C.

ELECT

THE FEDERAL GOVERNMENT

Based in Washington D.C., deals with matters of common concern to all the states, for example foreign relations, currency, the national economy, national defence.

CONGRESS
Congress is the United States parliament. It has two houses:

Senate
Two Senators per state, elected for six years.

House of Representatives
435 Congressmen, elected every two years.

PRESIDENT
• The Head of State (like the British Crown)
• Head of Government (like the British Prime Minister)
• Commander-in-Chief of the Armed Forces. Elected for a four-year term.

SUPREME COURT
Nine judges who make sure the President and Congress govern according to the constitution.

THE CABINET
A group of ministers, known as Secretaries, appointed by the President to run the major government departments.

On a local level all men* aged 21 and over can vote for the State Govenor, State Assembly and many local officials.

On a national level all men* aged 21 and over can vote for:
• The President (every 4 years)
• The Senate (every 6 years)
• The House of Representatives (every 2 years)

THE VOTERS

*Exceptions: in Alabama, Alaska, North and South Carolina, Georgia, Louisiana, Mississippi and Virginia, voters had to pass a literacy test or pay a poll tax to qualify for the right to vote. This prevented most black people from voting. In Colorado, Idaho, Utah and Wyoming, women had the right to vote.

How the United States was governed in 1900.

Weimar Republic after the town where it was born, its leaders drew up a constitution in 1919 to show how it would be governed.

When the Weimar constitution was published in 1919 people in many countries claimed that it made Germany a model democracy.

1 It gave all men and women over twenty the right to vote. Few other countries allowed women to vote at that time.
2 It used a method of election called proportional representation. This gave seats in the German parliament to parties in proportion to the number of votes they won. This seemed fairer than the methods used in other countries because it gave small as well as large parties a share of the seats.
3 The constitution guaranteed many human and civil rights. It gave Germans the right of free speech, freedom of movement, assembly and religious belief, equality before the law and many other rights.

Source 4

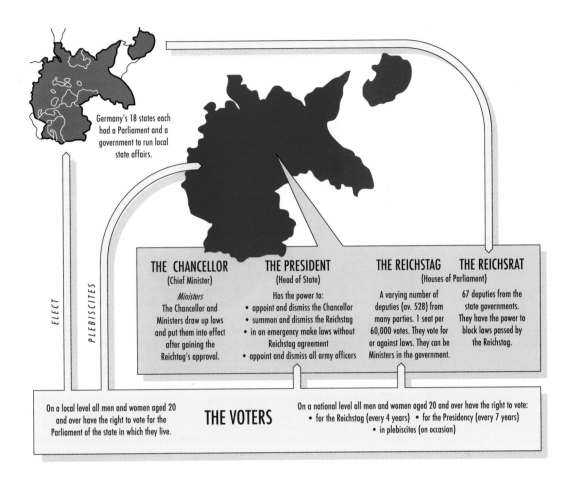

Germany's 18 states each had a Parliament and a government to run local state affairs.

ELECT

PLEBISCITES

THE CHANCELLOR
(Chief Minister)

Ministers
The Chancellor and Ministers draw up laws and put them into effect after gaining the Reichtag's approval.

THE PRESIDENT
(Head of State)

Has the power to:
• appoint and dismiss the Chancellor
• summon and dismiss the Reichstag
• in an emergency make laws without Reichstag agreement
• appoint and dismiss all army officers

THE REICHSTAG
(Houses of Parliament)

A varying number of deputies (av. 528) from many parties. 1 seat per 60,000 votes. They vote for or against laws. They can be Ministers in the government.

THE REICHSRAT

67 deputies from the state governments. They have the power to block laws passed by the Reichstag.

On a local level all men and women aged 20 and over have the right to vote for the Parliament of the state in which they live.

THE VOTERS

On a national level all men and women aged 20 and over have the right to vote:
• for the Reichstag (every 4 years)   • for the Presidency (every 7 years)
• in plebiscites (on occasion)

How Germany was governed in 1900.

4 Parliament had two houses. One, the Reichstag, was directly elected by all the people. The other, the Reichsrat, was made up of elected members of the eighteen regions into which Germany was divided. Many countries with parliaments, including Britain, had only one house elected by the people.

5 The German head of state, the President, was also elected by the people. Unlike Britain, where the crowned head of state inherited the post, the German President was directly elected by all the people.

Questions

1 Work in a group of four. One of you is a referee. The other three represent one country each: Britain, the United States and Germany. The year is 1920. Prepare a short talk, using the information in this section, in which you try to convince the referee that your country's system of government is more democratic than the other two.

2 After listening carefully to all three talks, the referee must say which of the three seems most democratic. The referee must explain clearly the reasons for his or her decision.

2 Party politics

When we vote in elections, we vote not just for the person we want to represent us. We vote also for the party to which he or she belongs.

Source 1

This postcard was produced during the 1905 general election, encouraging electors in Bristol West to vote for Sir Thomas Joseph Lennard.

1 How can you tell which party Lennard stood for?

2 What issues were voters being asked to think about?

A political party is a group of people who share similar ideas about how the country should be governed. Their aim is to get enough power to put their ideas into effect. They do so mainly through elections, when they aim to get more of their members into Parliament and local councils than any other party. It is usually the largest party in Parliament that forms the government.

Two party politics

For much of this century, three parties have dominated Parliament. As Source 2 shows, the Conservative, Labour and Liberal parties have been the largest parties since 1922. In nearly every election, however, one party has trailed a long way behind the other two. In practice, at any one time, two parties have had control of Parliament. For this reason the parliamentary system in Britain is often called a two-party system.

Decline of the Liberal Party

As Source 2 shows, the Conservative Party has always been one of the two largest parties. It has also been the party of government for longest. Of its two main rivals, the Liberal Party was powerful at the start of the century. The Liberals won the 1906 election and the government which they ran for the next ten years made many important reforms. A split between its two most important leaders, Prime Minister Asquith and Chancellor Lloyd George, during the First World War divided the party. It was weakened further after the war by a period of power-sharing with the Conservatives – the coalition government of 1918–1922 – and it fell into a decline from which it never recovered. New splits in the party in the 1930s continued to damage its chances, and after 1945 it never got more than 23 seats in Parliament.

Source 2

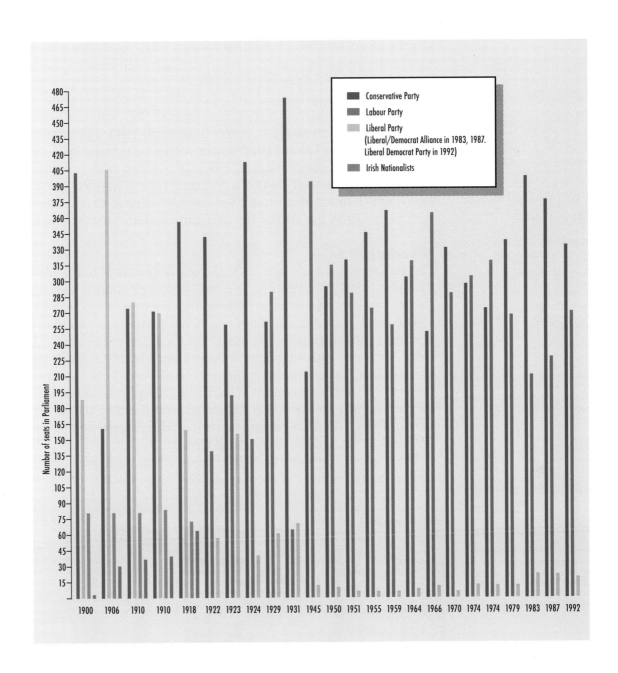

The three largest parties in Parliament, 1900–1992.

The rise of the Labour Party

From the 1920s onwards the Labour Party took the place of the Liberals in the two-party system.

The Labour Party was born in 1900 with the setting up of a Labour Representation Committee (LRC). The LRC was a combination of socialist groups which aimed to get better working conditions and greater equality of wealth for working people. In the 1906 election 29 LRC members were elected as MPs. Soon after, they renamed themselves the Labour Party, with Keir Hardie as their chairman.

For the next twelve years the Labour Party supported the Liberal government and joined in a coalition government with the Liberals during the First World War. At the end of the war, the party drew up a new set of aims. It declared that its aim was to create 'a new social order' based on the sharing of wealth and common ownership. This, combined with the setting up of party branches in every constituency, strengthened the Labour Party. By 1922 it had 142 seats in Parliament.

After two short and unsuccessful periods in government (1924 and 1929–31), Labour went into opposition against the National, or coalition Government which stayed in power from 1931–1945. The election of 1945 produced the first Labour government with a clear majority in Parliament. Clement Attlee's government of 1945–51 was the most productive of any Labour government. It created a National Health Service and introduced many other important reforms. Ever since, whether in or out of government, the Labour Party has shared the two-party system with the Conservatives.

Minority parties

The Conservative and Labour Parties are only two of hundreds of parties that have existed this century. In every general election at least seven small parties regularly win seats in Parliament.

The most important of these 'minority' parties are nationalist parties, aiming to gain more self-government for their part of the United Kingdom. Until Southern Ireland gained independence in 1922, there was a large group of Irish Nationalists in Parliament (see Source 2). Since then Northern Ireland, which remained a part of the United Kingdom, has been represented by parties such as the Ulster Unionists and the Social Democratic and Labour Party (SDLP). Scotland has often been represented by the Scottish National Party, and Wales by *Plaid Cymru*.

There have been some smaller extreme left or right wing parties which aim for major changes in the way society is run. On the left have been

Source 3

A certificate issued in 1914 by the Independent Labour Party, (one of the socialist groups that helped form the Labour Party), to commemorate its founding in 1893.

groups, such as the Communist Party, which want to change society by revolution. On the right have been nationalist and racist groups such as the British Union of Fascists in the 1930s or the National Front in the 1970s and 1980s.

Some parties exist to campaign for particular issues which they think are of special importance. The Green Party, for example, was set up to campaign for environmental issues. Usually these parties are very small, with only one or two candidates in the entire country, and they usually have limited aims. Such parties rarely win seats in Parliament.

Has the party system represented people fairly?

'First past the post'

In each constituency, the candidate who gains the most votes wins and becomes the Member of Parliament for that constituency. This is called the 'first past the post' system. Some people say that this system is unfair. In an election with three candidates, for example, one candidate can win with fewer than half the votes. Source 4 shows how this can happen.

Source 4

The Times Election Guide, February 1974.

Result of the general election in Halifax constituency, February 1974			
Candidate A	Dr Shirley Summerskill	(Labour)	20,970
Candidate B	S.R. Lyons	(Conservative)	17,967
Candidate C	A. Clegg	(Liberal)	12,300

Critics of the system also say that it gives the biggest party an unfair share of the seats in Parliament. Sources 5 illustrates this view. Source 5a shows the number and percentage of votes won by each party in the 1983 general election. You can easily see that the Conservative Party got most votes, followed by Labour and the Liberal Democrat Alliance with 16 million votes between them. Compare this with the number of seats each party had in Parliament (Source 5b). The Conservatives, with less than half the total number of votes, got more than half the seats in Parliament. Labour, with just over a quarter of the vote, got a third of the seats. The Liberal Democrats, also with a quarter of the vote, got only one thirtieth of the seats.

Source 5

Percentage of votes won by each party and the number of seats in Parliament won by each party in the 1983 general election.

(a)   (b)

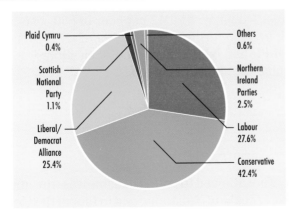 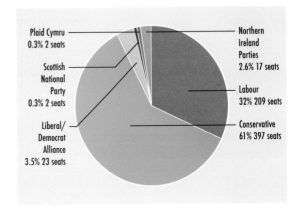

Proportional representation

Critics of the 'first past the post' system have often suggested that we should use a different method of election. The most favoured method is called proportional representation (PR). This means that parties would win seats in Parliament in the same proportion as the number of votes they won in an election. Try doing question 3 below to find out what difference this might make.

Some people disagree strongly with PR. They point out that countries which use the system often have parliaments which contain so many parties that it is hard for any one party to form a government. They often have to form coalition governments which find it difficult to agree on policies.

Is everybody represented?

People who disagree with PR also say that it is unnecessary. In the first past the post system, they say, the Member of Parliament represents everyone in the constituency, including people who voted for other parties.

A hundred years ago women did not have the right to vote. Most men said this did not matter, because MPs represented everyone, women as well as men. Why should women need to vote if they were already represented? Section 3 of this book looks at why many women disagreed with this, and at why they wanted to vote for their representative.

Questions

1 Look at Source 2.
 a Which party has won the largest number of general elections this century? Which has been in government for longest?
 b How has the number of MPs for (i) the Liberal Party, and (ii) the Labour Party changed over the course of the century?
 c Between which years did this change take place?

2 Look at Source 4.
 a Who won the Halifax election in February 1974?
 b How many people voted in the election?
 c With a calculator, work out the percentage of the electors who voted for the winning candidate.
 d How could it be argued that the result was unfair on many voters?

3 Look at the percentage of the vote won by each party in Source 5a.
 a With a calculator, find out how many seats each party would have won if they were in proportion to the percentage of the vote. For example, for the Conservative Party, find 42 per cent of 650 seats.
 b Make a pie chart like Source 5b to show the number of seats each party would have won if PR had been the method of election.
 c Which parties on your chart are most likely to favour PR? Why?

3 Votes for women!

In 1900 British women were not allowed to vote. The same was true almost everywhere else. Only in New Zealand, Australia, and in four of the United States, could women vote in general elections.

In many countries women campaigned for the right to vote. Fifty thousand British women belonged to the National Union of Women's Suffrage Societies. (Suffrage is an old-fashioned word for the right to vote.) They held meetings, gave out pamphlets, ran newspapers and sent petitions to Parliament. Some refused to pay taxes. In the United States, the National American Woman Suffrage Association used similar methods to demand the same voting rights as men. Similar organisations existed in Russia and in most European countries.

Why was voting so important to these women? What did they think would change if they could vote? Sources 1– 8 show some of the most common arguments used by women around a century ago.

Why did women want the vote?

One of the most basic arguments had been put forward when the campaign for votes first started in the nineteenth century. Source 1 shows how it was summed up by a leading campaigner in a magazine article in 1851.

Source 1

Harriet Taylor Mill, *The Enfranchisement of Women*, 1851.

The real question is whether it is right ... that one-half of the human race should pass through life in a state of forced subordination* to the other half ... (when) the only reason that can be given is, that men like it.

subordination Inferiority.

The women who found it hardest to accept their 'state of forced subordination' were often those who had jobs, money of their own, or an education. Their views can be seen in Source 2, a petition written by Russian women in 1906, and in Source 3, a British postcard of 1912.

Source 2

Petition of the Mutual Philanthropic Society, St Petersburg, 1906.

We work as equals in the fields and factories, in science, literature and art; in government, public and private organisations, as doctors and teachers, as rearers of the future generation. As taxpayers, workers and obeyers of the law in the same measure as men, we need the right to make those laws.

Source 3

What a woman may be ...' A postcard and poster produced in 1912 by a group of women artists, the Suffrage Atelier. Their aim was to produce 'picture propaganda for the Suffrage ... by supplying advertisements, banners and decorations'.

Women taxpayers in the United States had particularly strong views about the right to vote. The United States had been created by American colonists who objected to paying taxes to Britain when they had no MPs of their own in Britain's Parliament. 'No taxation without representation' was the slogan they used when they broke away from British rule in 1776. Over a century later, American women complained that:

Source 4

Declaration of Principles by the National American Woman Suffrage Association, 1904.

The women of the United States now pay taxes ... valued at billions of dollars. In a number of individual states their holdings amount to many millions. Everywhere they are accumulating property. In hundreds of places they form one-third of the taxpayers ... and yet they are absolutely without representation in the affairs of the nation, of the State, even of the community in which they live and pay taxes. We enter our protest against this injustice.

For many women, having the right to vote meant more than gaining a right. They wanted to use their votes to influence the government and to bring about changes. Sources 5 and 6 show one kind of change they hoped to achieve. Source 5 comes from a pamphlet written by a campaigner for women's rights. Source 6 is a poster designed in 1909.

Source 5

Mrs Wibaut, *Working Women and the Suffrage*, 1900.

The working woman does not need the suffrage to gain her independence from men. The employer has already made room for her in the factory and workshop and field. The working woman needs the suffrage ... in order to obtain better houses, better conditions of living, shorter hours of working, better care for her children.

Source 6

This poster was designed for an annual competition, held by a group called The Artists' Suffrage League, to find the best pro-suffrage propaganda. It appeared in 1909.

It wasn't only their working lives that women wanted to change with the vote. Many also believed that voting could change their home lives. In 1872, a campaigner for women's votes had written:

Source 7

Lydia E. Becker, *The Political Disabilities of Women*, 1872.

The franchise (vote) is needed as a protection for women from the ... savage passions of man. In the less cultivated classes of society these passions rage with terrific violence, and their effects fall chiefly on the unhappy wives .... There is not, we believe, any class so subjected to brutal personal violence as English wives ....

The sufferings and the wrongs of women will never be considered worthy of attention by the legislature (Parliament) until they are in possession of the suffrage ....

Similar views were being put forward in the 1900s by American campaigners. In Source 8, Susan Anthony, a leading campaigner for women's rights in the United States, said in a speech in 1900:

Source 8

Susan B. Anthony, *Statement to the National American Woman Suffrage Association*, 1900.

enfranchisement Giving the vote to.

There is an enemy of the homes of this nation and that enemy is drunkenness. Everyone concerned with the gambling house, the brothel and the saloon works and votes solidly against enfranchisement* for women, and, I say, if you believe in chastity, if you believe in honesty and integrity, then do what the enemy wants you not to do, which is to take the necessary steps to put the ballot in the hands of women.

Question

1 Sources 1–8 show several different reasons why women wanted the right to vote. These reasons were of two basic types:
1 they wanted equality with men,
2 they wanted to change women's lives.
Make a table like the one below to show what their reasons were, and what type of reason it was. Source 1 has been completed as an example.

	Reason for wanting the vote	Type of reason	
		Wanted equality with men	Wanted to change women's lives
Source 1	Being subjected to men was simply not right	✓	
Sources 2 and 3			
Source 4			
Sources 5 and 6			
Sources 7 and 8			

4   British women get the vote

By 1914 women in Britain had been campaigning for the vote for 50 years. They had not succeeded. No government supported their demands. Time after time, Parliament voted against reforming the electoral laws.

This changed suddenly. In 1918, Parliament passed a law which gave the vote to women over 30 who were householders or the wives of householders. What brought about this sudden change?

Why did women get the vote in 1918?

The suffragettes

An important event in women's campaign for the vote took place in 1903. Some women had become impatient with their lack of success so far. They felt that a more active campaign was needed. In 1903 Mrs Emmeline Pankhurst, with her daughters Christabel, Sylvia and Adela, formed the Women's Social and Political Union (WSPU). Their aim was to put pressure on the government by using militant protests.

Militant protesters use actions rather than words to get their point across. The Pankhursts began their campaign by shouting out slogans while a government minister was making a speech at a public meeting in 1905. When a policeman tried to throw them out, Christabel Pankhurst spat in his face. The women were arrested, and went to prison rather than pay the fine they were given for their behaviour. Newspapers gave headline coverage to the event, and the WSPU were soon the best-known campaigners for women's votes. The newspapers called them **suffragettes**.

Source 1

Militant action

In 1906 the Liberal Party won the general election and formed a government. This raised suffragettes' hopes because many Liberal MPs supported their cause. But the new government was divided on the issue and did nothing. The suffragettes therefore stepped up their militant action to try to force the government to act. They chained themselves to railings in public places and smashed windows in government offices. Source 1 shows one suffragette involved in militant action in 1909.

From 1909, suffragettes who were jailed for such actions went on hunger-strike. By starving themselves, they hoped to get so much publicity that the government would not dare keep them in prison. The government tried to avoid this by ordering that hunger-strikers must be fed by force. However, this only helped their cause. Stories of brutal forced feeding, illustrated by pictures like Source 2, attracted great public sympathy.

In 1910 the suffragettes called a halt to their campaign when the Prime Minister suggested that he would support a change in the voting laws. When he failed to do so in 1911 the suffragettes began a new campaign of violence and vandalism. They set fire to buildings and cut telephone wires. They slashed valuable paintings in art galleries, smashed shop windows and set fire to post boxes. They thought the government would eventually give them the vote simply in order to end the violence.

War and the vote

In 1914 Britain entered the First World War. The government promptly released over 1,000 jailed suffragettes, while the WSPU announced an end

Lady Constance Lytton, a leading suffragette, in Newcastle in 1909. Moments after the picture was taken she threw the stone in her hand at a car carrying Lloyd George to a public meeting. She was arrested for this attack. When she refused to pay a fine for it, she was sent to prison where she went on hunger strike.

Source 2

This poster, produced in 1910 by the WSPU, was an artist's impression, based on first-hand accounts, of how hunger-striking suffragettes were force-fed in prison.

■ This poster was produced during the 1910 election campaign. Who do you think the artist was hoping to influence?

TREATMENT OF POLITICAL PRISONERS UNDER A LIBERAL GOVERNMENT.

Produced by ARTCRAFT LTD 161 Strand W.C.   published by the WOMEN'S SOCIAL & POLITICAL UNION.

to the violence, so that it could concentrate on helping the war effort. While the government was at war with Germany, it was at peace with the suffragettes – for a while.

However, the question of votes for women did not stop being a problem for the government. The problem now was that a general election would have to take place when the war ended, but because the country was at war, it was impossible to draw up a list of registered voters. Men could vote only if they had lived at the same address for at least a year. Now several million men had left home to serve in the army. One man in five would not be able to vote.

In 1916 the government therefore had to draw up a new list of voters. When the suffragettes heard that it was planning to do so, they demanded that any new system of voting should include women as well as men.

By this time, more than 1 million women were doing war work – serving as nurses or as auxiliaries in the forces, or doing jobs left by men who had joined the forces. This changed public opinion. Many men who had disagreed with women having a vote now felt they had 'earned' the right to vote. As one opponent of the suffragettes said in March 1917:

Source 3

A.C. Morton, MP for Sutherlandshire, speech in the House of Commons, 28 March 1917.

Opinion ... is largely changing in favour of giving women a vote as soon as possible, and no doubt that is largely owing to the excellent work they have done for us and the country during the war.

On 10 January 1918, Parliament changed the voting laws by passing the Representation of the People Act. This gave the right to vote to all men over the age of 21, and to women over the age of 30 who were householders or married to householders.

Explaining the change

People at the time, as well as since, had different explanations for the government's change of heart. One explanation was put forward by Sylvia Pankhurst, the suffragette leader, in her autobiography. She wrote:

Source 4

Adapted from E. Sylvia Pankhurst, *The Suffragette Movement*, 1931.

Undoubtedly the large part taken by women during the war had proved a tremendous argument for giving them the vote. Yet the memory of the old militancy, and the certainty that it would happen again if the claims of women were set aside, was a much stronger factor.

Not every suffragette agreed with such views. One suffragette leader, Mrs Pethick-Lawrence, was thrown out of the WSPU in 1914 because she disagreed with the use of violence. She later wrote about Christabel Pankhurst's use of violence:

Source 5

Emmeline Pethick-Lawrence, *My Part in a Changing World*, 1938.

Where I think she was fundamentally wrong ... is in supposing that ... attacks directed more and more on the property of individuals would strengthen the movement and bring it to more speedy victory. So long as we attacked the government, and even when we attacked government property, we won wider and wider public support .... The further attacks on private property that developed in the course of the following two years roused a great deal of hostility.

■ How might Mrs Pethick-Lawrence (Source 6) have replied to Sylvia Pankhurst's explanation in Source 5?

One of the leading campaigners for women's votes was never a suffragette. Millicent Fawcett was leader of the moderate National Union of Women's Suffrage Societies, which did not agree with the use of violence:

Source 6

Millicent Fawcett, *Progress of the Women's Movement in the United Kingdom*, 1922.

I do not believe we should have won the vote just when we did, except for the fact that it was absolutely necessary ... to prevent many millions of men who had served their country from losing their vote .... Millions of the best men in the country had become disqualified through their war service by giving up their qualifying premises. Therefore by sheer necessity the government was forced to change the law dealing with the whole voting question as it affected the male voter ....

Questions

1 What did the women's campaign for votes achieve before the Pankhursts founded the WSPU in 1903?

2 a Briefly describe the Pankhursts' campaign for votes for women.
   b How did the outbreak of war in 1914 change the campaign?
   c Imagine that the war did not happen. What do you think the Pankhursts might have done after 1914?
   d What effect might this have had on the government?

3 Look at Source 3. Why should women's war work have changed public opinion in favour of giving them the vote?

4 Do you think the government would have changed the voting laws even if there had been no need to hold an election at the end of the war? Explain your answer.

5 a Read Sources 4, 5 and 6. Which, in your view, is the best explanation for women getting the vote in 1918?
   b Why is it difficult to explain why women got the vote in 1918 and not earlier?

5 Women and politics

The 1918 Representation of the People Act was quickly followed by another change in the electoral laws. The Eligibility of Women Act (1918) gave women the right to be elected as Members of Parliament. Ten years later, the Equal Franchise Act (1928) reduced the voting age for women to 21, and scrapped the rule which said they must be the wives of householders if they were not householders themselves.

Source 1

Two women in their early twenties walk out of a polling station after voting in the 1929 general election.

■ Why could a photographer not have taken a photograph like this during the elections of 1918, 1922, 1923 and 1924?

The voting laws then stayed largely unchanged for the next 40 years. Apart from some minor amendments in 1948, the only major change took place in 1969 when another Representation of the People Act reduced the voting age for men and women to 18.

Women, then, have been voting for 75 years. What effect has this had? Has it helped women in the ways that suffragettes and other campaigners hoped it would?

Did getting the vote change women's opportunities?

Let us begin by looking at the women who became Members of Parliament. Source 2 shows the number of women MPs elected in each of the 21 elections that have been held since 1918.

Source 2

The Times Guides to the House of Commons. 1929–1992.

* The one woman MP in 1918, the Countess Markiewitcz, was elected as a Sinn Féin candidate in Ireland. As she was in prison, accused of treason, she never took her seat in Parliament.

Women in British Parliamentary Elections 1918–1992

	Women MPs	Total MPs		Women MPs	Total MPs
1918	1*	707	1959	25	630
1922	2	615	1964	28	630
1923	8	615	1966	26	630
1924	4	615	1970	26	630
1929	14	615	1974 (Feb)	23	635
1931	15	615	1974 (Oct)	27	635
1935	9	615	1979	19	635
1945	24	640	1983	23	650
1950	21	625	1987	41	650
1951	17	625	1992	60	651
1955	24	630			

Now that women had the vote, did Parliament do anything that improved the lives of women? Source 3 shows the Acts of Parliament, introduced during the first ten years after women were given the vote, which concerned women.

Source 3

Martin Pugh, *Women and the Women's Movement in Britain, 1914–1959*, 1992.

Main Acts of Parliament dealing with women's issues, 1919–1929

The Sex Disqualification (Removal) Act (1919) said that being female or being married must not disqualify a person from getting a job in the government, in the law or any other profession.

The Nurses Registration Act (1919) set up a State Register of Nurses and recognised nursing as a profession.

The Infanticide Act (1922) said that a woman who killed her child while suffering from post-natal depression would not be charged with murder.

Criminal Law (Amendment) Act (1922) said that a man charged with sexual assault on a girl could no longer say in defence that he thought she was over sixteen.

The Law of Property Act (1922) allowed husband and wife to inherit equally each other's property.

Matrimonial Causes Act (1923) allowed a wife equal grounds for divorce (i.e. adultery) with a husband. A divorced husband was allowed access to the children only if he was considered a desirable influence.

The Widows, Orphans and Old Age Contributory Pensions Act (1925) gave a ten shillings weekly pension to widows, and to insured 65–70 year-old men and women. It also provided Children's Allowances for widows with dependent children.

The Married Women's Property Act (1925) required husband and wife to be treated as separate individuals in any action involving property.

The Separation and Maintenance Act (1925) extended the grounds on which a husband or wife could be separated to include (1) cruelty, (2) habitual drunkenness, (3) being made to have sex with a partner suffering from venereal disease.

Registration of Midwives and Maternity Homes Act (1926) provided for inspection and registration of both.

Representation of the People (Equal Franchise) Act (1928). See above.

Age of Marriage Act (1929) raised the age of marriage to 16.

1 For each of the Acts in Source 3, say whether it was concerned mainly with (a) political, (b) social, (c) family, (d) legal issues.

2 In which of those four categories did you put most of the Acts in Source 3?

Changing the law, however, did not always achieve what it was meant to achieve. For example, the Sex Disqualification Removal Act did not fully succeed in its aims. While it said that being married must not be a bar to getting a job in government, the law and the professions, it did not say that a woman could not be sacked from a job when she got married. This, combined with male prejudice against women, was one reason why the numbers of women in such jobs were slow to rise (Source 4).

Many women war workers had to give up their jobs when the soldiers returned from war after 1918. Women who tried to hold on to their jobs were attacked, verbally and even physically, by unemployed men.

Source 4

Lindsay Mackie and Polly Patullo, *Women at Work*, 1977.

Number of Women in the main professions in 1975		Number of women	Number of men
The Law	Barristers	252	3,386
	Solicitors	1,299	27,442
Medicine	Doctors	19,000	67,000
	Consultants	931	11,164
Education	Primary School heads	10,128	13,521
	Secondary school heads	1,050	4,295

The press ran hate campaigns against them. Women's working conditions did not improve for many years. Trade unions did little to help them and only one woman in seven belonged to a union in the 1930s. It wasn't until 1970 that an Equal Pay Act stopped women being paid less than men for the same work. Everywhere, women were more likely than men to work in part-time, or low-paid jobs.

Fifty years after women gained the vote, a new generation of women campaigners emerged. Known generally as 'Women's Liberation', they felt that voting had not brought the improvements that suffragettes had wanted. One of the best known campaigners, Germaine Greer, wrote this about the suffragettes:

Source 5

Germaine Greer, *The Female Eunuch*, 1970.

Marriage, the family, private property and the state were threatened by their actions, but they were anxious to allay the fears of conservatives, and in so doing the suffragettes betrayed their own cause .... Five years ago it seemed that emancipation had failed: the number of women in Parliament had settled at a low level; the number of professional women had stabilised as a tiny minority; the pattern of female employment had emerged as underpaid, menial and supportive.

Questions

1 How did women's political opportunities change in 1918?

2 How can Sources 2 and 4 be used to suggest that these changes did not lead to progress for women?

3 A woman who first voted, at the age of 21, in the 1929 election recalled many years later: 'No question that the vote made a difference for us. That feminist pioneer, Dame Margary Corbett Sashby, told me that before 1918, ministers and their civil servants just dropped all letters from women's organisations into the wastepaper basket. From 1918 onwards they replied courteously and received deputations cordially.' (Mary Stott in *The Guardian*, 6 February 1993.)

Using the information and sources in this section, say whether you agree or disagree with Mary Stott that the vote made a difference for women, explaining your answer clearly.

Review: Voters, parties and politics

1 Investigation

You have read that people's voting rights changed in 1918 and 1928, partly as a result of the activities of women campaigners. You can extend your knowledge and understanding of this topic by investigating the contribution that one of these women made to the campaign for votes:

a Choose a campaigner. You could choose one of the women featured in this book: a suffragette (e.g. one of the Pankhursts) or a suffragist (e.g. Millicent Fawcett). Or you could choose someone from another book (e.g. Emily Davison, who threw herself under the King's horse at the 1913 Derby). Whoever you choose, make sure you will have no difficulty in finding information about her. This will mean visiting your local or school library.

b Plan your investigation. Your task isn't to write a complete life history of your chosen person. It is to find out what she did in the campaign for votes and to decide how important her contribution was. Decide what exactly you are looking for by drawing up specific questions: for example, when and for how long did she campaign for the vote? In what ways did she campaign? How did people react to her efforts? What was the most important thing she did? And so on.

c Collect information and present results. Decide the most effective way to present the information you collect. You could use tape to present it as a radio programme, draw a storyboard for a TV documentary, or write notes for a museum display, for example.

2 Local study

Find out how people in your locality have voted in general elections during the twentieth century. You can find this information in *The Times Guides to the House of Commons* which is kept in many large libraries.

a Summarise the information in a chart or diagram.
b If one particular party has often won the election in your area, suggest why this has been so.
c If the results have been variable, suggest why this is so.

3 Essay

Answer one of the following essay questions:
a   During the twentieth century the laws on voting have been changed several times.
(i)   Describe these changes.
(ii) Which of these changes did most to make Britain more democratic?

b   The voting system used in British elections is called 'First Past the Post (FPTP)'.
(i)   Explain how the FPTP system works.
(ii) Opponents of this system sometimes say that FPTP also means 'Forever Power to the Tory Party.' Why should they say this?
(iii) What alternatives are there to the FPTP voting system? What are the arguments for and against using these alternatives in Britain?

Focus study · The impact of the Depression

This photograph of an unemployed man in Wigan in 1939 is one of the most famous photographs taken in Britain during the Depression. However, this was not an ordinary scene which the photographer came across by chance. The picture was carefully posed.

People everywhere spend much of their time working, making things, consuming them or trading them. We use the word economy to describe all these activities. A country's industry, farming, trade, banking and commerce are all parts of its economy.

In good times a country may produce a large number of goods and make a profit from its trade. Many of its people will have work and reasonable living standards, but good times never last. Throughout history, countries have gone through periods of economic depression. In a depression, production falls, trade dwindles, people earn and spend less money, and many lose their jobs. Countries which trade together are often all affected by the same depression.

One of the worst depressions in history began in 1929 and lasted until the mid 1930s. Known as the Great Depression, it affected nearly every country. Trade between them slumped. Thousands of companies went out of business. At least 25 million people lost their jobs and many also lost their homes.

This focus study describes how the Great Depression of the 1930s affected the people of Britain and Germany. It shows how the Depression changed the way they voted, how they thought about political matters, and how this destroyed the democratic system of Germany.

1 How were British people affected by the Depression?

In the 1920s most British workers paid unemployment insurance out of their wages every week. This meant that when they lost their jobs they got unemployment benefit for fifteen weeks. If they had not found a new job after fifteen weeks, they could then claim 32 weeks extra payment from government funds. This came from money collected in taxes and was known as the dole. Source 1, written by an out-of-work printer, gives us an idea of what dole money could buy.

Source 1

H.L. Beales and R.S. Lambert, *Memoirs of the Unemployed*, 1934.

8 shillings = 40 pence. In 1994 prices, that would be worth about £12.   6d = 6 old pennies or $2^1/_2$ pence, worth about 75p in 1994 prices.

letters for situations Letters applying for jobs.

second hand flannels Second hand trousers.

...I pay eight shillings* for a furnished room, which includes laundry. Gas costs 6d* weekly; letters for situations* 6d; razor blades, soap, blacking, haircuts, etc., average 3d; and 6d a week I save to help buy boots, second-hand flannels, etc. This leaves me 5s 6d a week for food .... My breakfast consists of three slices of bread and jam, and a cup of tea. Dinner, two slices of bread and about 2 oz of cheese. Tea, two boiled eggs, or $^1/_2$ lb of tomatoes, or a tin of baked beans.

As the number of out-of-work people soared, so did the cost of the dole. In an effort to save money, the government in 1931 cut the dole by 10 per cent and said that people claiming the dole must take a 'means test'. This meant that officials visited them in their homes to ask them about their earnings. If they had any savings they could not get any dole until they spent the savings. If they had children earning money – for example, by doing a paper round – the dole was cut. Source 2 describes some of the effects of the means test. It is from an interview with a former Welsh miner.

Source 2

Nigel Gray, *The Worst of Times. An Oral History of the Great Depression in Britain*, 1985.

If somebody had a decent home, the man from the Means Test came and made a list of what you had. Then you were told to sell a wardrobe this week, some chairs next week, some pictures the week after, until you perhaps only had your bed, two chairs and a table left. Only then would you able to claim off the Public Assistance.

It wasn't only unemployed people who were affected by the Depression. Source 3 shows one of the ways in which it also affected people in work and in business. It is part of a conversation between the owner of a shop in Glasgow and a politician who was touring Britain in 1932.

Source 3

Fenner Brockway, *Hungry England*, 1932. The author was leader of the Independent Labour Party. He toured Britain in 1932 to investigate the effects of the Depression on people's lives.

24lbs 24 pounds in weight, equivalent to around 10 kg.

'Can you tell me how much your business has dropped since the Means Test came into operation?' I ask ....
   'Last October I took £19 16s 10d (£19.84) a week for bread. Last week I took £7 7s 6d. I now sell 24 lbs* of margarine a week; I used to sell twelve lbs a day. I am not selling any cheese at all, nor practically any tea ... I used to sell four cases of milk, containing 24 pints, a day; now I sell one in three weeks. You see that row of jam jars?... I don't remember the last time I sold a jar ....'.

Many of the unemployed left home to look for work in better-off parts of the country. Source 4 describes a family that did so.

Source 4

Frank Cousins, leader of the Transport and General Workers Union, talking in a television interview in the 1960s.

Shields A town at the mouth of the River Tyne, 450 kilometres from London.

I happened to be in a transport cafe on the Great North Road, when a young couple came in with a child in a nearly broken-down pram. They were walking from Shields* because the man understood he could get a job in London. They came into the cafe and sat down, and they fetched a baby's feeding bottle out and it had water in. They fed the baby with water, and then sort of lifted the kiddy's dress up ...and it had a newspaper nappy on. They took this off and sort of wiped the baby's bottom with the nappy they'd taken off and then picked up another newspaper and put that on for another nappy. And I think if ever I felt resentment against the system it was on that occasion. I thought somebody ought to do something about it.

Older people and people with family commitments could not move to find a job. Unable to find work and unable to move, the long-term unemployed suffered poverty and hardship for many years. Source 5 describes one such family and Source 6 shows a scene that was common in many towns.

Source 5

From a radio broadcast in 1935 in which the wife of an unemployed worker described their situation.

My husband never changes his dole money, but although he doesn't keep a halfpenny pocket money, we still can't manage. And we don't waste nothing. And there's no enjoyment comes out of our money – no pictures, no papers, no sports. Everything is patched and mended in our house .... I haven't had a holiday for thirteen years. My husband's never been to a football match.

Source 6

This photograph, taken in 1936, shows unemployed men on a street corner with nothing to do.

Questions

1 The man in Source 1 could have saved 3d a week by growing a beard, not having his hair cut, not blacking his shoes, etc. Why do you think he spent money on these things?

2 Read Source 3. What effect might this shop owner's fall in sales have had on local bakeries, dairies and other such businesses?

3 Read Source 4. What was it that shocked Frank Cousins so much?

4 Roughly how old do you think were the men in Source 6? Why were men of that age likely to be unemployed for a long time?

5 Using Sources 1–6, write a paragraph or prepare a short talk describing how unemployment affected people's lives during the Depression.

2 Depths of Depression

Source 1 is from a radio discussion broadcast in 1933. It was about slum housing in Britain. One of the speakers got out a newspaper parcel while he was speaking, and pulled from it a large, dead rat. He said:

Source 1

Quoted in Wilfred Fienburgh, *25 Momentous Years. A 25th Anniversary in the History of the Daily Herald*, 1955.

> I live in a house in which there are six families in seven rooms, 31 people in all. My family live in a damp basement. There are seven of us, all sleeping in one room. It is in such repair that we cannot leave the babies alone because of the rats. We hear them scratching at night. I brought one along with me. We caught it in the gas oven this afternoon.

Now look at Source 2 – two advertisements from a weekly magazine in one of the worst years of the Depression. Does this mean that some people were not affectd by it? If so, why did some people escape the Depression, but not others?

Source 2

From the *Illustrated London News*, a weekly magazine aimed at middle and upper class readers, 27 May 1933. The advertisement on the right is for flats to rent in a fashionable area of London. The other shows how you might have furnished such a flat.

■ How much would an unfurnished flat in Source 2 have cost to rent each week? How does this compare with the rent in Source 1?

CONSULT **LIBERTY's**
FOR ADVICE ON ALL MATTERS CONCERNED WITH THE EQUIPMENT OF A HOUSE OR OF ONE APARTMENT
DESIGNS AND ESTIMATES AT COMPETITIVE PRICES FREE
LIBERTY & CO. REGENT ST. LONDON W.1

LONDON FLATS

The Entrance Hall, 2, Weymouth Street.

2, WEYMOUTH STREET, W.1, within fifty yards of Portland Place, is an imposing block of SERVICE FLATS. Central Heating and Constant Hot Water are installed throughout. Meals may be taken in the flats or in the charming restaurant.

The accommodation is varied and rentals range from £275 p.a. for Unfurnished Flats; 6 guineas per week for Furnished Flats.

For details of this building and others similar, owned by Associated London Properties Ltd. write for illustrated booklet to ST. ERMIN'S, Westminster, S.W.1, or 'Phone Victoria 1723.

A series of advertisements giving information of other properties owned by Associated London Properties Ltd. will be published on this page fortnightly.

Why did the Depression not harm everybody?

The Depression put many people out of work. However, unemployment was not a new problem started by the Depression. There was severe unemployment in Britain's traditional industries throughout the 1920s. This was because the usual pattern of trade, in which Britain sold textiles, ships and machinery to non-industrial countries in return for raw materials and food, was disrupted by the First World War. Coalmines, shipyards, and iron and steel plants never fully recovered. Workers in these industries steadily lost their jobs.

When the Depression began in 1929 the worst effects were felt in the industries that were already struggling. Source 3 shows how workers in the old industries were affected in comparison with the country as a whole.

Many of the unemployed left the old industrial areas to look for work in the Midlands and the South-East. There, new factories making such things

Source 3

Percentage of people out of work in the old industries, compared to the national average

	1929	1932	1936
Coal	18	41	25
Cotton	14.5	31	15
Shipbuilding	23	59.5	31
Iron & steel	20	48.5	29.5
National average	10	23	12.5

Source 4

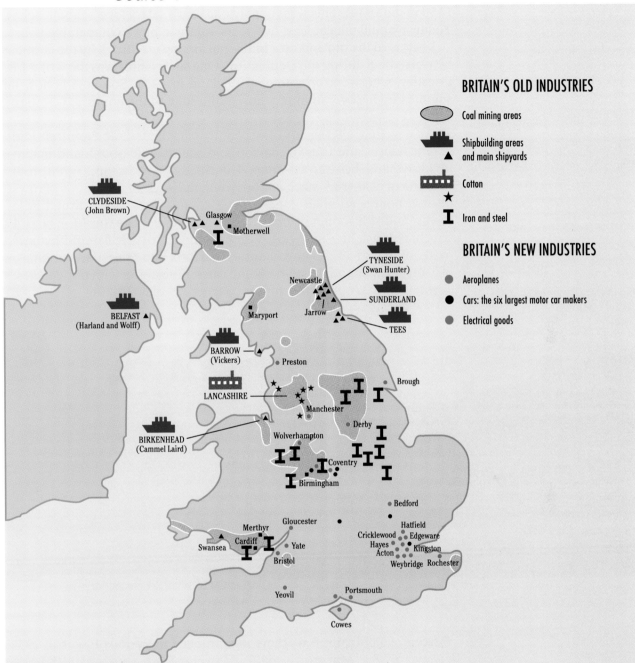

BRITAIN'S OLD INDUSTRIES

- Coal mining areas
- Shipbuilding areas and main shipyards ▲
- Cotton
- ★ Iron and steel
- I Iron and steel

BRITAIN'S NEW INDUSTRIES

- Aeroplanes
- Cars: the six largest motor car makers
- Electrical goods

Britain's industries between the wars.

as cars and electrical goods had opened in the past twenty years. There was little unemployment in these new industries before the Depression began, and new factories continued to open during the Depression. In Greater London alone, 532 new factories opened between 1932 and 1937.

Most workers who had jobs in the Depression had to go without pay rises. There was less overtime and more short-time working, so many earned less than before the slump. Some even had their pay cut. The fall in people's earnings was not as disastrous as it might seem. The prices of goods also fell during the 1930s. This meant that many people's earnings rose in real value, even if their pay had been cut. This was especially true of middle-class people with secure jobs. They could afford to spend more than ever before on housing, cars, household equipment and holidays.

A new semi-detached house in the London area, for example, cost around £450 in the 1930s. This was roughly one year's salary for a schoolteacher. Today it would take at least five years' salary to buy a comparable house.

Visitors to the old and new industrial areas were struck by the contrast between them during the Depression. One such visitor was the writer J.B. Priestley, who went on a tour of England in 1933. Source 5 is how he summed up his overall impression of the state of the country.

Source 5

J.B. Priestley, *English Journey*, 1934.

There was, first, old England, the country of cathedrals and minsters and manor houses and inns, of parson and squire; guide-book and quaint highways and byways .... Then, I decided, there is the ... industrial England of coal, iron, steel, cotton, wool, railways; of thousands of rows of little houses all alike ... devastated countryside, sooty, dismal little towns, and still sootier grim fortress-like cities .... The third England, I concluded, was the new post-war England .... of arterial and by-pass roads, of filling stations and factories that look like exhibition buildings, of giant cinemas and dance-halls and cafes, bungalows with tiny garages, cocktail bars, Woolworths, motor coaches, wireless, hiking ....

Source 6

New, 'semi-detached' houses nearing completion in Southgate.

Source 7 A street in Wigan, Lancashire, in 1939.

Questions

1   **Percentage of insured workers unemployed in various towns in 1934**

| Jarrow | 67.8 | Maryport | 57.0 | Coventry | 5.1 | Oxford | 5.1 |
| Merthyr | 61.9 | Motherwell | 37.4 | Luton | 7.7 | St Albans | 3.9 |

Look carefully at the figures above. Using Sources 3 and 4, as well as the information in the text, suggest why the figures on the left were so much greater than the figures on the right.

2   Look at Sources 6 and 7, then read Source 5 again.

a J. B. Priestley wrote that there were three Englands in the 1930s. Explain in your own words what he meant by this.

b Which of the 'three Englands' do you think (i) Source 6, (ii) Source 7 belonged to?

c Sources 6 and 7 show great differences in life-style and housing during the Depression. How might these differences be explained?

3 Politicians and the Slump 1929–32

Out-of-work people expected their governments to help them. When they failed to do so, some took direct action or joined extreme political parties to try to change things.

Why did politicians find it so difficult to deal with the Depression? Why couldn't they provide work for the unemployed? This section describes how the British and German governments reacted to the Depression between 1929 and 1933, and how both failed to overcome it.

Why couldn't governments overcome the Depression?

The British government

The Depression began shortly after Labour won the general election of 1929. Led by Ramsay Macdonald, the new Labour government promised to help the unemployed. Although Labour had most seats in the House of Commons (287) it did not have more than the Conservatives (261) and Liberals (51) combined. This meant that Conservatives and Liberals could vote together to stop Labour introducing measures they did not like. Labour therefore could not take any action on unemployment which the other parties disliked. By 1931 nearly 3 million people were out of work and the government had done little to reduce the number.

The 1931 budget crisis

This led to a political crisis. The more unemployed people there were, the more money the government had to spend on paying them the dole. Yet the more unemployed there were, the fewer workers there were to pay taxes to the government. A huge gap opened up between what the government spent and what it earned.

The problem grew worse in 1930 when banks in Germany and Austria went bankrupt as a result of the Depression. Worried foreigners who had big savings in the Bank of England started to withdraw their money, in gold. To cover such big withdrawals, the Bank of England needed to borrow gold from the United States and France. However, French and American banks did not want to lend money to Britain while it was spending more than it earned. They wanted to be sure that Britain could repay any money it borrowed.

To close the gap between spending and income, a government committee advised that cuts of around 10 per cent were needed in the pay of everyone paid from government funds. This included not only workers such as police, teachers, soldiers and sailors, but also everyone on the dole. Half the ministers in the government refused to agree to such big cuts and so the government broke up.

The National Government

Ramsay Macdonald did not resign, despite the collapse of his government. Instead he formed a coalition government with four Labour, four Conservative and two Liberal ministers. It was known as the National Government. Quickly they agreed on pay cuts. They cut police pay by 5 per cent, the armed forces by 10 per cent and teachers by 15 per cent. Insurance benefits and the dole were cut by 10 per cent.

Source 1

A poster for the General Election of October 1931 asks voters to support the National Government set up two months earlier.

Smokeless Chimneys and—
ANXIOUS MOTHERS!

THE REMEDY

VOTE FOR THE **NATIONAL GOVERNMENT**

The cuts achieved the government's aim, which was to borrow money from abroad. French and American bankers lent £19 million. This did not stop foreigners from losing confidence in Britain and withdrawing their money. Their confidence was shattered when 12,000 sailors at the Royal Navy base in Invergordon, mutinied in protest against their pay cuts. Foreign investors panicked and the flow of money out of Britain became a flood. In September 1931, as a result, the government had to take Britain off the Gold Standard and devalue the pound.

For the next few years the main aim of the National Government was to restore business confidence and to close the gap between government spending and income. Spending money on helping the unemployed was seen as a low priority. Amongst the government's few measures were a scheme for the unemployed to grow vegetables on allotments, and a programme of physical education for out-of-work men.

The German government

Germany was hit harder by the Depression than almost any other country. Germany had borrowed huge amounts of money from the United States in the 1920s. After the Wall Street Crash of 1929, American banks demanded repayment of these loans. German companies which had borrowed heavily were ruined, putting their employees out of work.

After losing their jobs, German workers were paid unemployment benefit for 26 weeks. After that, they had to depend on 'crisis payments' from the government, then on charity. As the number of unemployed rose, the government was paying much more on benefits to the unemployed than it was receiving in tax. Like the British government, it had to think of a way of closing the gap between its earnings and its spending.

A divided government

Germany's system of voting was proportional representation (see page 50). This gave many parties seats in the Reichstag – the German parliament. Often there were so many parties that no single party had enough seats to form a government. This is what had happened in an election in 1928. No single party had a majority in the Reichstag, so five parties joined together to form a coalition government. These parties, however, disagreed almost every time they had to make a decision.

When they met in 1930 to discuss how to close the gap between income and spending, three of the parties suggested cutting unemployment pay. The Social Democratic Party strongly disagreed, and resigned from the coalition. As it was the largest party in the Reichstag, the government could not continue to function without its support.

Government by decree

The solution to this problem lay in the President's hands, for he had the power to make laws by decree in an emergency. In this emergency, the President asked the leader of a smaller party, Heinrich Brüning, to head a new government without the SPD. He would use his power to make laws by decree to put Brüning's decisions into effect.

Helped by the President, Brüning reduced government spending, cut the pay of government workers and increased taxes. These measures were unpopular. However, when the Reichstag voted against them, the President simply dismissed it and ordered elections for a new Parliament.

The election did not help Brüning. Millions of unemployed voters voted for extreme parties which promised work if they came to power. Adolf Hitler's National Socialist, or Nazi Party, did especially well. The Nazis increased their seats from twelve to 107, becoming the second largest party in the Reichstag.

For the next two years, Brüning had to continue making laws by decree. He made further cuts in government spending and raised taxes again. These harsh measures started to close the gap between government spending and income, but they did nothing to help the jobless. The number of people registered as unemployed rose from 1.6 million in October 1929 to 6.13 million in 1932. In addition there were between 1 and 3 million jobless people not on the registers. Altogether between 7 and 9 million Germans were out of work by 1932 (Source 2).

Source 2

Unemployed, homeless men living on waste ground in Berlin in 1930. One of them is shaving in front of a broken piece of mirror. The writing on the wall says 'Golden Corner Boarding House'.

Questions

1 Look at Source 1.
   a What was the National Government?
   b Which party had been in government before it?
   c What was the main reason why that government had not been able to solve the problem shown in the poster?
   d Why did the National Government also fail to solve the problem?

2 In Britain and Germany, neither government had an overall majority in Parliament. How did this affect the way each tackled the Depression?

4 Politics and the unemployed

To try to force their governments into action, some unemployed people joined protest movements. Others joined political parties to campaign for change. In elections, many voted for parties which promised to provide work if they won.

The result was that protest groups and extremist parties grew in size and influence in·many countries. Often they used direct action such as street demonstrations to achieve their aims. Sometimes they turned to violence, with rival groups fighting each other in the streets. In this section you can find out about the British people who became activists during the Depression. As you read about their feelings and experiences, ask yourself what made these people behave in these ways.

What did the activists want?

Demonstrating in the street is something that most people do not do. This was as true 50 years ago as it is today. In Source 1 Max Cohen, an unemployed Londoner, described how he felt when he unexpectedly came across a large street demonstration in 1931.

Source 1

Max Cohen, *I Was One of the Unemployed*, 1941.

I had never seen such a large crowd .... A vast elemental roar smote the sky, re-echoed and vibrated from the tall buildings.
  'Not-a-penny-off-the-dole!'
  'Not-a-man-off-benefit!'
  'Down-with-the-Means-Test!'
For a moment I hesitated on the pavement as the river of people swept past me, and then I plunged into it.

Many protests took the form of 'hunger marches' in which out-of-work people marched long distances to London to give petitions to the government or to Parliament. The most famous hunger march of all was organised by Ellen Wilkinson, the MP for Jarrow, a shipbuilding town on the River Tyne. Jarrow depended entirely on shipbuilding for jobs. After Hunter's shipyard there closed down, four men out of every five were unemployed. To draw attention to their desperate situation, 200 men marched 450 kilometres from Jarrow to London where they presented a petition to Parliament. According to the police who followed them, the petition said:

Source 2

Special Branch report on the Jarrow March, 6 November 1936.

During the last fifteen years Jarrow has passed through a period of depression without parallel in the town's history. Its shipyard is closed. Its steelworks have been denied the right to reopen. Where formerly 8,000 people ...were employed, only 100 men are now employed on a temporary scheme. The town cannot be derelict, and therefore your petitioners humbly pray that His Majesty's government ...should realise the urgent need that work should be found without further delay.

When they reached London the marchers were given tea in the House of Commons and taken on a sight-seeing trip, but the petition achieved nothing. The government did nothing to revive industry in the town.

Source 3

Marchers on the Jarrow Crusade pass through a village near Bedford, in rain on 27 October 1936.

Source 4

Police fight with 'hunger marchers' of the NUWM in Bristol in 1931. Fighting started when police stopped the marchers from entering a hall where the Trades Union Congress was meeting. The marchers were protesting against the TUC's refusal to support their march.

When the marchers returned to Jarrow, they found that their dole had been cut for the time they were away. They had, however, won great public sympathy for Jarrow, and their crusade is one of the best remembered events of the 1930s.

With the exception of the Jarrow Crusade, the hunger marches of the 1930s were organised by the National Unemployed Workers' Movement (NUWM). Because the NUWM was led by Communists, the police kept a close watch on its marches and often tried to break them up. Other workers' organisations, such as the Trades Union Congress, also mistrusted the NUWM's Communist leaders and refused to support the hunger marches. Source 4 shows what happened when unemployed miners in the NUWM marched from South Wales to Bristol to demonstrate against the TUC.

Source 4 was not typical of the NUWM's hunger marches. Most of their protests were peaceful. However, some organisations which sprang up during the Depression regularly used violence. The most violent new political group was the British Union of Fascists, founded in 1932 by Oswald Mosley. A young man who joined the BUF in 1932 explains his reasons for doing so in Source 5.

Source 5

Jeffrey Hamm, *Action Replay. An autobiography*, 1983. The author became a leading member of the British Union of Fascists and of later extreme right wing groups in the 1950s and 1960s.

I used to go every Saturday morning to the ... magistrate's court in Pontypool, where I listened to the most extraordinary cases. Man after man would shuffle into the dock, to hear the charge ... 'Stealing a quantity of coal, to the value of one shilling'. The 'criminal' was an unemployed miner who had gone to a railway siding where hundreds of rusting trucks were standing, piled high with coal for which there was no market. He had taken a quantity of coal, and was running home with it, to light a fire in his empty grate for his wife and children, when he had been arrested. Ridiculous fines would be imposed on these unhappy men which of course they could not pay. In default, they trooped off to Cardiff prison, week after week ....

It was in revolt against this state of things that I ... turned to Fascism, which was to me, as to so many others, basically an economic creed.

The British Union of Fascists imitated the German Nazi Party and the Italian Fascist Party by wearing black uniforms. Like the Nazis, they were anti-semitic, attacking Jews and their property especially in the East End of London, where many Jews lived. From 1935 onwards the black-uniformed Fascists regularly held meetings and staged marches through the East End, terrorising the Jewish population. In reply, Communists and various Jewish organisations staged anti-Fascist demonstrations. An anti-Fascist, named Gladys Gibson, later described one such demonstration:

Source 6

Gladys Gibson, an investigator for the Unemployment Assistance Board, quoted in Nigel Gray, *The Worst of Times*, 1985.

Yids London slang for Jews.

I marched with the anti-Fascists, passing many blocks of flats bristling with Union Jacks, with women at their windows screaming that we were traitors and Jewish scum. The police were there in force to keep the two crowds apart. After a wild meeting we reformed our ranks and were very glad of police protection as the Blackshirts ran alongside shouting 'The Yids*. The Yids. We gotta get rid of the Yids' and trying to get at us. Many a citizen of Jewish appearance who had been an onlooker was glad to join us to escape the rage of the Fascists who, only a week before, had thrown a Jewish baby through a plate-glass window.

Questions

1 Look at Source 1. What were these people protesting about?

2 Look at Source 3:
   a What were the Crusades of the Middle Ages?
   b Suggest why the Jarrow workers called their march a crusade.
   c There was great public support and sympathy for the Jarrow Crusade. How do Sources 2 and 3 help us to understand why?
   d Nobody in Jarrow got a job as a result of the Jarrow Crusade. If it was such a failure, why do you think it was remembered for so long?

3 a According to Source 5, what was the main reason why people joined the British Union of Fascists?
   b Judging by Source 6, what other reasons did people have for supporting the Fascists?

5 Depression and dictatorship

In Germany, so many people supported the extremist Nazi Party that its leader, Adolf Hitler, was able to come to power in 1933 and set up a dictatorship. In Britain there was no threat to democracy. Despite the activities of extremists the National Government stayed in power throughout the 1930s. This section asks why democracy was destroyed in Germany, but not in Britain, even though they suffered similar problems.

The Nazi rise to power

From 1930–1932 the German Chancellor, Brüning, cut spending and raised taxes. Although this closed the gap between what the government spent and what it earned, it sent the jobless figures soaring to over 6 million. In 1932 Brüning decided he could safely spend government money on creating jobs for some of the unemployed. By this time, however, he was very unpopular. A senior army officer, General Schleicher, took advantage of his unpopularity to plot against him. He persuaded President Hindenburg to sack Brüning and replace him with another Centre Party politician, Franz von Papen.

Like Brüning, Papen did not have enough supporters in the Reichstag to get his measures made into law. So he organised another election in July 1932, hoping to get more seats. This did not happen. So many of the unemployed voted for the Nazis that they doubled their vote and became the biggest party in the Reichstag.

As leader of the biggest party, Hitler demanded the post of Chancellor. President Hindenburg refused. He mistrusted Hitler and thought the Nazis were too violent. Instead, Hindenburg asked Papen to stay as Chancellor and said he would issue decrees to make Papen's decisions into law.

Papen tried to provide work for some of the unemployed by creating a National Labour Service. This gave work to young men on projects that required heavy manual labour, such as digging ditches on farms. He also created jobs with a road-building programme. However, the Reichstag did not support his government and voted in September 1932 that it had no confidence in him. Faced with this no-confidence vote, Papen arranged yet another election, hoping to get a Reichstag that supported him.

Source 1

Many unemployed Germans joined the Nazi Party as uniformed Stormtroopers. This photograph shows Stormtroopers at a Nazi rally in Dortmund in 1931.

The November election gave Papen's Centre Party a few more seats, but the Nazis were still the biggest party in the Reichstag. Papen would therefore have to rely on the President making decrees for him. At this point, however, General Schleicher put a new obstacle in Papen's way. Schleicher told the President that the army would not agree to Papen staying in power. As no government can exist without the army's support, Papen had to resign. Schleicher himself took over as Chancellor.

Schleicher lasted only two months. He too could not get the Reichstag to agree to his decisions. He too had to ask Hindenburg to make laws for him by decree. Not surprisingly, Hindenburg was suspicious. Only weeks before, Schleicher had warned that the army would not support a government that ruled by decree. Now he was wanting to do exactly that. Hindenburg refused and asked Schleicher to resign.

Two Chancellors had come and gone in the past eight months. Hindenburg had no alternative but to offer the post to the leader of the largest party in the Reichstag, Adolf Hitler. He made Hitler Chancellor on 30 January 1933. A man who hated the democratic system was now the leader of Germany.

The British Fascists

You read in section 3 that Britain had a party similar to the German Nazi Party. The British Union of Fascists, formed in 1932 by Sir Oswald Mosley, aimed to provide 'national reconstruction' through corporations which would replace Parliament. The Fascists attracted support mainly through public meetings, rallies and uniformed parades (Source 2).

Source 2

Blackshirted members of the British Union of Fascists parade in a street in Manchester in February 1934.

From the start, meetings of the BUF often led to fighting between blackshirted Fascists and left-wing groups such as the Communist Party. From 1935 onwards there was a great deal of fighting in London's East End, where the Fascists held marches and rallies to intimidate the Jewish population. The worst fighting took place on Sunday, 4 October 1936 when Communists, Jewish groups and members of the NUWM decided to halt a Fascist march through the East End. In the 'Battle of Cable Street' that day, 70 people were injured in street fighting.

Why wasn't there a Fascist takeover in Britain?

Many people feared that such violence would lead to a revolution in Britain. However, not everybody was a Fascist or an anti-Fascist. According to a survey of unemployed people made between 1936 and 1939:

Source 3

Carnegie Trust, *Disinherited Youth*, 1943. A survey of unemployed young people in Liverpool, Cardiff and Glasgow between 1936 and 1939.

Out of a total of 1,490 young unemployed men for whom information was available, only twenty ... were attached to one or other of the political organisations .... At least 10 per cent of the young men did not even know the names of the various political parties.... The overwhelming majority of the men had no political convictions whatsoever.

Source 4 gives a clue to why many young men felt like that:

Source 4

An unemployed labourer quoted in H.L. Beales and R.S. Lambert, *Memoirs of the Unemployed*, 1934.

Politics do not interest me very much. I see a paper now and again and the politicians seem to be saying the same words over and over again. They always seem to be saying things will get better next month. Any improvement in conditions won't be due to them. I worry over my position and try to think what I can do. But I can never see a way out.

People used the word 'apathy' to describe that kind of mood among the unemployed, but apathy wasn't the only reason why people didn't join revolutionary groups. An American researcher in London noted that 'talk of revolution is conspicuous by its absence'. He explained that:

Source 5

E.W. Bakke, *The Unemployed Man. A Social Study*, 1933.

The Scheme (unemployment insurance) has ... kept diet from falling to unhealthy levels; it has kept the workers from falling into arrears on their rent; it has made it unnecessary to dispose of home furnishings to the extent that would have been necessary without it; ... it has kept unrest to a minimum.

Source 6

The BUF never published its membership figures. The figures here are estimates made by senior members of the BUF, by the British Press and by the police.

Source 6 throws further light on why the British Fascists were less successful than the German Nazis during the Depression. It compares the rates of unemployment in the two countries with the support for each party.

Year	No of unemployed in Britain (monthly average)	Membership of British Union of Fascists	No of unemployed in Germany (monthly average)	Membership of the Nazi Party * estimate
1929	1,216,000		2,543,000	96,918
1930	1,917,000		4,169,000	129,563
1931	2,630,000		5,550,000	200,000*
1932	2,745,000		6,071,000	450,000
1933	2,521,000	17,000	5,006,000	849,009
1934	2,159,000	50,000	3,480,000	1,700,000*
1935	2,036,000	5,000	2,725,000	2,493,890
1936	1,755,000	15,500	2,150,000	2,600,000*
1937	1,484,000	16,000	1,450,000	2,793,890
1938	1,791,000	16,500	775,000	4,985,400
1939	1,514,000	22,500	275,000	5,339,567

In an attempt to stop street battles such as the 'Battle of Cable Street', the British government introduced a Public Order Act in 1937. This gave the police the power to forbid processions and it banned the wearing of uniforms at political meetings. Source 7 shows the effect this had on the British Union of Fascists.

Source 7

A march by the BUF through the East End in 1937, shortly after the introduction of the Public Order Act.

Questions

1 How can Source 6 be used to explain why the BUF was less successful than the German Nazi Party?

2 a Look at Sources 1 and 2. What similarities can you see between the German Nazi Party and the British Union of Fascists?

  b What difference is there between the Fascist parades in Source 2 and Source 7? What was the reason for this difference?
   Use sources 3–7 to give as many reasons why the British Union of Fascists did not become as big a party as the Nazi Party.

3 Look back at the information in this section and on pages 74–75 about how Hitler and the Nazis came to power in 1933.

  a What policy did Chancellor Brüning follow between 1930–1932?

  b How might these events have been different if Brüning had spent money on job creation schemes instead of following that policy?

  c How might events have been different if Germany had not used proportional representation in elections?

6 Overcoming the Depression 1933–39

You have read that governments in Britain and Germany did not want to spend much money on helping the unemployed. Their main aim was to balance their earnings with their spending, so as to avoid inflation.

In Germany Hitler and the Nazi Party came to power in 1933, and started spending large amounts of money on creating jobs for the unemployed. Britain's National Government did not do so. This section compares Germany's job creation schemes with Britain's approach, and invites you to judge how effective these policies were.

How effective was job creation?

Germany

Adolf Hitler, leader of the Nazi Party, became Chancellor of Germany in January 1933. One of the promises he had made in his election campaigns was to give Germany's jobless 'work and bread'.

Fortunately for Hitler, the previous government had already started creating jobs for the unemployed (see page 79). Papen had set up a National Labour Service to give young men jobs on projects that needed manual labour, such as digging drainage ditches on farms. Hitler took over the National Labour Service and expanded it. The men in it were put into uniform and sent away to work camps. There they received pocket money instead of wages, and did military training as well as work. In 1935 a Labour Service Law said that all men aged eighteen to 25 must spend six months in the service. With hundreds of thousands of young Germans entering the camps, the jobless figures dropped sharply.

Hitler also took over Papen's road building programme. He expanded it in June 1933 by ordering the creation of a network of motorways, linking Germany's major cities. This gave work to never fewer than 80,000 men over the next five years. Also in June 1933, a Law to Reduce Unemployment gave government grants for building new homes, schools, hospitals and other public services. To make sure that as many people as possible had work, the law said that all building work should be done by hand: machinery should be used only when absolutely necessary.

Source 1

Equipped only with spades, thousands of men give the Nazi salute as they prepare to start work, building a motorway in Germany in 1934.

■ Suggest why the government paid men with spades to build a motorway instead of using earth-moving machinery.

One of Hitler's aims was to build up Germany's armed forces. This too had a big impact on the unemployment figures. From March 1935 onwards, all eighteen to 25 year olds had to do military service for two years. The armed forces grew from 100,000 in 1933 to 1,400,000 in 1939, cutting over a million from the unemployment registers.

Source 2 shows what happened to the jobless figures in Germany after Hitler came to power.

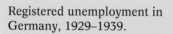

Source 2

Registered unemployment in Germany, 1929–1939.

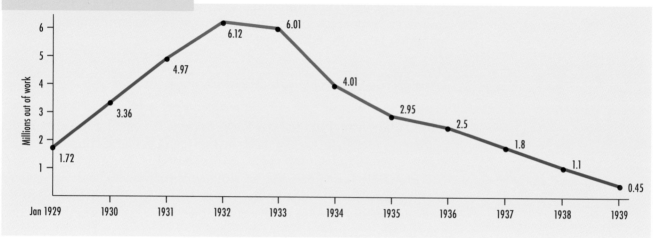

Britain

The British government spent much less money than the Germans on overcoming the Depression. Its main job-creation measure was a Special Areas Act in 1934. This gave grants to local authorities and voluntary agencies in four 'Distressed Areas': South Wales, Tyneside, West Cumberland and Scotland. The grants could be spent on improvement schemes for such things as hospitals and water supplies. Grants were also used for several large projects, including a new steel works at Ebbw Vale in South Wales. By 1938 the Act had provided grants of about £8.5 million, creating around 15,000 jobs.

The government also gave help to the industry which had been hardest hit by the slump. In 1935 it started a 'scrap and build' scheme for the shipbuilding industry. This gave loans to shipping companies to scrap old ships and order new ones. The government also lent money to the Cunard shipping company to buy two new ocean liners, the Queen Mary and the Queen Elizabeth, from John Brown's shipyard on the Clyde.

Source 3

'Work at last', a *Daily Express* cartoon, 1937.

'Work at last'

From 1935 onwards, the biggest boost to jobs came from Hitler's Germany. As Hitler increased his armed forces and stocks of weapons, so British armed forces spent more on weapons, in case of a future war with Germany. Between 1935–1939 spending on arms rose threefold. This created jobs especially in the steel and engineering industries.

Source 4

Unemployed people in Britain, 1929–1939.

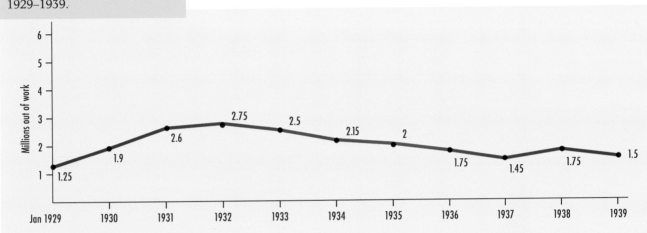

Questions

1 a Add these notes to a copy of Source 2: Brüning's government, Papen's government, Hitler's government, National Labour Service set up, motorway building programme started, National Labour Service Law, compulsory military service introduced.

   b Add these notes to a copy of Source 4: Labour Government 1929–31, National Government 1931–1945, Special Areas Act, start of the scrap and build scheme.

   c Compare Sources 2 and 4. In which country did unemployment drop fastest? Which of the notes on your graphs best explain the drop?

2 The German Government did something that created jobs which the British Government did not do. What was it?

3 Look at Source 3.
   a What and where were the 'Distressed areas?'
   b What does the cartoon suggest about the effect of the Special Areas Act on the Distressed Areas?
   c What is the machine made of? Why is it labelled 'work'?
   b What point do you think the cartoonist was trying to make?

Review: Slump

Many writers and photographers have portrayed the 1930s as a time of deep depression. The strongest images in books about the 1930s are usually those of unemployed men (page 69), of the Jarrow marchers (page 77), and of black-shirted Fascists (page 80). How accurate are these images?

Wal Hannington, who organised many of the hunger marches of the 1930s, portrayed the Depression in his autobiography published in 1967:

Source 1

Wal Hannington, *Never on our knees*, 1967. Wal Hannington was a Communist who helped organise the hunger marches of the 1930s.

The unemployed did not quietly suffer their degradation and poverty. They were hungry; their wives and children were hungry. They marched on the streets with mighty protest demonstrations .... If history is to be truly recorded, our future historians must include this feature of the 'Hungry Thirties'.

In the last twenty years, historians have added new features to their portrayals of the 1930s. John Stevenson, one of Britain's leading social historians, stated his views in Source 2.

Source 2

J. Stevenson, *Myth and Reality. Britain in the 1930s*, 1976.

Beside the pictures of the dole queues and the hunger marches must be placed those of another Britain, of new industries, prosperous suburbs and a rising standard of living .... For those in work, the Thirties was a period of rising living standards and new standards of consumption ....

The writer of Source 3, Nigel Gray, would strongly disagree with Source 2. In the introduction to his book about the Depression, he wrote:

Source 3

Nigel Gray, *The Worst of Times. An Oral history of the Great Depression*, 1985.

This book came about as a result of the anger I felt when I first encountered the arguments of ...historians who claim there was no Great Depression in Britain between the wars. ... This seems to me so glib that it is an insult to millions .... For people involved in older industries like mining, steel, cotton, ship-building, agriculture, the Twenties and Thirties were years not of increasing wealth, but of uncertainty, long-term unemployment, continual humiliation and deep poverty.

Questions

1 Look back though this focus study (pages 67–85).
   a Find sources which support Wal Hannington's views (Source 1).
   b Find sources which support John Stevenson's view (Source 2).

2 Which of the two views, Hannington's or Stevenson's, do you think is best supported by the sources you have found? Why?

3 Is there anything about Hannington's or Stevenson's backgrounds that might have affected their views? How?

4 The photograph on page 67 is a posed photograph. It is also one of the most famous and widely used pictures of the Depression. Why should a posed photograph be so widely used?

5 Read Source 3.
   a Why do you think the arguments of 'historians who claim there was no Great Depression' made Nigel Gray so angry?
   b Nigel Gray did his own research into the depression because of the anger he felt. He interviewed many people who had lived in the 1930s and wrote 'an oral history of the Great Depression'. What difficulties do you think he would have faced in trying to make his book accurate and objective?

BRITAIN IN THE TWENTIETH CENTURY

A Caring People

JOSH BROOMAN

General Editor: Josh Brooman

Contents

Changing care and welfare

1 Rich and poor in the 1900s   91

2 Thinking about the poor   95

3 The Liberal Reforms of 1906–1914   98

4 State care between the wars   102

5 A growing nation   105

   Review: Changing care and welfare   109

Focus study · Creating the Welfare State

1 The eve of the Welfare State   111

2 War and welfare   113

3 The birth of the Welfare State   117

4 Bevan and the doctors   120

5 Problems and achievements of the Welfare State 123

   Review: The Welfare State   127

Longman Group UK Limited
Longman House, Burnt Mill, Harlow, Essex
CM20 2JE, England and Associated Companies throughout the World.

First published 1994

ISBN 0582 245974

Set in Concorde and Tekton

Printed in Great Britain
by Butler and Tanner Ltd, Frome and London

The Publishers' policy is to use paper manufactured from sustainable forests.

Design and production by Hart McLeod

Illustrations by Stephen Hawes

Cover photograph *Ancoats Hospital Outpatients Department 1952*, by L.S. Lowry. © Mrs Carol Ann Danes/Whitworth Art Gallery.

Acknowledgements

The written sources in this book are taken from many different kinds of published material. Some were originally written in old-fashioned or unusual language. This has not been altered, but in most cases, unusual or difficult words are explained in the margin. In many of the sources words have been left out. A cut in the middle of a sentence is shown like this ...; and at the end of a sentence like this ....

We are grateful to the following for permission to reproduce photographs. The numbers refer to page numbers.

From the *Daily Herald*, 6 July 1948, 127; Hulton-Deutsch Collection, 115 below, 121; Imperial War Museum, London (neg. no. Q.33,682), 103; Liverpool City Council, Development & Environmental Services Dept., 94; Mansell Collection, 97; National Museum of Labour History, Manchester, 116; from the *News Chronicle*, 7 August 1945, courtesy Associated Newspapers Group, 122; from *Picture Post*, 112 (21 January 1939), 115 above (4 January 1941); Popperfoto, 124; Royal Holloway and Bedford New College, Surrey (Photo: Bridgeman Art Library), 89; Salvation Army, 90; from George Sims: *Living London* Vol. 2, 1903, 98; Suffolk Record Office, 101; Chris Thomond, 126; Topham Picture Source, 108, 110, 120.

We are indebted to the Central Statistical Office for permission to reproduce the figures on p105 from material in *Social Trends* 23 p97, HMSO 1991 and *Annual Abstract of Statistics* p40, 1992.

We have been unable to trace the copyright holder of the figure on p126 (Peacock and Wiseman 1961; CSO 1977 and earlier equivalents) and would appreciate any information which would enable us to do so.

Changing care and welfare

Britain before the Welfare State: a painting by Sir Luke Fildes shows homeless people queuing to get into a workhouse in London in 1874.

In every society there are people who are poor. Some are people who cannot survive without help: widows or orphans, people who are disabled or ill, and people who do not have work. Others may be poor through lack of opportunity, lack of ability or effort, or perhaps through bad luck.

Every society has its own views about how to care for the helpless and the poor. In Britain 100 years ago much less care was available than there is today. Few people expected the government or local authorities to provide any more than the bare minimum needed to stop the poor from starving. They expected charities rather than the government to care for them.

These attitudes began to change in the early years of this century. The Liberal government of 1906–1914 introduced new laws to help children, old people, the ill, and the unemployed. Later governments added to these measures in the Twenties and Thirties. Between 1945–1951 the Labour government introduced such a wide range of new measures that people described Britain as a 'Welfare State'.

This book describes how Britain became a Welfare State in the twentieth century. It asks why governments started to involve themselves in the care and welfare of people and their families. It shows how that involvement grew during the first half of the century and it examines some of the consequences.

Source 1

This picture appeared at the front of William Booth's book *Darkest England and the Way Out*, 1890.

1 Rich and poor in the 1900s

Source 1 is taken from a book written in 1890 by William Booth, leader of the Salvation Army. It shows, in Booth's words, 'the appalling extent of the misery and poverty existing in Great Britain.... In the raging sea, surrounding the Salvation lighthouse, are to be seen the victims of vice and poverty'. The scenes above the sea show how the Salvation Army tried to help the poor.

Poverty had existed throughout the nineteenth century. Groups such as the Salvation Army did what they could to help the poor but poverty was still widespread when the twentieth century began. In the early 1900s the view began to spread that helping the poor shouldn't be left only to volunteers. Instead the government should do more to help. In section 2 you will find out why this view gained ground. First let us look at the problem of poverty as people saw it at the start of this century.

A divided society

In 1905 a wealthy Member of Parliament published a book called *Riches and Poverty*. On the first page of the book he put the diagram opposite (Source 2).

It was only one of many books published in the 1900s on the subject of poverty and wealth. Dozens of books like it showed that British society was deeply divided between the poor and the rich.

Source 3 is taken from one of those books. It was by an American writer, Jack London, who spent the summer of 1902 living rough in the East End of London, posing as an out-of-work seaman. He wanted to find out how the poor in London lived. In this extract he describes walking along a crowded street with two other out-of-work men, looking for a place to sleep for the night.

Source 2

BRITISH INCOMES IN 1904

RICH 1,250,000 persons £585,000,000	COMFORTABLE 3,750,000 persons £245,000,000
POOR 38,000,000 PERSONS £880,000,000	

'British incomes in 1904'. This diagram appeared in *Riches and Poverty* by L.G. Chiozza Money, a Liberal Member of Parliament, in 1904.

Source 3

Jack London, *The People of the Abyss*, 1903. Note how he used italic type to emphasise his description.

Both kept their eyes on the pavement as they walked and talked, and every now and then one or the other would stoop and pick something up .... I thought it was cigar and cigarette stumps they were collecting, and for some time took no notice. Then I did notice.

From the slimy, spittle-drenched sidewalk, they were picking up bits of orange peel, apple skin, and grape stems, and they were eating them .... They picked up stray crumbs of bread the size of peas, apple cores so black and dirty one would not take them to be apple cores, and these things these two men took into their mouths, and chewed them, and swallowed them; and this, between six and seven o'clock in the evening of 20 August, year of our Lord 1902, in the heart of the greatest, wealthiest and most powerful empire the world has ever seen.

Poverty didn't exist only in London. In 1901 Seebohm Rowntree, son of the famous chocolate maker, published a survey on poverty in York. One of his findings was that four out of every ten wage-earners had to spend everything they earned on the bare necessities of life. All their wages, which averaged eighteen to 21 shillings (90p to £1.05), went on food, rent, clothing and fuel. In Source 4 he described what such people could not afford to buy.

Source 4

B. Seebohm Rowntree, *Poverty, A Study of Town Life*, 1901.

(They) must never spend a penny on railway fare or omnibus. They must never go into the country unless they walk. They must never purchase a halfpenny newspaper or spend a penny to buy a ticket for a popular concert .... They cannot save, nor can they join a sick club or Trade Union, because they cannot pay the necessary subscriptions. The children must have no pocket money for dolls, marbles or sweets. The father must smoke no tobacco, and must drink no beer. The mother must never buy any pretty clothes for herself or for her children .... Finally, the wage earner must never be absent from his work for a single day.

If any of these conditions are broken, the extra expenditure involved is met, and can only be met, by limiting the diet.

Rowntree included in his book many examples of the diet of poor people in York. Source 5 helps us to understand what he was saying. It is a list of the meals eaten in a week by the family of a carter earning twenty shillings (£1) a week.

Source 5

B. Seebohm Rowntree, *Poverty, A Study in Town Life*, 1901.

	Breakfast	Dinner	Tea	Supper
Friday	Bread, butter, tea	Bread, butter, toast, tea	Bread, butter, tea	
Saturday	Bread, bacon, coffee	Bacon, potatoes, pudding, tea	Bread, butter, shortcake, tea	Tea, bread, kippers
Sunday	Bread, butter, shortcake, coffee	Pork, onions, potatoes, Yorkshire pudding	Bread, butter, shortcake, tea	Bread and meat
Monday	Bread, bacon, butter, tea	Pork, potatoes, pudding, tea	Bread, butter, tea	One cup of tea
Tuesday	Bread, bacon, butter, coffee	Pork, bread, tea	Bread, butter, boiled eggs, tea	Bread, bacon butter, tea
Wednesday	Bread, bacon, butter, tea	Bacon, eggs, potatoes, bread, tea	Bread, butter, tea	
Thursday	Bread, butter, coffee	Bread, bacon, tea	Bread, butter, tea	

Writers like Rowntree and London drew attention to the terrible poverty that existed in parts of Britain. There were also writers who described another Britain inhabited by rich people. In a book published in 1909 a young aristocrat compared the lifestyles of poor people with those of some of his acquaintances. Source 6 is one of the comparisons he made.

Source 6

Arthur Ponsonby, *The Camel and the Needle's Eye*, 1909.

A single meal:

Bread	1d
Cheese	1d
1/4 lb of meat	3d
Potatoes and onions	2d
Jam	1d
1/2 pint of beer	2d
Total	10d*

Another meal:

Cantaloup Glacé	(Chilled melon)
Tortue Claire	(Turtle soup)
or Bisque Nantua	(Seafood soup)
Truites Saumonées Michigan	(Salmon-trout)
Mousse de Jambon a l'Escurial	(Ham pate)
Selle d'Agneau Montefiore	(Saddle of lamb)
Poularde Strasbourgeoise	(Chicken)
Salade Indienne	(Rice salad)
Cailles flanqués d'Ortolans	(Quails and buntings)
Asperges Verts. Sauce Mousseuse	(Asparagus. Sauce)
Pêches Framboisines	(Peaches in raspberry liqueur)
Friandises	(Sweets)
Fanchonettes Suisses	(Cream and meringue gateaux)

Hock, Claret, Port, Coffee and Liqueurs.

This dinner for twenty people cost £60, or £3* a head, without wine ...

10d (roughly 4p) in 1909 was worth about £1.40 in 1994 prices.
£3 was worth about £105 in 1994 prices.

Rich and poor not only ate very different meals but also lived in very different homes. Arthur Ponsonby reported that:

Source 7

Arthur Ponsonby, *The Camel and the Needle's Eye*, 1909.

In a house consisting of living-room, bedroom, and a small scullery live father, mother, three sons, also three children under ten and two men lodgers. Seven sleep in the bedroom ... and five sleep in the living-room; the only window of the latter room will not open ....

The landlord and lord of the manor of this district lives with his wife and family in a house containing over one hundred rooms, and is attended by a staff of 44 indoor servants. He has the choice of three other country residences and a town house, and owns over 186,000 acres.

People's housing and living conditions were being recorded in the 1900s not only by writers like Rowntree, London and Ponsonby, but also by local councils. Source 8 is a photograph taken by Liverpool City Council of a courtyard of houses in the city.

Source 8

Houses in Liverpool, photographed by the city council in 1906. The water pump in the courtyard was the only water supply for all the houses.

Questions

1 Look at Source 1. What does the writing on the pillars and on the sea tell you about (i) the causes, and (ii) the effects of poverty in Britain at the end of the nineteenth century?

2 **a** Look at Source 2. Use a calculator to find the average earnings in 1904 of (i) a 'poor' person, (ii) a 'comfortable' person, and (iii) a 'rich' person. (Divide the £ shown in each box by the number of persons shown in each box.)
   b £1 in 1904 bought roughly the same as £35 today. Find the present day values of these average earnings by multiplying them by 35.

3 Read Source 3 again. Why might reading this description have made people think that something should be done to help the poor in London?

4 In source 4, Rowntree said that the only way a poor family could afford things like bus fares, toys, newspapers, beer, was to limit their diets.
   a On what occasions might a family want to buy such things?
   b Read the diet in Source 5. What part of it do you think the family could have limited in order to afford such things?

5 Arthur Ponsonby (Sources 6 and 7) was a wealthy man. Why do you think he recorded these comparisons between the diet and housing of rich and poor people?

2 Thinking about the poor

Books like Seebohm Rowntree's *Poverty* made a strong impression on many readers. Poverty became a leading subject for discussion among the ruling class. Newspapers and magazines frequently ran stories and features on the subject.

Why this sudden interest in poverty? There had been poverty in Britain for hundreds of years. Why did it become a major issue in the 1900s and not before? The sources in this section should help you to find three answers to that question.

Why did poverty become an issue in the 1900s?

One of the many people who read Rowntree's book was a 27-year-old Member of Parliament, Winston Churchill He wrote:

Source 1

Winston Churchill, letter written on 23 December 1901 to a Conservative Party politician in Birmingham.

I have lately been reading a book by Mr Rowntree called *Poverty* which has impressed me very much. It is quite evident ... that the American labourer is a stronger, larger, healthier, better fed and consequently more efficient animal than a large proportion of our population, and this is surely a fact which our unbridled Imperialists (keen suppporters of the British Empire) ...should not lose sight of. For my part, I can see little glory in an Empire which can rule the waves, and is unable to flush the sewers.

Rowntree's *Poverty* was published at a time when Britain was at war. Since 1899 the British army had been fighting the rebel Boers in South Africa. It took the British three years to win this war against much smaller, untrained forces. In 1902 the army had to turn down two out of every three men who volunteered to fight in the war, because they were unfit. Fears grew among the ruling class that the British people were being weakened by 'race degeneration' brought about by poverty. To investigate these fears, the government set up a Committee on Physical Deterioration in 1904. This recommended the introduction of medical inspections and free school meals in schools run by local authorities.

The following year, in 1905, the government set up a more general enquiry into the subject of poverty. Source 2 gives the conclusions of the enquiry, which lasted five years and covered the entire country.

Source 2

Adapted from the report of the Royal Commission on the *Poor Laws and Relief of Distress*, 1905–9.

Our investigations prove the existence in our midst of a class whose condition and environment is a peril to the whole community ....

No country, however rich, can permanently hold its own in the race of international competition, if hampered by an increasing load of this dead weight; or can successfully run an overseas empire if its own folk at home are sinking below the civilisation of its subject races abroad.

Views about how to deal with the problem of poverty differed widely. Some were harsh and unforgiving. One writer who was horrified by the poor health of army recruits, demanded that:

Source 3

Adapted from Arnold White, *Efficiency and Empire*, 1901.

We must abandon the idea that ... every poor man in need of help is an innocent victim .... A sterner attitude by the average man towards paupers is essential if England is to begin to deal with her unfit. Consider the army of 26,000 tramps who infest the high roads of England .... Get rid of them by locking them up for life .... Until we are content to see the idle perish ... little change for the better in the health of the people can be looked for.

The sight of poverty could also provoke great sympathy. A young man in Oxford at the turn of the century describes in Source 4 how the sight of poverty made him join the Labour Party.

Source 4

Interview with the son of a bricklayer's labourer, in Paul Thompson, *The Edwardians*, 1975, a book based on 444 interviews with old people remembering their youth in the 1900s.

I'll tell you what made me turn a Socialist .... I've seen boys when I went to school, I've seen one or two boys before they went into school at nine o'clock go round this back yard ... and the people who lived in the back, if they had some stale bread, they'd chuck the stale bread in pieces to the birds out on to the grass, you see. Two of the boys used to come out early, pick up that bread and eat it, cause they'd got nothing to eat to go to school. When I realised that, I thought to myself, well, England is supposed to be – it was – the most powerful and richest country in the world, and yet – nothing could be done. Why not? I tried to be a Socialist, and have been ever since.

Socialists in Britain came together in 1900 to form the Labour Party. They aimed to get better working conditions and greater equality of wealth for working people. Some members of the Liberal Party feared that the new Labour Party would take support away from themselves. In 1905, a leading member of the Liberal Party, David Lloyd George, spoke about what they must do to avoid losing support:

Source 5

David Lloyd George, speech on *Liberalism and the Labour Party*, 11 October 1906.

If at the end of an average term of office it were found that a Liberal Parliament had done nothing to cope seriously with the social condition of the people, to remove the national degradation of slums and widespread poverty and destitution in a land glittering with wealth ... then would a cry arise for a new party.

Over the next ten years, David Lloyd George was to take a leading part in social reform. However, it wasn't simply fear of losing support to the Labour Party that made him do this. Source 6 shows another, deeper motive for wanting to help the poor.

Source 6

David Lloyd George, speech on *Social Reform*, 1 October 1908.

I have had ... letters ... from people whose cases I have investigated – honest workmen thrown out of work, tramping the streets ... begging for work as they would for charity, and at the end of the day trudging home, disheartened and empty-handed, to be greeted by faces, and some of them little faces, haggard and pinched with starvation and anxiety. The day will come, and it is not far distant, that this country will shudder at its toleration of that state of things when it was rolling in wealth. I say again, that apart from its inhumanity and its essential injustice, it is robbery, it is confiscation of what is the workman's share of the riches of the land.

Source 7

David Lloyd George (left) and Winston Churchill (right) in 1908. Lloyd George was Chancellor of the Exchequer and Churchill was President of the Board of Trade.

Questions

1 Read Sources 5 and 6. If the Labour Party had not been formed, do you think Lloyd George would have wanted to help the poor? Explain your answer.

2 The sources in this section show several kinds of reasons for helping the poor. One reason is to do with the British economy. One is to do with politics. Another is to do with social justice and yet another with race. Which sources show each kind of reason?

3 The Liberal reforms of 1906–1914

In 1906 the Liberal Party won a landslide victory in the general election. There were now 400 Liberals in Parliament, compared with 157 Conservatives. There were also 83 Irish Nationalists and 30 Labour MPs, who all supported the Liberals. This huge majority gave an opportunity to Liberals like David Lloyd George and Winston Churchill to introduce daring new laws on social reform. This section describes those reforms and asks whether, as many people said, they led to a revolution in care.

The shadow of the workhouse: care before 1906

Before 1906 the only state-run social service was 'poor relief'. Using tests laid down by the Poor Law of 1834, Poor Law guardians could give tiny cash payments called 'outdoor relief' to people who were destitute through ill health, disablement, or old age. Those who did not pass the test, for example able-bodied unemployed people, could only get indoor relief – in a workhouse.

The workhouse was a kind of prison where poor people who had nowhere else to go lived under military discipline in return for basic meals and a bed. The poor hated and feared the workhouse, old people especially. Couples who had been married all their adult lives risked ending their days sleeping in separate dormitories and eating in silent, uniformed ranks. Source 1 gives an idea of why the workhouse was so hated.

Source 1

A meal time at the workhouse in Marylebone, London, in 1900.

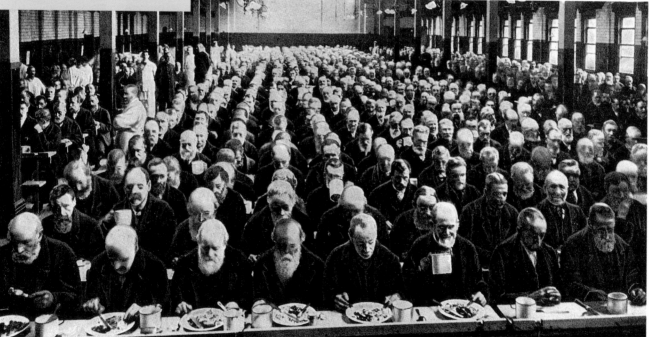

Moving away from the Poor Law

The reforms which the Liberals introduced went far beyond the provisions of the Poor Law:

Children

• **Free school meals (1906).** Free school meals for poor children could now be paid for out of local council rates. This meant that parents did not have to ask the Poor Law guardians for help.

- **School medical service (1907)**. Doctors went to schools to give children medical tests and to recommend treatment where needed.

- **The Children's Act (1908)** made it a legal offence for parents to neglect their children. Also, children could no longer be sent to prison under the age of fourteen. Instead, young offenders could be sent to Borstal, a kind of prison school named after the village where the first one opened.

- **School clinics (1912)**. Many families could not afford a visit to the doctor when the School Medical Service recommended treatment. In 1912 the government therefore opened school clinics where children could be treated.

The elderly

- **The Pensions Act of 1908** said that men and women over 70 were entitled to a weekly pension paid out of government funds. The pension was tiny – five shillings (25p) a week for a single person and 7s 6d (37$\frac{1}{2}$ p) for couples – about £8 and £12 in today's prices. Moreover, you could only draw the pension if you earned less than £26 a year (for single people; £39 for couples). However, small though it was, the pension came from government funds and people did not have to undergo a Poor Law test.

Workers

- **Labour Exchanges**. Unemployment pay was paid through a network of Labour Exchanges, set up in 1910 by Winston Churchill, President of the Board of Trade. As well as giving out unemployment pay, they provided information about job vacancies, so that workers looking for jobs no longer had to walk from one factory to the next looking for work.

- **The National Insurance Act (1911)** set up a National Insurance scheme. All workers in manual jobs or low-paid white-collar jobs had to join it. Each week they paid fourpence for insurance stamps to stick on a card. The employer added threepence and the government twopence. In return, an ill worker got sick pay of 10 shillings a week for 26 weeks as well as free medical treatment. This was provided by doctors who belonged to a 'panel' in each district. Doctors received a fee from the insurance fund for each 'panel' patient they treated.

- **The second part of the National Insurance Act**. This came into force in 1912. It gave unemployment insurance to 2$\frac{1}{4}$ million workers in jobs liable to heavy seasonal unemployment, for example, building work. The workers, employers and the government each paid for 2$\frac{1}{2}$ pence worth of insurance stamps a week. In return, an unemployed worker could receive seven shillings a week for a maximum of fifteen weeks in any one year.

The People's Budget

The Conservatives bitterly opposed many of these measures. This led to a major crisis over the way the country was governed. The crisis began in 1909 when the Chancellor, David Lloyd George, produced a budget to pay for the National Insurance scheme (see above).

The budget is a statement which the Chancellor makes to Parliament each year. In it, the Chancellor describes how the government will raise money to pay for its spending plans for the coming year. Lloyd George's budget was designed to raise £16 million for spending on insurance. This would be done by increasing income tax for the rich, by taxing profits on the sale of land, and by putting new taxes on petrol, cars, alcohol and tobacco.

The Conservatives in Parliament hated these proposals. They especially hated the tax on land, for many of them were landowners. Although they were in a minority in the House of Commons, they had a majority in the House of Lords. At that time, bills had to be approved by both Houses before they could become law. The Lords refused to pass the budget.

Parliament in crisis

For two centuries decisions about taxation had always been made by the Commons, with the Lords giving approval without question. The Liberal government said that the budget was therefore not a matter for the Lords to decide. They called an election to ask the people for their views. When the Liberals won this election, the Lords backed down and voted for the budget.

The government now decided that the Lords' powers must be reduced. It drew up a Parliament Bill saying that the Lords could have no say in money matters and could block other laws for no more than two years. Not surprisingly, the Lords refused to agree to this. After long arguments with the Lords, the Prime Minister decided on drastic action. He asked the king to add 500 Liberals to the House of Lords, giving the Liberals a majority there. When the king agreed, the Lords saw that they had lost and voted for the bill. It became the Parliament Act of 1911.

Reform or revolution?

At the time and since, people have disagreed about the importance of the Liberal reforms of 1906–14. Some see these reforms as a major break with the past which laid the foundations of the Welfare State. Flora Thompson, a Post Office worker in 1908, gave out some of the first old age pensions ever issued. She later wrote in her autobiography about what pensions meant to the old people of Lark Rise, where she lived:

Source 2

Flora Thompson, *Lark Rise*, 1939.

There were one or two poorer couples, just holding on to their homes, but in daily fear of the workhouse. The Poor Law authorities allowed old people past work a small weekly sum as outdoor relief; but it was not sufficient to live upon.... When, twenty years later, the Old Age Pensions began, life was transformed for such aged cottagers. They were relieved of anxiety. They were suddenly rich. Independent for life! At first when they went to the Post Office to draw it, tears of gratitude would run down the cheeks of some, and they would say as they picked up their money 'God bless that Lord George!' (for they could not believe that one so powerful and munificent (generous) could be a plain 'Mr') and God bless you, miss!...

Some historians are not impressed by the Liberal reforms:

Source 3

Arthur Marwick, *Britain in our Century*, 1984.

In my view these reforms fall within a limited, filling the gaps tradition, bearing no more than the faintest distant relationship to the idea of a comprehensive Welfare State.

Other historians have commented more favourably:

Source 4

Colin Cross, *The New British*, *The Observer*, July 1973.

David Lloyd George with his 'people's budget' of 1909 and his national health and unemployment insurance of 1911, inaugurated (started) a new political morality, now shared by all parties, that the state should intervene against gross poverty. His reforms were continued after the Second World War with the creation of what was termed 'the Welfare State'.

Source 5

Pensioners outside the post office in Wickhambrook, Suffolk, on 6 January 1908, the first day of old age pensions.

Questions

1 Read the information on pages 98–99 and make notes about the Liberal reforms of 1906–14 under the following headings. You should be able to find information about eight reforms.

Date	Reform	What the reform did	Who was helped by it

2 In Source 3, Arthur Marwick claims that the reforms were 'limited, filling the gaps...' Which parts of your completed table agree with this view?

3 Read Source 2.
   a How could Source 2, by itself, be used as evidence that the Pensions Act transformed the lives of the poor?
   b Look at the information on page 11 about the Pensions Act of 1909. How does this suggest that Flora Thompson's description of old age pensions was exaggerated?
   c If Flora Thompson was exaggerating, is there anything useful that Source 2 can tell us about old age pensions in 1909?

4 In Source 4, Colin Cross says that Lloyd George started 'a new political morality (way of thinking) ... that the state should intervene against gross poverty'. Judging by what you have read in Sections 1 and 2, do you think it is fair to give Lloyd George the credit for starting this way of thinking?

4 State care between the wars

The Liberal reforms of 1906–14 were halted when the First World War began. From 1914–1918 the government turned its efforts to surviving and winning the biggest war the country had ever fought. At the end of the war the government returned to the issues of care and welfare, but now with greater urgency. Over the next twenty years a mass of new laws gave the government an increasingly important part in people's lives. This section looks at how and why the state's involvement in people's welfare grew so rapidly between the two world wars.

Why and how did state care grow between the wars?

Wartime controls

During the First World War the government gained powers to control people's lives which it did not have before. The first of these powers came from the Defence of the Realm Act, or 'DORA' as people called it. Dora allowed the government to do almost anything it wanted to help it fight the war. Some of the things it did interfered in people's personal lives. For example, it changed the laws on drinking: pubs had to close in the afternoons, beer was watered down, and customers were not allowed to buy each other drinks. This was because the government believed that drunkenness was reducing the output of factory workers.

This was just one way in which the government controlled people's behaviour. Lives were also changed by the Military Service Act of 1916, which brought in compulsory service in the armed forces for men aged eighteen to 41. In 1917 the government took control of what people could eat when it introduced food rationing. It also intervened in people's working lives when it allowed women to do industrial jobs normally done by men.

Although many of these arrangements were scrapped when the war ended, people were now used to the idea that the government had a right to control certain aspects of their lives if it was in the national interest. Equally, the government became used to the idea that it could intervene in people's lives in ways it had not thought of doing before the war.

The war and pensions

The government had begun paying old age pensions in 1908. The First World War forced it into a new area of pensions. About four soldiers in every ten who saw active service in the war received wounds which disabled them (Source 1). By 1928 almost $2\frac{1}{2}$ million ex-soldiers were receiving army pensions for war wounds and disabilities.

In 1925 a new Pensions Act for old people set up a pension fund to which individuals and the government contributed. Workers paid a sum out of their weekly wage while the government made a contribution which equalled the total paid by all workers. An insured person received ten shillings (50p) a week between the ages of 65 and 70. There were also pensions for widows, children's allowances for widows, and payments for orphans.

Source 1

Disabled soldiers having artificial legs fitted at Roehampton hospital in 1918.

'Moulding a better world'

Long before the fighting ended, the government was making plans for the reconstruction of Britain at the end of the war. The Prime Minister, Lloyd George, and other ministers saw the war as an opportunity to break with the past. They said that their task was 'not so much a question of rebuilding society as it was before the war, but of moulding a better world ....' In a famous speech in 1918 Lloyd George promised 'Homes fit for heroes' for the soldiers who would shortly return from the war.

For a while it seemed that the government would succeed in 'moulding a better world'. An Education Act in 1918 provided for full-time schooling for all children aged five to fourteen: up until then eight out of ten children were finding jobs and leaving school at thirteen. Also in 1918 a Maternity and Child Welfare Act led to the building of child welfare and ante-natal clinics. In 1919 a Housing Act gave government funds to local authorities as well as private builders to build new houses. Also in 1919 a Ministry of Health was created to look after public health and health insurance.

Unemployment and state intervention

In 1920, however, Britain went into a slump. Trade dwindled and unemployment shot up. The government was forced to cut its spending on housing, health and welfare. So many workers lost their jobs that it had to alter the system of unemployment insurance it had set up in 1911. The 1911 Act covered only $2\frac{1}{4}$ out of 19 million workers, and those only for fifteen weeks in a year. After that, if they were still out of work, they had to ask the Poor Law guardians for relief.

In 1920 therefore, the government brought in a new Unemployment Insurance Act which gave benefits to all workers. In 1921 it scrapped the fifteen-week limit on payments and gave extra benefits to the wives and children of unemployed men.

The Great Depression of the 1930s put even more people out of work. By 1931, the government was spending so much on unemployment benefit (£120 million a year) that there was a financial crisis which led to the collapse of the Labour government. This was followed by cuts in benefit and the introduction of the hated means test. Testing was done by local Public Assistance Committees which took over from the Poor Law guardians in 1929.

In 1934, with unemployment still very high, the government created an Unemployment Assistance Board to take responsibility for workers who had been out of work for more than 26 weeks. This replaced the locally-run Public Assistance Committees and put the care of the long-term unemployed into the government's hands.

Planning

By the mid-1930s many people took it for granted that the government involved itself in their welfare. There was a general expectation that social problems could be dealt with by state authorities. In order to provide the services that were expected of it, the government put more and more effort into what it called 'planning'.

The idea of planning had started in the Soviet Union, whose government was taken over by Communists in 1917. One of the aims of Communism is to share a country's wealth equally among its people. The Soviet government tried to do this by planning the country's industry, agriculture, trade, and transport. A government organisation called Gosplan estimated the likely output of the country's factories and farms, and worked out ways of increasing it. From 1928 onwards, this was done through ambitious 'five-year plans' which set targets for every branch of the economy.

Governments in many countries followed the example of the Soviet Union. In Britain, many leading politicians and thinkers favoured the idea of planning because it seemed the only way to overcome the Depression and to build a fair, efficient society.

Questions

1   Look at these figures:

The percentage of the national income spent by the government on health, pensions, unemployment insurance and other social services:		
1913 5.5%	1924 10.3%	1931 15.8%

Using the information in this section, suggest reasons for the increase in these figures.

2   How did (i) the First World War, (ii) unemployment, help to bring about more government involvement in the care and welfare of British people? Which do you think was the more important in doing so?

5 A growing nation

While all these changes were taking place, the population of Britain was growing. This added to the pressure on governments to provide more care and welfare.

As Source 1 shows there are many more of us now than at the start of the century. Our numbers have risen from 38.2 million in 1901 to 55.5 million in 1991. Yet, as Source 2 shows, the average family is smaller now than in 1901. It doesn't seem to make sense. The main reason for this apparent contradiction is that people's life expectancy has steadily increased during the century (Source 3). In other words, people, are living longer than they used to. Why?

Source 1

The population of the United Kingdom, as counted in each census, 1901–1991.

Source 2

The average size of a family, 1901–1991.

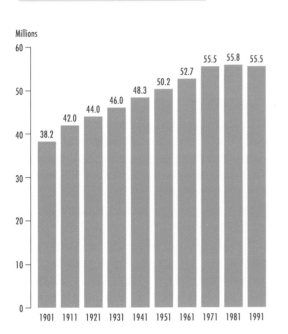
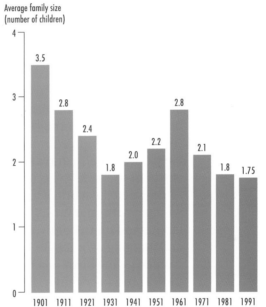

Source 3

The expectation of life at birth in the United Kingdom, 1901–1991.

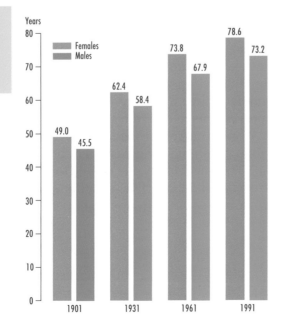

Source 4

Infant mortality in the United Kingdom, 1900–1990. (Deaths of infants under one year old per 1000 live births.)

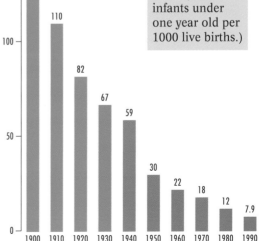

Why are people living longer?

Infant care

People are living longer firstly because the infant mortality rate has dropped. Infant mortality means the death of a baby before its first birthday. As Source 4 shows, babies at the start of the century were ten times more likely to die before their first birthday than they are today. Source 5 helps us to understand one reason why this was so. It is a description by a Glasgow midwife of the first birth she attended.

Source 5

Mary Thomson, *Stork's Nest*, an unpublished autobiography.

My first call took me to a vermin-infested building where babies slept side by side with dogs, cats, rats, bugs, fleas and lice .... I was ushered into a room about five feet square. The patient lay on a bed built into a recess in the wall, and a line of washing – under which I had to duck – spread itself across the room. Two dogs ... occupied the space in front of the fire .... The room smelt strongly of soapsuds, bad fish, cat and dog ....

As you have read on page 95, there was a growing fear in the 1900s that the British people were becoming 'degenerate'. Both the government and local authorities took steps to improve the health of young children. In 1907 the Notification of Births Act said that the local medical officer for health must be told as soon as possible that a baby had been born. The medical officer then had to arrange for a health visitor to call on the mother and baby to check their health and arrange help if there was any problem. This system is still in use today.

Between the world wars, some local authorities provided poor pregnant women with 'maternity bags' containing all that was needed for their labour and for the delivery of the baby. More common was the practice of encouraging women to have their babies in hospital. The number of women giving birth in a hospital or maternity home rose from 15 per cent in 1927 to 54 per cent in 1946 and to 95 per cent by 1974. Although hospital delivery was often less pleasant for the mother than a home delivery, it was generally safer for the baby. Specialised help was also available if complications developed.

Child care

Children as well as babies benefited from government welfare. The act of 1906 encouraged local authorities to give poor children free school meals. Another act in 1907 set up a school medical service to provide medical inspections and, later, free treatment in schools.

Further improvements in children's health care came about during the Second World War. To make sure that children did not suffer malnutrition as a result of food rationing, the government brought in a National Milk Scheme in 1940. This gave a daily pint of milk to every pregnant or nursing mother and to every child under five (see photograph on page 110). From 1942 it also provided free vitamin supplements in the form of cod-liver oil, rose-hip syrup and orange juice.

Vaccination

People's life expectancy has been greatly increased by advances in medicine and medical care. Medicine has prolonged life firstly by preventing diseases. In the first half of the century tuberculosis (TB) was the country's biggest killer. More people died of TB than from all the other infectious diseases put together. One surgical operation in every six was to repair bones and glands rotted by TB. A major step towards fighting this awful disease was taken in 1922 when the Ministry of Health ordered that all milk be pasteurised so that TB could not be passed from dairy cattle to humans. Further progress was made after the Second World War when mobile x-ray units started touring the country to detect signs of the illness at an early stage. From the 1950s onwards, local health authorities also carried out mass vaccination campaigns, using the newly-developed BCG vaccine.

From the 1930s vaccination was also used to combat diphtheria, an often fatal infection of the throat and chest. Later, local health authorities also introduced mass vaccination against whooping cough, smallpox, scarlet fever, measles and polio. As a result of these measures, the number of people dying from infectious diseases dropped from 50 per thousand in the 1920s to less than one in a thousand in the 1970s.

New cures

From the 1930s doctors were increasingly able to cure as well as prevent killer diseases. In 1910 a German scientist developed a drug called Salvarsan to cure the sexually-transmitted disease syphilis. It was the first selective germ-killing drug. Building on the success of Salvarsan, scientists in the 1920s and 1930s developed chemical germ killers which worked in the same way – by bonding themselves to germs and killing them. Known as sulpha drugs, they could cure infectious diseases which until then usually killed people, especially the old.

Sulpha drugs, which killed one kind of germ, led to the development of a drug which could kill a wide range of germs – penicillin. Discovered by Alexander Fleming in 1928 and developed between 1938–1942 by Ernst Chain and Howard Florey, penicillin came into widespread use in 1943. Penicillin is an antibiotic drug – a substance produced by a microbe that can kill another microbe. Since the Second World War a wide range of antibiotic drugs has been developed, allowing doctors to treat most infectious diseases. Antibiotics have also made surgical operations safer by reducing the risk of post-operative infection.

Better living conditions

Compare the photograph on page 20 with the photograph on page 6. This shows us another reason why people's life expectancy increased in the twentieth century. Homes became healthier, cleaner and more comfortable as new flats and houses replaced old houses and slums. One of the most important improvements in these new homes was the provision of running water and of sewage disposal. By 1950 most homes in Britain's towns were connected to sewers and water mains, making it easier to keep them clean, to prepare food and to maintain personal hygiene.

Many people's health was also improved by a better diet. As you read on page 4, poor people in York at the start of the century mostly ate cheap 'fillers' such as bread, potatoes, stewed meat and evaporated milk. As the century went on, more and more people were able to afford fresh vegetables, fresh milk, eggs and fruit. People not only ate better, they also had to work less hard. As working hours got shorter people could spend more time on leisure activities, helping them to relax or to get exercise.

Source 6

The kitchen of a newly-built council flat in London in 1948. The flat, which was considered luxurious, had three bedrooms, a living room, bathroom and kitchen. The rent was 16s.6d. (82.5p) a week.

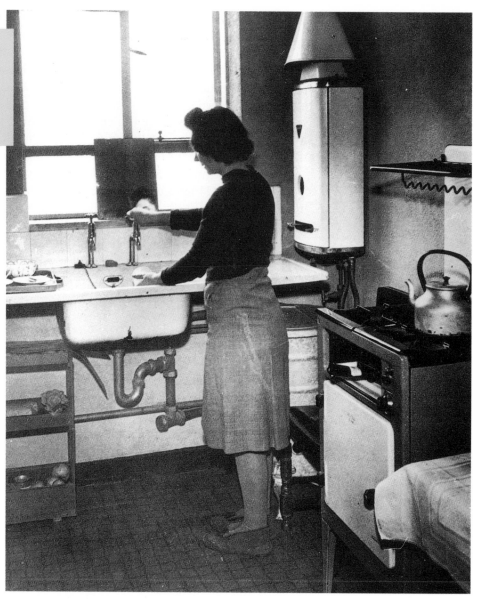

Questions

1 What dangers to the life of a baby can you find in Source 5?

2 Look at Source 4.
   a How many pupils are there in your year at your school?
   b If you had all been born in 1901 how many of you would have died before reaching the age of one?
   c Assume that there will be the same number of pupils in your year at your school in fifteen years time. How many of them are likely to die before reaching their fifteenth birthday?

3 Look at Source 7 and at Source 8 on pages 93–94.
   a Make a note of everything you do at home which involves the use of water.
   b If you did not have running water to do these things, how might your health be affected?
   c Why was the woman in Source 6 likely to have a healthier life than the woman in the picture on page 94?

Review: Changing care and welfare

1 Reasons for change

In 1914 a well-known economist said:

Source 1

A.C. Pigou, *Lectures on Housing*, 1914.

> The position I start from is this. It is the duty of a civilised state to lay down certain minimum conditions in every department of life, below which it does not allow any of its free citizens to fall. There must be a minimum standard of conditions in factories, a minimum standard of leisure, of dwelling accommodation, of education, of medical treatment in case of illness, and of wholesome food and clothing …. The standards must be upheld all along the line.

a What arguments can you think of to support the idea that the state (or government) has a 'duty' to provide people with minimum standards of housing, education, health, etc?

b Why did many people at the start of this century disagree with the argument that the state had this 'duty'?

c Between 1900 and 1939 the government took action to improve conditions especially for children, the elderly and the unemployed. Using pages 89–108 of this book, list the ways in which each of these three groups was helped by government action.

d There are many reasons why the government involved itself more and more in the welfare of such people. Find as many reasons as you can to explain this. Group them under these headings: political reasons; reasons to do with the economy; reasons to do with national strength; reasons to do with social justice; reasons to do with the First World War.

2 Investigation

The issues you have read about in the first part of this book are still of great concern today. Hardly a day goes by without television or newspapers carrying stories about problems connected with poverty, unemployment and welfare. Why do these problems still exist? Does it mean that little has changed since the start of the century? You can use the material in this book as the starting point for an investigation into the historical background of one of these issues.

a Begin by identifying a particular issue concerned with poverty. (For example, why are there homeless young people begging on the streets of many British cities today?) Make a collection of newspaper cuttings or video recordings about this issue.

b Try to decide why the story has got so much press coverage: why is it seen as an important issue?

c Using the material in the first part of this book, find out what similarities and differences there were between the problem of poverty today and the problem in the first part of the century?

d Display the results of your investigation e.g. mount newspaper cuttings in a wall display and write brief labels to go with them explaining the similarities and differences between the situation then and the situation today.

Focus study · Creating the Welfare State

Children of the welfare state. Five-year-olds drinking free school milk in 1947.

You have read how governments took more and more responsibility for the care and welfare of people and their families between 1900–1935. In the 1940s this led to the making of what people called the Welfare State.

In the 1940s when people talked about the Welfare State they meant a country in which the government would take a leading part in helping people to deal with any social problems that affected them. The most difficult of those problems, as we have seen, was poverty, especially when it was made worse by unemployment, old age, illness, or disability. In the Welfare State, the government would give income support, or 'social security', to help people in these situations.

Poverty was closely linked to several other social problems, especially poor health and bad housing. Helping people who lived in poverty meant dealing with these problems as well. Good, affordable medical care and decent housing were therefore also part of the Welfare State.

Underlying all these problems was the issue of work. What was the point of providing welfare benefits, free medical care and good housing if people had no jobs? In the Welfare State the government was expected to have policies which helped to provide work and avoid unemployment.

This focus study looks first at why a Welfare State was needed. The government already had welfare schemes for pensions and unemployment insurance: why were these not sufficient? We will then look at why the Welfare State was created in the 1940s and not sooner, or later; what was special about the 1940s that made it happen then? After studying the new welfare measures which the government introduced between 1945 and 1951, we ask how important these changes were, and whether they were successful.

1   The eve of the Welfare State

The picture on page 90 shows a nation wrecked by poverty. If William Booth, whose vision it was, could have seen Britain 50 years on, would he have seen any improvement? How much had changed by 1940?

How effective was welfare cover by 1940?

You have read that social insurance changed a great deal. The National Insurance scheme, started in 1911, gave health and unemployment insurance to around 12 million workers. In 1925 widows, orphans and the over-65s were included in health insurance. Further laws in the 1920s and 1930s spread health insurance cover to some 20 million people and unemployment cover to 14 million.

These insurance schemes were far from comprehensive. Health insurance entitled workers, but not their families to treatment from a panel doctor (see page 99). Workers who could afford it could pay into private insurance funds, as a Mrs Carter recalled in an interview in 1985:

Source 1

Paul Addison, *Now the War is Over*, 1985.

> My husband used to pay a stamp of one and sixpence a week, a health insurance stamp for himself only, for the doctor or any medication he would need and he also paid a scheme at work, threepence a week, which was called a hospital scheme and that covered the whole family for any hospitalisation that was needed, but not maternity. I paid threepence a week into a medical aid for my son, but I was in good health so I didn't bother about myself.

Many people could not keep up the payments on private insurance schemes. People without insurance cover therefore avoided visits to the doctor unless it was absolutely necessary. The wife of a Yorkshire miner, talking in the 1980s, remembered:

Source 2

Stuart Archer and Nigel Shepley, *Witnessing History*, 1988

> I had my daughter before the 1939 war. At the maternity home we had to pay £2 deposit and another ten shillings when she came. I got up at six in the morning and said to my husband, 'Come on, we're ready'. I had to walk down to the maternity home with a hole in my shoe ....
>
> I never went to the doctor's. There was a post-natal clinic, but I didn't go .... We got no help at all with anything.

Women who neglected their health because they could not afford treatment often suffered later in life. A Scottish doctor, looking back to the 1940s, remembered that:

Source 3

Doctor Alastair Clarke, *The Independent*, 4 July 1988.

gynaecological problems
Diseases and disorders of the female reproductive system.

> People always managed to find the money to bring in their children. But the mothers would go without. When the National Health Service (and free medical treatment) came in, all that emerged. Within six months I had 30 or 40 women come in who had been suffering gynaecological problems*, many of them for years ....

It wasn't only doctors who were too expensive for many people to visit. Dentists' fees were so high that people usually only went to get aching teeth pulled out, not to have check-ups. Opticians' fees were so high that people who needed glasses had to buy them in shops like Woolworths. In Source 4, a Mr Law remembers his father buying spectacles from Woolworths in Manchester Piccadilly.

Source 4

Paul Addison, *Now the War is Over*, 1985.

Stacked on the counter were spectacles with a large card with a large A going down to a small Z ... and I can see my father now, trying on different pairs of glasses, looking at the card, putting down, picking another pair up, until he got the selected pair he required, then he would look at me, he would ask me how he looked. I'd say, 'You look smashing, Dad,' and then we'd just go out of the store.

Source 5

A page from one of a series of feature articles about unemployment in *Picture Post* magazine in 1939. It followed unemployed Alfred Smith in his search for work.

PICTURE POST

Vol. 2.   No. 3.   January 21, 1939

Before the Labour Exchange : One of 1,830,000 Workless
There are over 1,830,000 Unemployed in Great Britain. From a group outside Peckham Labour Exchange we picked out one, Alfred Smith (X) and followed him with the camera. On the following pages is the story of his daily routine.

UNEMPLOYED!

Britain is a rich country. But at the beginning of this year, it had 1,831,372 registered unemployed, and many more not registered. This was 3,269 more than in November, 1938, 165,965 more than a year ago. In two years, the figures have risen by 207,770. Is this volume of unemployment necessary?

ALFRED SMITH lives at 52, Leo Street, Peckham. He is a little man, thin, but wiry, with the pale face and bright eyes of a real Londoner. He wears a cloth cap and white muffler, old brown jacket and corduroy trousers. He talks animatedly, likes a joke, walks with his hands in his pockets, shoulders bent, head slightly forward. And he looks down as he walks—the typical walk of an unemployed man. His face is lined, and his cheeks are sunken, because he has no teeth. He is only 35 years old. He has a wife and four children.

He has not had a regular job for three years. When Alfred Smith married 12 years ago, he was a skilled workman, a spray enamel maker, earning good wages. Things went well with him for nine years. But then the chemicals used in this work made his teeth rot, so that they had to be

Like health insurance, unemployment insurance had its limitations. After receiving sixteen weeks of benefit, an unemployed worker had to go on the 'dole', like Alfred Smith in Source 5. This was hard enough, but unemployed people who had no insurance could only get help from the local Public Assistance Committees (PAC) which took over from the Poor Law Guardians in 1929. In an interview in 1988 Violet Harris remembered the help her family got from the PAC in Lambeth in London:

Source 6

Mary Chamberlain, *Growing up in Lambeth*, 1989.

They used to give you what they called parish relief, served it out on the premises, along the Kennington Lane, right opposite the police station there. They used to give you some meat, black as your hat. True. Potatoes, with whiskers all growing out of them. Black sugar. Black, almost, bread. Yards of treacle and blooming old car grease supposed to be margarine, you know. But you never got a penny off them.

When the Depression began, the only people who got to know about the misery of unemployment were the unemployed and their families and neighbours. By the late 1930s, most people knew something about it. Newspapers and magazines increasingly gave space to the social problems of the Depression. Magazines like *Picture Post* used what they called 'photojournalism' to give these stories maximum impact. The photograph opposite, which appeared in *Picture Post* in 1939, was typical of the new photojournalism, and helped to create an unforgettable image of the Depression for the magazine's readers.

Questions

1 Judging by Sources 1–6 in this section what gaps and shortcomings were there in welfare provision in the 1930s?

2 Why did more people know about poverty and other social problems in 1939 than in 1900?

2 War and welfare

By 1939 public opinion was firmly in favour of a major expansion of social services. Opinion did not change when Britain went to war with Germany in September 1939. In fact the opposite happened. Over the next five and a half years of war, demands for government action on social problems grew louder and louder. The government could not ignore these demands, and drew up plans for new health and insurance schemes. Between 1944 and 1948 these plans were put into practice with the passing of major new National Insurance, National Health, and National Assistance Acts. These acts together created 'the Welfare State'.

It might seem surprising that the Welfare State was planned and partly created during the Second World War. You might expect the government to have dropped welfare plans so that it could concentrate on the war effort. Why did the war speed up instead of slow down the expansion of the social services?

How did the war help to accelerate reform?

The changing mood of the nation

The Second World War changed the way in which British people thought about their society and about the future of the country. Public opinion surveys showed that most people hoped for a better world after the war than the depressed world of the 1930s. This new mood can be explained by several wartime developments.

1 The war brought people together. For five and a half years millions of men and women shared experiences such as evacuation or service in the Home Guard or rescue services. They shared hardships such as food rationing and they sheltered together during air raids. This not only broke down the barriers between people of different social classes. It also gave people a sense of fighting together in a common cause.

2 The war forced the government to involve itself more closely in social services. For example, to make sure that hospitals could cope with war casualties, the government brought most hospitals under its control through the Emergency Hospital Scheme. It also introduced food supplements to protect children from malnutrition as a result of food rationing. From 1940 onwards it provided children with free school milk and later with free orange juice, cod-liver oil and vitamin tablets.

3 The war opened many people's eyes to the poverty of Britain's cities. Many of the 1.5 million women and children evacuated in 1939 were from poor working class families. Source 1 describes the condition of some of the children.

Source 1

The National Federation of Women's Institutes, *Town Children Through Country Eyes*, 1941.

In practically every batch of children there were some who suffered from head-lice, skin diseases and bed-wetting .... Some children (from Manchester) had never slept in beds before .... One boy (from Salford) had never had a bath before .... The state of the children (from Liverpool) was such that the school had to be fumigated after reception .... Few (Manchester) children would eat food that demanded the use of teeth – could only eat with a teaspoon .... One little girl of five (from Liverpool) remarked that she would like to have beer and cheese for supper .... Some (Gosport) children had never used a knife and fork ....

People's hopes for a better world were reflected in a huge number of plans, drawn up during the war, for postwar reconstruction. Political parties, churches, universities and local councils drew up detailed plans for postwar Britain. One such plan was put forward by the popular magazine, *Picture Post*, in January 1941. It demanded a job for everybody, minimum wages, child allowances, social insurance, a health service and new housing. Source 2, taken from its housing plan, gives us an idea of how some people saw the future in 1941.

The Beveridge Plan

The most famous wartime plan was an instant bestseller when it came out in December 1942. One hundred thousand copies of Sir William Beveridge's *Social Insurance and Allied Services* were bought in December alone. Beveridge was a senior civil servant who had been involved in social policy

Source 2

A drawing in *Picture Post's* new year issue in 1941, *A Plan for Britain*, shows its proposals for the rebuilding of Britain's towns and cities.

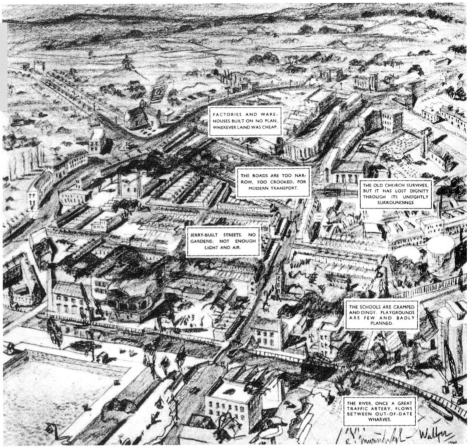

Source 3

Sir William Beveridge making a speech about his Social Insurance proposals at a Liberal Party meeting in 1943.

for many years. He had, for example, helped to set up the National Insurance scheme of 1912. In 1941 he was made chairman of a government Committee on Social Insurance to look into the various insurance schemes that existed and to suggest how to improve them. In his report, however, Beveridge made suggestions about more than just insurance. In the famous introduction to the Report, he explained that social problems were all linked:

Source 4

Report by Sir William Beveridge, *Social Insurance and Allied Services*, 1942.

> A revolutionary moment in the world's history is a time for revolutions, not for patching.
>
> ...Social insurance should be treated as one part only of a comprehensive policy of social progress. Social insurance fully developed may provide income security; it is an attack on Want. But Want is only one of five giants on the road of reconstruction and in some ways the easiest to attack. The others are Disease, Ignorance, Squalor and Idleness.

In his report, Beveridge went on to say that there should be a single insurance system. People should make weekly contributions to a government-run insurance scheme that would protect them 'from the cradle to the grave'. The scheme would provide:

- benefits for the unemployed, sick and disabled
- pensions and benefits for old people, widows and orphans
- funeral grants
- maternity benefits.

Anybody not covered by the scheme would be maintained by a system of National Assistance. Underpinning all this, Beveridge expected that the government would provide family allowances, create a national health service and maintain full employment.

However, the government did not act immediately to put the Beveridge Plan into operation. The Prime Minister, Winston Churchill, worried not only about the cost, but also that the plan would 'raise false hopes'. Nevertheless, the plan was so popular that the government was forced to set up a Reconstruction Committee to plan Britain's post-war future. From 1943-45 this committee brought out a series of White Papers, proposing major changes in education, health, employment policy, social insurance and housing.

Source 5

A Labour Party election poster of 1945 uses the famous wartime V for victory symbol to encourage voters to 'win the peace'.

The 1945 election

Throughout the war the government of Britain was a coalition, led from May 1940 onwards by Winston Churchill. The idea was that the Conservative, Labour and Liberal parties would put aside their differences for as long as the war lasted to work together for the war effort.

In May 1945 Germany surrendered, bringing the war in Europe to an end. Churchill and the Labour leader, Clement Attlee, agreed to hold a general election without delay. The date was fixed for 5 July 1945.

In the election campaign, the Conservatives promised that they would introduce all the measures outlined in the White Papers of 1945. However, Churchill warned voters that the country was in a difficult economic position and that introducing these measures quickly would be hard. In contrast, the Labour Party promised to enact the White Paper proposals without delay. It also promised other measures designed to modernise Britain: the nationalisation of coal, gas, electricity, the railways, iron and steel.

The election result was a landslide victory for the Labour Party. Labour won 393 seats against the Conservatives 213. With a majority of 183 over all other parties put together, it was able to start putting its promises into effect without delay.

Questions

1 Read Source 1. How might the experience of looking after children like these have changed the way people thought about the subject of poverty?

2 Look at Source 2. What does this drawing tell you about the kind of Britain some people hoped for at the end of the war?

3 a In Source 4, Beveridge identified five 'giants': what were they?
  b These were rather old fashioned words to describe modern problems: suggest five modern words which mean the same.
  c Why should Beveridge have thought that 1942 was 'a revolutionary moment in the world's history'?

4 Beveridge was not a good speech-maker (Source 3), yet he was asked to give many speeches in 1942–43. Suggest why he was in such demand.

5 Using the sources and information in this section, give as many reasons as you can to explain why the war led to demands for more state provision of welfare.

3 The birth of the Welfare State

Source 1

A mother collects the Family Allowance from a post office in 1946.

The new Labour government's first action was to put into effect an act of the wartime coalition government, the Family Allowances Act. All mothers were issued with books of coupons which they could cash at the local post office (Source 1). The coupons were worth five shillings (25p) a week for each child after the first.

The rest of Beveridge's proposals were made into law by four Acts of Parliament:

- The National Insurance Act, 1946
- The National Health Service Act, 1946
- The Industrial Injuries Act, 1946
- The National Assistance Act, 1946

Much complex planning was needed before these Acts could be put into operation. The date fixed for the start of a new National Insurance scheme, a National Health Service and a National Assistance Board was 5 July 1948. The government called it 'The Appointed Day'. Ever since it has been taken as the day when the Welfare State was born – a key date and a key event in Britain's history.

'The Appointed Day': a turning point?

People at the time believed that something was about to change on 'the Appointed Day':

Source 2

The Daily Mail, 3 July 1948.

> On Monday morning you will wake up in a New Britain, in a State which 'takes over' its citizens six months before they are born, providing care and free services for their birth, for their early years, their schooling, sickness, workless days, widowhood, and retirement. Finally, it helps defray the cost of their departure. All this, with free doctoring, dentistry and medicine – free bath chairs, too, if needed – for 4s 11d out of your weekly pay packet. You begin paying next Friday.

National Insurance

The payments of 4s 11d (25p) were contributions to a National Insurance scheme. After the 'Appointed Day', all workers (except married women) had to pay for a weekly insurance stamp costing 4s 11d which was stuck onto his or her National Insurance card. The government and the employer also paid contributions towards the stamp. Having a paid-up card entitled the holder to sickness and unemployment benefits, retirement and widows' pensions, maternity benefit and a funeral allowance. The benefits were all flat-rate, meaning that everyone got the same amounts. For pensioners this was 42 shillings a week for a married couple, compared with 20 shillings before. Unemployment pay for a man was 26 shillings a week, with a further sixteen shillings a week for a wife and 7s 6d for each child. James Griffiths, the Minister of National Insurance, said that this was 'the best and cheapest insurance policy offered to any people anywhere'.

With 25 million workers in Britain in 1948, this scheme was on a gigantic scale. The Ministry of National Insurance which ran it had 40,000 staff in newly-built offices in Newcastle. The records of insured workers were kept on 25 million sheets stored in 100 rooms. (Computers had not yet been invented to store such information.) Among those records were the details of 650,000 men and women named Smith, of whom 8,000 were all called John Smith. Throughout the country 992 local offices handled claims for benefit and passed them on to the headquarters in Newcastle.

National Assistance

People not in paid work – for example, the disabled, the homeless, or unmarried mothers – could not receive National Insurance benefits, nor could workers with insufficient stamps. These people could apply for help to a new National Assistance Board. Although there was a means test for help, it was a test on the claimant only, not the whole family. As one minister in the government said, 'At last we have buried the old Poor Law'.

The National Health Service

The National Health Service which came into existence on 5 July 1948 made four major changes to the existing system of health care.

- **All medical treatment was to be free** for everybody, whether or not they had National Insurance stamps.

• **Doctors were to be paid by the state**: hospital doctors received a salary, while General Practitioners received a fee for every patient on their lists, whether or not they treated them.

• **Three thousand hospitals were nationalised** and put under the control of fourteen regional hospital groups.

• **Local authorities had to provide free medical services**; for example, home nurses, midwives, infant care, immunisation, and ambulance services.

The impact of the Welfare State

These new welfare measures took rapid effect. Source 3 describes how the introduction of the National Health Service affected a family in Leeds.

Source 3

Mrs Clare Bond, from Leeds, interviewed in 1985 in Paul Addison, *Now the War is Over*, 1985.

gas and air Nitrous oxide and oxygen – a recently introduced form of pain relief used in childbirth.

... oh, it was fantastic. My mother and dad had been having problems with their teeth for ages, and I think they were first at the dentist, as soon as he opened .... Instead of having just a few teeth out, they had the complete set out, and free dentures. You know? Thought it was wonderful .... My sister had had school-supply steel-rimmed spectacles for ages .... As soon as the NHS started she was there, (at the) optician. Marvellous NHS spectacles, you know, some style about them .... And then I had another sister, she'd had one baby and it was rather bad, she had to pay 12s 6d for a midwife, no gas and air*, anything like this, and just after the NHS started she had her second baby, at home .... Then she thought it was absolutely wonderful, because besides having a free midwife, she had a nurse come in every day ... bathed the baby, showed her how to look after it.

At a press conference in October 1949 the Minister for Health, Aneurin Bevan, gave figures to show what use had been made of the National Health Service since the 'Appointed Day'.

• 187 million prescriptions had been dispensed at 2s9d (14p) each.
• 5.25 million pairs of glasses had been supplied. Three million more were on order.
• 8.5 million dental patients had been accepted for treatment.

Seebohm Rowntree, whose research into poverty in York in 1901 you read about on page 92, conducted further surveys of poverty in York over the following half century, the last in 1951. The results were startling:

Source 4

Seebohm Rowntree, *Poverty. A Study of Town Life*, 1901, and Seebohm Rowntree and G.R. Lavers, 1951.

Poverty in York 1901–1951		
	Percentage of working-class families living in poverty	Percentage of the whole population of York living in poverty
1901	43.4%	27.8
1936	31.1%	18.0
1951	2.8%	1.5

Source 5

An optician fits a schoolgirl with free National Health Service spectacles in February 1951.

Questions

1 In Source 2 the *Daily Mail* told its readers that they would wake up in 'a New Britain' on 5 July 1948. Using the information in this section, say what changed in Britain on 5 July 1948.

2 How can the information in this section be used to support the idea that 'a New Britain' was born on 5 July 1948?

4   Bevan and the doctors

After reading how patients flocked to use the National Health Service in 1948, you might think that doctors welcomed the birth of the Welfare State. Not so. There were doctors who angrily opposed the NHS from the moment the Beveridge Plan first appeared in 1942. From 1942–1948 they fought a fierce battle to stop the creation of the health service.

The main target of the doctors' attacks was the Labour Minister for Health from 1945–1951, Aneurin Bevan. For three years Bevan and the doctors argued angrily about the future of the country's health. What was at stake? Why could they not agree on an issue that seemed to be in everybody's interests? Why were their arguments so heated?

The National Health Service: for and against

At first the doctors had been in favour of a National Health Service. They set up a Medical Planning Commission during the war and in 1942 issued a report calling for a health service covering the whole country. This was to include the building of health centres, the payment of doctors by the state, and the reorganisation of hospitals.

However, their attitude changed after the Beveridge Report appeared in 1942. When they learned in 1943 that the government was planning to create a health service along the lines suggested by Beveridge, they protested:

Source 1

British Medical Journal, 1943.

If this happens, then doctors will no longer be an independent, learned and liberal profession, but will instead form a service of technicians controlled by bureaucrats and by local men and women entirely ignorant of medical matters.

Up to 1945 the ideas for creating a national health service came from a Conservative Minister of Health. The Labour victory in the 1945 general election put the Ministry of Health under Labour control. The new Minister of Health was Aneurin Bevan, MP for Ebbw Vale in Wales.

Source 2

Aneurin Bevan, Minister of Health from 1945–48, visiting the tuberculosis centre at Papworth Hospital in May 1948.

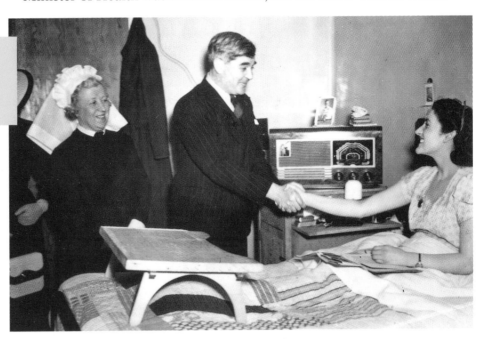

Aneurin Bevan

Aneurin Bevan – or Nye as he was known – was born in 1897 in the mining town of Tredegar in South Wales. He was the sixth of ten children, but only eight of his brothers and sisters survived infancy and only six reached adulthood. He left school at the age of thirteen to work in the local coal mine, and worked at the coal face for the next nine years.

The experience of working in the pit – of danger, long hours and low pay – made him despise the mine owners. He joined the miners' trade union and, at nineteen, became leader of the local branch. He quickly gained a reputation as a militant and in 1926 he led the Welsh miners in the General Strike. During the 1920s he was also out of work for two years.

Bevan's dislike of the mine owners grew when his father died of pneumoconiosis in 1925. This lung disease, which cements up the air passages in the lungs, was caused by a lifetime of breathing coal dust beneath the ground. Bevan later wrote in his autobiography:

Source 3

Aneurin Bevan, *In Place of Fear*, 1952.

No compensation was paid him by the mine owners; in those days it was not scheduled as an industrial disease under the Workmen's Compensation Acts.

In 1929 Bevan became a Member of Parliament, first as a member of the Independent Labour Party, then after 1931 as a member of the more moderate Labour Party. He became Minister of Health following the Labour election victory of 1945. He did not, however, forget his experiences as a young man. In a famous speech in 1948, he told Labour supporters about the time when he was unemployed in the 1920s He went on:

Source 4

Speech in Manchester, reported in *The Times*, 5 July 1948.

> That is why no amount of cajolery (sweet-talking) ... can eradicate from my heart a deep burning hatred for the Tory Party that inflicted these experiences on me. So far as I am concerned they are lower than vermin. They condemned millions of first-class people to semi-starvation.

The NHS Bill

In 1945 Bevan drew up a National Health Service bill. Bevan's bill went further than the plans of his Conservative predecessor. Four new proposals alarmed the doctors. Bevan planned to put all hospitals under the control of thirteen regional boards directed by the Ministry of Health. He wanted doctors to be paid a salary rather than fees for each of their patients. He wanted to stop doctors setting up new practices in areas where there were already enough doctors, and to encourage them into areas with too few doctors. He also wanted to abolish the right of doctors to buy and sell practices (and thus patients.) The cartoon in Source 5 reflects the worries of the doctors.

Source 5

A cartoon by 'Vicky' shows Aneurin Bevan, the new Minister of Health, walking along Harley Street, the famous London street where wealthy medical specialists and consultants have their practices.

HERE HE COMES, BOYS!

These proposals so angered the doctors that Bevan decided he had to tone them down. He began by making concessions to the most powerful doctors, the consultants who belonged to the Royal Colleges of Surgeons, Physicians and Obstetricians. He said they would be able to work part-time in the NHS, that they could charge fees to their private patients, and that they could have private hospital beds for their private patients in NHS hospitals. Privately, Bevan said he was 'stuffing their mouths with gold'.

This left the 51,000 general practitioners of the British Medical Association to deal with. Some members of the BMA were deeply suspicious of Bevan. Source 6 tell what one of them said about the NHS Bill.

Source 6

Michael Foot, *Aneurin Bevan*. Volume 2 1945–60 (1973).

The Bill can be written in two lines: "I hereby take powers to do what I like about the medical service of the country – signed Nye Bevan, fuehrer.*

Fuehrer The official title of Adolf Hitler, Nazi dictator of Germany from 1933 to 1945.

The BMA could not stop Parliament from making the NHS Bill into law in 1946, but it could try to stop its members from joining the NHS. In 1947 it organised a vote of its members in which 40,814 doctors voted against the Act and only 4,735 in favour. The NHS could not possibly work with only 4,735 doctors, so Bevan was forced to make a concession. He announced that he would add to the NHS Act a promise that doctors would never be paid wholly by salaries. At the same time he started a publicity campaign to persuade people to register with a NHS doctor. A doctor who refused to accept registrations risked losing patients to a doctor who would.

In these ways, Bevan persuaded many doctors to drop their opposition to the NHS. By the 'appointed day' for the start of the NHS, nine out of every ten GPs had joined it.

Questions

1   How does Bevan's early life help us to understand why he wanted a National Health Service under state control?

2   What do Sources 1 and 6 tell us about why the British Medical Association opposed the creation of the National Health Service?

5   Problems and achievements of the Welfare State

The arguments about the National Health Service did not stop after it was created in 1948. The NHS was immediately faced with many difficult problems. The social security schemes of National Insurance and National Assistance also ran into difficulties. This section looks at why the newly-formed Welfare State faced so many problems, and asks whether this meant that it was a failure.

Did the Welfare State succeed?

Problems of the NHS

The planners who created the NHS assumed that there was a backlog of untreated illnesses which could be cleared up very quickly – people with bad teeth or poor eyesight, for example. Once these had been treated, the planners thought, the number of patients would quickly fall.

They were wrong. Patients came in growing numbers throughout the 1950s to receive free medical treatment. One reason for this was that the

Source 1

Nine months after the creation of the NHS, out-patients at the London Hospital in Whitechapel queue to see doctors, to make appointments and to collect prescriptions.

people most likely to need medical treatment – children and old people – were increasing in numbers faster than the rest of the population. In the case of pensioners, this was because new drugs and advances in surgery helped to cure old people of illnesses such as pneumonia that previously would have killed them. Source 1 shows one of the National Health Service's biggest problems – too many patients.

The huge demand for treatment led to an explosion in the costs of the NHS. Medicines especially cost more than expected. Instead of an expected 50 million, doctors wrote 227 million prescriptions for drugs in 1951. NHS spending rose so fast that the government decided in 1951 to charge patients for part of the cost of glasses and false teeth. In 1952 it also introduced charges for prescriptions and dental treatment.

The introduction of health charges did not reduce the demand for medical care. During the 1950s and 1960s there were many advances in what doctors could do for their patients. New drugs such as penicillin allowed them to control infections. New anaesthetics allowed surgeons to perform longer and more complex operations. Naturally, the more that doctors were able to do, the more their patients came to them for treatment.

In the 1950s the government tried to keep tight control of all its spending and it limited pay increases for many state-paid workers. This had a serious effect on the NHS. While long waiting lists for hospital treatment built up, 57,000 hospital beds were empty because there was a shortage of nurses, caused mainly by low pay. Government controls on its spending also meant that no new hospitals were built during the 1950s.

Despite its problems, few people wanted to turn the clock back. A public opinion survey of 1956 found that 90 per cent of the population thought the NHS was a good service, with 7 per cent undecided and only 3 per cent against it. On the tenth anniversary of the NHS, *The Times* newspaper said that:

Source 2

The Times, 7 July 1958.

... it has been criticised in detail, but the concept as such has not been seriously challenged. Mistakes have been made, but an impartial review of the past ten years indicates that the nation has good reason to be proud of the Health Service.

Problems of social security

The social security schemes of 1948 (National Insurance and National Assistance) also ran into difficulties. The first problem was that the cash benefits provided by National Insurance were too small for many people to live on, especially the old. When they were introduced in 1948 they were already smaller than the benefits Beveridge had recommended in his Report. In the 1950s inflation reduced their value further. By 1953 one in four widows and old people were having to ask for National Assistance to supplement their pensions.

Benefits were not only small but also flat-rate: everyone got the same regardless of their needs. While poor people were getting benefits too small to live on, people who did not really need them also had a right to the same benefits. The Conservative governments of the 1950s questioned whether this was a good use of government money. Source 3, written by a leading economist, summed up this view:

Source 3

W. Hagenbuch, *The Rationale of the Social Services*, 1953.

Social services were originally intended to provide services for the poorest members of the community; now they have become the providers of universal services, free for everyone, on an ever-increasing scale.

In 1959 the government therefore brought in graduated insurance payments. Instead of paying flat-rate contributions, workers now paid according to their earnings. The more they earned, the bigger their contributions; and the bigger the contribution, the bigger the pension. In this way the government was able to increase pensions without having to spend more.

The next major change to social security came in 1966 when a Labour government scrapped the National Assistance Board and replaced it with a Supplementary Benefits scheme. This was meant to give benefits to those who most needed them. Supplementary Benefits increased claimants' incomes on a scale that took into account such things as the number and age of their children, and gave them a rent allowance. By 1980 more than 5 million people receiving National Insurance were also drawing Supplementary Benefits.

The cost of welfare

The cost of welfare was enormous. Source 4 shows how spending on social services has increased during the twentieth century. You can easily see that spending has risen faster and faster since the introduction of the Welfare State.

The most expensive of those services was social security. The rocketing costs of social security led some people, especially those in the Conservative Party, to question its very existence. They also argued that the Welfare State was taking away from many people a sense of responsibility for looking after themselves and their families. The example they gave most often to illustrate this problem was the 'social security scrounger'. From the 1950s

Source 4

The percentage of Britain's income used to pay for health, social security, education, housing and other social services.

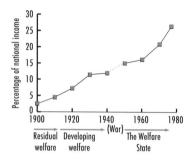

onwards, stories went round of people claiming benefits they were not entitled to. Such stories became common after the introduction of Supplementary Benefits in 1966 when, despite complex rules to ensure against it, some people found they could earn nearly as much in benefits as they could if they were working.

In 1980 the Conservative government declared that public spending was the main cause of Britain's economic difficulties. Social services was the biggest item of spending, and the government therefore set about reducing it. In 1980, for example, it stopped increasing old age pensions at the same rate of inflation, saving 4 billion pounds a year.

Despite such cuts, in 1990 the Welfare State was still receiving the same share of Britain's income as it was in 1980. As Source 4 shows, half the government's spending was on social services. This was because a massive rise in unemployment led to several million more people claiming unemployment benefits. At the same time, it seemed to many people that poverty was becoming more serious and more widespread than at any time since the start of the Welfare State. Scenes like that in Source 5 seem to show that poverty in Britain in the 1990s is still a major social problem.

Source 5

This photograph appeared in *The Guardian*, a left-of-centre newspaper, in June 1993. It showed 22-year-old James Flood, unemployed since leaving school, begging in a street in Manchester.

Questions

1 *The Times* (Source 2) said that 'mistakes have been made' in the National Health Service.

   a Use the information in this section to give examples of 'mistakes' in the first ten years of the NHS.

   b An opinion poll in 1956 found that 90 per cent of the British people supported the NHS. In view of the 'mistakes' you have listed, how might this be explained?

2 Source 5 shows a man begging in the street. Does this prove that the Welfare State has not succeeded in wiping out poverty in Britain?

Review: The Welfare State

Historians do not always agree about the history of the Welfare State. They differ chiefly on two questions. First, was the creation of the Welfare State a revolution, or was it created by a gradual process? In other words, was it the product of revolution or evolution? Second, who, if anyone, deserves the credit for creating it?

Revolution or evolution?

Forty years after the start of the Welfare State, a civil servant looked back to when he started work in the newly-created Ministry of Health:

Source 1

Patrick Benner, *The Early Years of the National Health Service – an Insider's View*, 1989.

> To me … it seemed at the time that the process must have been revolutionary rather than evolutionary, and that there was a great cataclysm in 1946–48 as a result of which an entirely new service had been brought to birth.

In 1990 a historian wrote:

Source 2

Michael Rawcliffe. *The Welfare State*, 1990.

> The Welfare State was essentially the culmination of half a century of piecemeal social reform now carried to its logical conclusion.

1. Look at pages 118–119. What was there about the National Health Service in 1948 that could be described as 'entirely new'?

2. Look at pages 99, 106 and 107. What health services already existed by 1948?

3. Look at pages 98–99, 102–104 and 112. Give examples of 'social reforms' that had been made over the half century before 1948.

4. How much progress do you consider these reforms made in the provision of welfare? Explain your answer.

5. Using the information in this book, say whether you agree with Source 1 (that the Welfare State was a revolution) or with Source 2 (that it was a result of evolution.) Explain your answer.

Source 3

This cartoon appeared on 5 July 1948 in *The Daily Herald*, a left-wing newspaper which supported the Labour Party.

BRITAIN'S QUADS: *First family album picture*

Who created the Welfare State?

In this book you have read about the involvement of many people in the subject of welfare. Some were politicians. Some were writers who drew attention to the subject of poverty and some were civil servants. There were also many less famous people; doctors, researchers and journalists, for example. Which, if any, played the biggest part in creating the Welfare State?

Source 3 gives one answer. The cartoonist George Whitelaw showed Aneurin Bevan, the Minister of Health, and James Griffiths, the Minister of National Insurance, as the proud fathers of the Welfare State.

Another newspaper, *The Times*, which claimed not to support any one party, wrote on the tenth anniversary of the National Health Service:

Source 4

The Times Supplement on the National Health Service, 7 July 1958.

Conceived by a Liberal, nurtured by a Coalition government under a Conservative Prime Minister, and brought to health by a Labour government, the National Health Service can justly claim to be a national institution.

Credit for creating the Welfare State could also be given to individuals much earlier in the century (Source 5).

Source 5

Colin Cross, Making a start on the Welfare State, in The Observer Magazine, July 1973.

Probably the greatest contribution ever made to British society by an individual politician has been that of David Lloyd George.

Professor Ben Pimlott wrote that:

Source 6

Ben Pimlott, review in The Guardian, 31 October 1992.

It is an amusing parlour game to guess what might have happened but for (the Second World War); presumably the Tories would have won an election in 1939 or 1940 and there would have been no Welfare State .... The wartime shake-up in Whitehall (was) 'Hitler's revolution'. There is certainly a sense in which it was Hitler's Beveridge Report; and today ... we still benefit from the Führer's council houses and secondary schools, social services and free hospital care.

Questions

1   Look at Source 3. What did Griffiths and Bevan do to change welfare provision in 1948?

2   **a** Read Source 4. Using pages 116, 122 and 127, identify (i) the 'Liberal', (ii) the 'Conservative Prime Minister', (iii) the Labour government   ministers who played a part in creating the National Health Service.
   b Did all the people you have identified play an equally important part in creating the Welfare State? Explain your answer.

3   Look back to pages 98-99. What did Lloyd George do between 1908 and 1912 to improve welfare provision?

4   Which of Sources 3, 4 and 5 do you think gives the best assessment of individuals' contributions to the Welfare State? Explain your answer.

5   Sources 3, 4 and 5 are taken from newspapers:
   a *The Daily Herald*, in which Source 3 appeared, supported the Labour Party. Griffiths and Bevan were Labour ministers. Might this have affected the way the cartoon portrayed the creation of the Welfare State?
   b *The Times*, from which Source 4 is taken, claimed that it did not support any political party. Might this have affected the view expressed in Source 4?
   c Source 5 comes from *The Observer*, at that time a Liberal newspaper. How might this have affected its point of view?

6   **a** Explain in your own words why Professor Pimlott suggests that the Welfare State was 'Hitler's revolution'.
   b Does this mean that Hitler can be considered as one of the people who created the Welfare State? Explain your answer.

A Changing Nation

JOSH BROOMAN

General Editor: Josh Brooman

Contents

National identities

1 Migration: a nation on the move   132

2 The experience of immigration   136

3 Doors open and close: towards a multicultural Britain   139

4 Nationalism in Britain   143

   Review: National identities   147

Focus study · Conflict and co-operation in Northern Ireland

1 Ireland becomes a free state   149

2 Northern Ireland after partition   153

3 A divided people   156

4 1969: the Troubles start   159

5 Men of violence   163

6 Sharing power   166

   Review: Conflict and co-operation in Northern Ireland   170

Longman Group UK Limited
Longman House, Burnt Mill, Harlow, Essex
CM20 2JE, England and Associated Companies throughout the World.

First published 1994

ISBN 0582 24594X

Set in Concorde and Tekton

Printed in Great Britain
by Butler and Tanner Ltd, Frome and London

The Publishers' policy is to use paper manufactured from sustainable forests.

Design and production by Hart McLeod

Illustrations by Stephen Hawes

Cover photograph *Are you angry or are you boring, 1977* ? by Gilbert and
George. © Gilbert and George/Van Abbemuseum, Eindhoven.

Acknowledgements

The written sources in this book are taken from many different kinds of
published material. Some were originally written in old-fashioned or unusual
language. This has not been altered, but in most cases, unusual or difficult
words are explained in the margin. In many of the sources words have been
left out. A cut in the middle of a sentence is shown like this ...; and at the end
of a sentence like this ....

We are grateful to the following for permission to reproduce photographs.
The numbers refer to page numbers.

Associated Newspapers Group, 138; Camera Press, 165; Express Newspapers,
169; Eye Ubiquitous/Trisha Rafferty, 157 right; Gwynedd Archives Service,
144; reproduced with permission of the controller's of Her Majesty's
Stationary Office (University of London Library), 154; Hulton-Deutsch
Collection, 136, 150, 153; Impact Photos/Alain le Garsmeur, 148; from *The
Fight Against Racism*, Institute of Race Relations, 1986, 133; Clive Limpkin,
159, 169; Magnum Photos, 162 (Bruno Barbey), 164 (Don McCullin); Barry
Lewis/Network, 157 left; Pacemaker Press, 158, 168; Press Association, 131,
134; Tegwyn Roberts, 145; Syndication International, 135, 152; courtesy
Martyn Turner/Irish Times/C & W Syndicate. Private collection, reproduced
from the front cover of *Troubled Times: Fortnight Magazine and the
Troubles in Northern Ireland*, Blackstaff Press, 1991, 170.

National identities

In 1966 England won the World Cup in a final against West Germany. Here, England supporters show their loyalty by waving the Union Jack – a combination of the English, Welsh and Scottish crosses.

Most of you reading this book are citizens of a country called the United Kingdom of Great Britain and Northern Ireland. This means you are British.

For many people this is important. They are proud to be British and they like their country. But what does being British really mean? There are many situations in which the answer isn't clear. In team sport, for example, we do not have many British teams. Football is played by English, Irish, Scottish and Welsh sides, cricket by an English eleven. One of the few teams that calls itself British is the British Lions rugby fifteen – but that includes players from the Irish Republic, which isn't part of the United Kingdom. When English football fans cheer the English team, they usually wave the Union Jack, Britain's flag, not the English Cross of St George.

Sport isn't the only thing which divides the British. The laws of Scotland differ from those of England and Wales. The British army has Scottish, Irish, Welsh and English regiments. There is a Church of England and a Church of Scotland. Schoolchildren in Scotland do not follow the same courses or take the same examinations as schoolchildren south of the border, while those in England, Wales and Northern Ireland have their own different versions of the National Curriculum.

Being Welsh, Scottish, Irish and English aren't the only variations on being British. People who live in Cardiff will probably say they are Welsh, and people in Edinburgh may say they are Scottish, but people in Newcastle are as likely to say they are Geordie as English.

It is sometimes said that we are united by the language we speak – English. Even this is only partly true. A recent survey of schools in London showed that pupils there speak 147 different languages. One pupil in six speaks English as his or her second language. Even in parts of the country where everybody speaks English, understanding it can be difficult. Southerners find it difficult to understand Geordie, while Geordies strain to understand cockney. Expressions which everyone understands in Glasgow can be meaningless in Gloucester.

So being British isn't as simple as it sounds. This book looks more closely at the British people – at where we come from and at some of the things which unite as well as divide us.

1 Migration: a nation on the move

Throughout the twentieth century the British people have been changing as a result of migration. Between 1900 and 1993 around four million Britons left the country to settle abroad, while two million arrived from overseas to settle in Britain. This section looks at the people who came to Britain and at some of their reasons for doing so.

Who settled in Britain, and why?

Jewish emigration from Russia

Source 1 shows the parts of the world that most immigrants have come from. They came in four main stages. The first took place around the turn of the century when the Russian government began to persecute the Jews of Russia, Poland and the Baltic States (Poland and the Baltic States were then part of the Russian Empire). It restricted Jews to certain parts of the country and encouraged non-Jews to kill Jews in attacks known as pogroms. Several million Jews left Russia to escape this persecution. Between 1880 and 1905 some 200,000 came to Britain. Most settled in London's East End, the rest in Manchester and Leeds.

Immigration in the era of the Second World War

The second main phase of immigration took place around the time of the Second World War. It began in the 1930s when the Nazi government persecuted the Jews of Germany and Austria (which came under German control in 1938). By 1940 some 80,000 Jews had escaped to Britain.

Immigration continued during the war when allies of Britain who had been defeated sought refuge in Britain. Many were from Poland. Around 190,000 Poles arrived between 1939 and 1945 and many served alongside the British armed forces. At the end of the war, Poles who did not want to return to Poland, now occupied by Soviet forces, were allowed to stay. Around 45,000 settled in Britain.

After the war had ended Britain needed large numbers of extra workers to rebuild the war-damaged cities, to staff new government bodies such as

Source 1

Main countries of migration to Britain in the twentieth century.

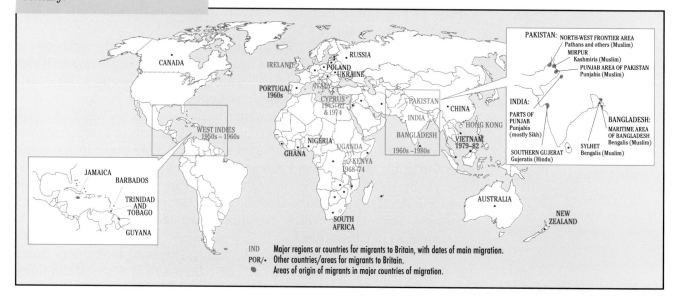

PAKISTAN: NORTH-WEST FRONTIER AREA
Pathans and others (Muslim)
MIRPUR
Kashmiris (Muslim)
PUNJAB AREA OF PAKISTAN
Punjabis (Muslim)

INDIA:
PARTS OF PUNJAB
Punjabis (mostly Sikh)
SOUTHERN GUJERAT
Gujeratis (Hindu)

BANGLADESH:
MARITIME AREA OF BANGLADESH
Bengalis (Muslim)
SYLHET
Bengalis (Muslim)

IND   Major regions or countries for migrants to Britain, with dates of main migration.
POR/·   Other countries/areas for migrants to Britain.
●   Areas of origin of migrants in major countries of migration.

the National Health Service, and to work in factories. The government found many of these extra workers by setting up recruitment agencies in foreign countries. Around 100,000 were recruited from Ireland. 'European voluntary workers' were also recruited from refugee camps in Germany and Austria. These included many Italians and people from eastern European countries that had come under Soviet control at the end of the war.

Immigration from the Commonwealth

The third major phase of immigration was also a result of the post-war labour shortage. The European and Irish workers who arrived after the war did not solve the shortage. Employers therefore looked further afield. London Transport and the National Health Service, for example, advertised jobs in the British West Indies. At that time these islands were colonies of the British Commonwealth so people there had British colonial passports. The Nationality Act of 1948 gave British citizenship to citizens of Britain's colonies and former colonies, so their passports gave them the right to come to Britain and to stay for as long as they liked.

There was no shortage of applicants for such jobs. One man who decided to work in Britain had been out of work for two years. He later explained:

Source 2

Wallace Collins, *Jamaican Migrant*, 1965. Wallace was 22 when he left Jamaica in February 1954.

I lost my job late in 1952 and stayed unemployed for over a year .... I thought and thought, and I could not invent anything else but to migrate .... I was fatherless and at one time or other the sole contributor in my family .... Migration to the UK seemed to me to be an urgent necessity. I could then support my mother and younger brothers. I could pay off her mortgage and everything would be all right.

The first post-war settlers from the Caribbean arrived in 1948 (Sources 3 and 4). Over the next ten years growing numbers of workers emigrated to Britain: 9,000 in 1954, rising to 30,000 in 1956 and to 66,000 in 1961. Later in the 1950s they were joined by workers from other colonies and ex-colonies, especially India and Pakistan, Hong Kong and Malaysia, Cyprus and parts of Africa. Most of these migrants came to do industrial jobs so they settled largely in industrial cities. Usually they could afford only cheap housing so they tended to settle in the poorer, inner areas of these cities.

Source 3

An advertisement in a Jamaican newspaper for a one-way journey to Britain.

THE SPACIOUS - COMFORTABLE - LUXURIOUS -
"Santa Maria"
SAILS AUGUST 26th!
via VIGO, SPAIN
FROM WHICH PORT PASSENGERS WILL BE TRANSPORTED BY TRAIN TO LONDON, ENGLAND at NO EXTRA COST!
BOOK NOW FOR ENGLAND
KINGSTON TO LONDON FOR ONLY £75
SEE YOUR TRAVEL AGENT IMMEDIATELY!
H. MACAULAY ORRETT LTD, 507 KING ST. KINGSTON
GENERAL AGENTS FOR: COMPANHIA COLONIAL DE NAVEGAÇÃO

Source 4

West Indian families arriving in Britain in 1948.

Many workers from the Commonwealth came not to settle, but to make money so that they could buy land or their own businesses when they returned home. An Indian called Rampal described how he felt when he saw such people returning home after working in the UK:

Source 5

Ursula Sharma, *Rampal and his Family*, 1971.

Vilayat is the origin of the word 'Blighty' and means 'abroad', especially England.

For everyone in India life was a struggle to earn his daily bread .... Those who are employed by others sweat in order to earn a 100 rupees or even 200 – seldom more. With that wage they have to keep their families for a whole month.

On the other hand, as I saw for myself, those people who had been to England came back wearing brand new suits and loaded with money. And all those who had daughters to marry would rush to their doors .... And those who had been to vilayat* to work could send money home each month and still afford to buy land or build a fine house in India on their return. Surely if they could do all this I could do the same.

For many people the opportunity to return home with a fortune never arose. They stayed in Britain, and saved to bring their families and relatives to join them. The number of 'dependants', as families and relatives were known, rose sharply during the 1960s. By 1967 nearly nine immigrants out of ten were arriving in order to join the head of the family.

East African Asians

The last major phase of immigration took place during the early 1970s. The migrants in this case were Asians living in Kenya and Uganda.

Source 6

A family of refugees from Uganda waiting for a train at Bishop's Stortford after arriving at Stansted Airport in 1972.

Kenya was a British colony until 1963. Over 100,000 people living there were Asians who long ago had left the Indian sub-continent to settle in Africa. When Kenya became independent in 1963, the Asians were given a choice of becoming Kenyans or remaining British. Around 95,000 decided to stay British and thus kept their UK passports.

The Asians in Kenya had for long been unpopular. Many were business or professional people, better-off than most black Kenyans. In 1967 the government declared that all non-Kenyan citizens would be treated as foreigners. This meant that they could live and work in Kenya only on a temporary basis. Many decided to leave the country for Britain.

Similar events took place in Uganda. As in Kenya, Uganda had a large Asian population that was envied and disliked by black Africans because they owned so many of the country's shops and businesses. In 1972 the Ugandan President announced that all Asians with British passports must leave the country immediately. Faced with threats of violence if they did not do so, the British government airlifted many thousands of Ugandan Asians out of the country. In all, some 71,000 Kenyan and Ugandan Asians arrived in Britain between 1968 and 1974.

Questions

1 Look at Source 3.
   a Use an atlas and its index to find the places mentioned in Source 3, then trace the journey from Kingston (Jamaica) to London of migrants on the *Santa Maria*.
   b The cost of the ticket, £75, would be about £750, today. Suggest why many Jamaicans were prepared to pay large sums of money for a difficult journey like this.

2 a What similarities are there between Wallace Collins' reasons for migrating to Britain (Source 2) and those of Rampal (Source 5)?
   b How do their reasons differ?

3 What reasons for migrating to Britain do you think the family in Source 6 had? Explain your answer.

2 The experience of immigration

Source 1

A recently arrived migrant from the West Indies walks the streets of Birmingham in 1949, looking for somewhere to live.

Many immigrants found that the advantages of living in Britain came at a cost. Whether they were from Africa or Asia, Europe or the Caribbean, immigrants often met hostility from people already living in Britain. This section investigates that hostility and looks at some of the ways in which immigrants reacted to it.

'White rejection, black withdrawal'

Source 2 is taken from the memory of a Polish woman whose family came to Britain at the end of the Second World War.

Source 2

A Polish interviewer working for the Adult Language Use Survey, quoted in ALUS, *The Other Languages of England*, 1985.

I attended an English school and most of my friends were English, but there was almost complete division between my Polish life and my English life .... If I said I was Polish, I would be asked when I had come here, or I would be told, 'No, you are not, you're British!' But I was also told that I had a funny name, that my family ate horrible foreign food, that we spoke a peculiar language, and that we had Christmas on the wrong day*.

Christmas on the wrong day
Polish people traditionally celebrate Christmas on 24 December.

As Source 2 suggests, a European who spoke good English was likely to be thought of as British. Non-Europeans were less likely to be treated as British because of their skin colour. Many immigrants from Asia, Africa and the West Indies found that the colour of their skins provoked unfriendly reactions. Theresa McClean, a Jamaican who came to Britain in 1963 when she was twelve, wrote this about her early experiences:

Source 3

Desmond Mason (Ed), From *Where I Stand. Minority experiences of life in Britain*, 1986.

I myself experienced things like going into a shop and having the shopkeeper totally ignore my presence, while they served people who came into the shop after me; or going to the Post Office to cash my giro or family allowance, and hearing somebody behind me refer to niggers who come to this country to scrounge, or niggers who have colour TVs and drive big cars while they are on the dole. It is hard to describe the emotions I experience at these times: emotions ranging from intense hate to cold indifference.

As you have read, most Asians, Africans and West Indians came to Britain in order to work. Despite the desperate labour shortage in the 1940s and 1950s, many found it difficult to get good jobs. More than half the West Indians who arrived in the 1950s had to accept jobs that were less skilled and worse paid than those for which they were qualified. A Mr Johnson, recalling his first weeks in London, described what always seemed to happen when he applied for a job:

Source 4

Donald Hinds, *Journey to an Illusion*, 1966.

Lyons The largest chain of restaurants in Britain in the 1950s.

They were all nice when they told me that they had nothing for me. Sometimes they would tell me that if I had come just that morning they would have taken me on, but as it was I was just a few hours too late. Boy, the Englishman can be the nicest man out when he is telling you no .... Back home I used to work as a welder. It didn't take me long to realise that I couldn't get a job in that trade .... So I start to ask for anything which would take me off the dole .... At last I went to Lyons*, and get a job there as a porter. I sweep and clean their place for four years.

When they did find work, Asian and West Indian immigrants were often treated badly by other workers. In Source 5 a Pakistani described an early experience.

Source 5

A Pakistani shopkeeper, quoted in Chris Mullard, *Black Britain*, 1973.

We were treated like filth, not good enough to lick their arses. I remember being told at an engineering firm I worked for ... to clean out the toilets. I told the chargehand it wasn't my job and that I wouldn't do it. The next thing I knew I was pounced on by half a dozen louts, kicked in the balls and thrown down the toilet.

Immigrants also found it difficult to obtain good housing. There were two problems. First, most immigrants could afford only cheap accommodation, and they needed to live close to where they worked. This meant living in poor, inner-city areas where housing was cheap. Second, many landlords refused to let their property to non-white people. The few houses that were available to rent or to buy therefore tended to be overcrowded.

The experience of racial discrimination led many immigrants to group together in small areas of towns and cities where they could find safety and friendship. Areas like Brixton in London or Handsworth in Birmingham quickly became 'ethnic enclaves' in which most residents were immigrants or the children of immigrants. As the years went by, and the immigrants saved money, more and more of them bought housing in these areas. Source 6 describes how Sikh immigrants bought houses in a street in Gravesend, in Kent.

Source 6

Arthur Wesley Helweg, *Sikhs in England*, 1986. The author, a social scientist, spent seven months living in the Sikh community in Gravesend in 1970–71, collecting information about the lives, culture and conditions of Sikhs.

In 1950, Baljit Singh ... came to Gravesend accompanied by his wife's cousin, ... Prakash Singh ... and his wife's nephew, Ajit Singh .... Prakash Singh's father had been living in Gravesend since 1949, and with him, Baljit Singh and Prakash Singh bought the house at 48 Pier Road. They lived as bachelors there until 1952, when Baljit Singh's brother, Sital Singh, arrived. At that time two English sisters in number 76, moving out to the country, sold their house to Baljit Singh and Sital Singh. When elderly Mrs Johnson migrated to Canada to be with her daughter, Sital Singh bought number 78 from her and moved with his family into the house, along with his wife's cousin and his wife ....

In the areas where large numbers of immigrants lived, racial tensions sometimes led to violence and rioting. The worst violence took place in the summer of 1958. It started in a pub in Nottingham with fights between West Indian and white men. The fights grew into a riot in which 1,500 whites attacked black people with razors, knives and bottles. In London, news of the Nottingham riot led to similar outrages in the poor black area of Notting Hill. During the first two weeks of September 1959, mobs of young white people made organised attacks on black people in the streets and smashed and burned their homes:

Source 7

Young white people running from police during the Notting Hill riots of 1958.

The race riots of 1958 hardened the attitudes of black and white people towards each other. One West Indian leader later said:

Source 8

Quoted in Dilip Hiro, *Black British, White British*, 1971.

The Notting Hill riots taught us one bitter lesson; we were black first and British last.

For many years to come, the issue of colour and British nationality would arouse ugly emotions in some white people, as Source 9 shows. It is an anonymous letter received by a West Indian race relations worker after he wrote an article about race relations in *The Times* in 1967:

Source 9

Chris Mullard, *Black Britain*, 1973.

Get out of our country Black Rubbish! You can never, never be English.

We shall always hate you, because blacks are lazy, immoral, savage, drug-taking, stinking bastards and we will never integrate with you.

Beware, Britons never, never, shall be slaves – especially to Niggers. So you will be turned out, and our fair land will be free from the black scum spreading over it.

How dare you presume to call yourself English – Black Apes and Cannibals not so long ago.

Questions

1 Look at Source 1. Suggest why:
   a the man is looking for somewhere to live in an inner city area of Birmingham, rather than a suburb;
   b why, although he is smartly dressed, he is finding it difficult to get accommodation.

2 According to Source 2, what were the things about being Polish that English people found unusual?

   a How do the experiences of the Jamaican woman in Source 3 differ from those of the Polish woman in Source 2?
   b Suggest a reason for the difference.

3 Suggest why the members of the Singh family (Source 6) bought so many houses in Pier Road rather than other streets in Gravesend.

4 Using the sources and information in this section, give reasons why:
   a many black people were living together in 'ethnic enclaves' in cities, rather than spread across the country.
   b this led to violence and rioting in some of these areas.

3 Doors open and close: towards a multicultural Britain

The race riots of 1958 showed that Britain had a worsening problem of race relations. Governments in the 1960s came under pressure to take action on immigration and race relations. They tackled these issues in three ways. The first was to limit the number of immigrants coming to Britain. The second was to try to assure equal rights for those already living here. The third was to encourage immigrants to integrate with the rest of the community. It was a policy of closing doors between Britain and the Commonwealth, while trying to open doors inside Britain itself.

Closing the doors: controls on immigration
The 1948 Nationality Act gave UK citizenship to citizens of Britain and to those in Britain's former colonies. A British passport allowed citizens of

these Commonwealth countries the unrestricted right to settle in Britain.

Following the racial violence of the 1950s, the government restricted this right. A Commonwealth Immigrants Act in 1962 took away the automatic right of entry from British passport holders, and limited the number of entrants by a quota of job vouchers. This did not, however, apply to the Dominions of the Commonwealth – Canada, Australia and New Zealand – whose citizens were mostly white. It applied only to the 'New Commonwealth' countries such as India and Pakistan, which had gained their independence since the Second World War.

Immigration was further restricted by the 1971 Immigration Act. This said that the right to live in the UK belonged only to people who were born in the UK or whose father or grandfather was born here. Anyone else needed a work permit to enter the country. These would be issued only for specific, mostly skilled jobs, for a stated length of time.

Many people said the act was racist because it treated white and black immigrants differently. White people from Australia or Canada were more likely to have British-born parents or grandparents than black people from the 'New Commonwealth' countries. The government defended the act by saying that smaller numbers of coloured immigrants would make it easier for white people to adjust to a multi-racial society.

Opening doors? Race relations policies

Government attempts to improve race relations began with a Race Relations Act in 1965. This made it illegal for public places such as pubs and dancehalls to turn people away because of their colour or race. It made it unlawful to say or to publish anything that incited racial hatred and it set up a Race Relations Board to deal with complaints.

The 1965 Act did nothing about two key areas of racial discrimination – housing and jobs. A second Race Relations Act in 1968 made it illegal for landlords and estate agents to discriminate against people on racial grounds. It said that refusal to employ, to train or to promote someone on grounds of race or colour was unlawful. It also made it illegal to show advertisements that discriminated on grounds of colour or race. Finally, the 1968 Act set up a Community Relations Commission.

A third Race Relations Act in 1976 was more far-reaching than the first two acts. First, it outlawed indirect discrimination. In the field of work, this meant that employers could no longer lay down conditions which resulted in black people not getting a job – for example, by saying that employees must have gone to school in Britain. Second, the Act set up a Commission for Racial Equality to replace the Community Relations Commission. This new body had powers which the earlier body did not have. It could, for example, look for cases of discrimination rather than just deal with complaints. Third, the Act also required local and national government to promote better race relations and to provide equal opportunities for black and white people.

Integration or disintegration?

The government hoped that its immigration and race relations policies would lead to the integration of immigrants into British society. If numbers of immigrants were limited, white Britons would more readily accept the presence of ethnic groups. How far did this work?

From the early 1950s onwards, well-meaning people formed local groups to promote harmony between ethnic communities and their white 'hosts'. Groups such as 'international friendship councils' tried to create a climate of tolerance by organising social events and by providing advice and information. Source 1 shows some of the difficulties involved in this approach. In it Chris Mullard, a black Englishman, describes how the international friendship group he joined in the 1960s organised 'home culture evenings'. At these events, African, West Indian, Asian and English members took turns to present aspects of their culture:

Source 1

Chris Mullard, *Black Britain*, 1973.

Every now and then white members insisted on displaying samples of home-grown culture to their guests. One of the first such evenings I attended began with a display of sword dancing, quickly followed by folk-singing turns, party games, old tyme dancing and a conjuror, building up to the climax of the evening – Knees Up, Mother Brown ....

After too many months of this I ceased going to group meetings. The group could not accept that I was a black man born in England and therefore English. It could not package me off as one of its overseas members. A threat to their own identity, their purpose, the whites saw me as a spy, untrustworthy ....

People who worked for racial integration put many of their hopes in education. By learning and playing together, they hoped, children would grow up in a common culture, speaking a common language. Some migrants, however, doubted whether this was a good thing. Source 2 was written by a Greek Cypriot who helped to set up a Greek language school in London. In it he explains the dangers that the average Greek Cypriot parent saw in this kind of 'assimilation'.

Source 2

Adamos Adamantos, *The Work of the Cyprus Educational Mission*, in *Cyprus Week in Camden*, 1972.

He is scared of the influence of the environment on his children .... They are neither Cypriot nor British. They are not Cypriot because ... their ways, aspects, beliefs are those of English boys and girls. They are not English, they have peculiar long names, their parents are foreigners, they are not always accepted by their peers and society. Parents want an identity for their children .... They will never accept assimilation.

In the 1970s some schools tried to tackle issues of immigrant culture by altering the school curriculum. Children were taught about the Hindu and Muslim religions as well as about Christianity. History and geography lessons looked beyond Britain to the Caribbean, Africa and Asia. Such efforts did not seem to succeed. There was growing evidence by 1980 that black children were underachieving in most schools, and that lessons, books and teaching materials reflected white, English attitudes. Moreover, as Source 3 suggests, multicultural education often went no further than the classroom:

Source 3

Ian Jack, *Before the Oil Ran Out. Britain 1977–1987*, 1989. Interview with the leader of the Southall Youth Movement in London, 1981.

We believe in our own culture. The communities here are already segregated. The Asians go to Asian shops, the English go to English shops, there's no mixing after school. Multiracialism and multiculturalism are figments of the imagination.

During the 1980s many local education authorities adopted anti-racist policies to improve the school performance of ethnic minorities. Through the appointment and training of teachers and the production of new teaching materials, schools tried to overcome racist attitudes and to make sure that the curriculum reflected the needs of ethnic minority groups.

By the end of the 1980s it was commonplace to hear Britain described as a multiracial, multicultural society. Source 4 illustrates this. It is a page from a history book published as a tribute to the Queen on her 60th birthday in 1986. However, the progress made in schools was not matched in all other public services. Police forces especially seemed to harbour racist attitudes and behaviour. This led to a breakdown of relations in many inner city areas between police and ethnic minority groups. There was also growing evidence that black people continued to suffer from discrimination

Source 4

A page from Philip Ziegler's *Elizabeth's Britain 1926–1986*, 1986.

By the sixtieth year of the Queen's life Britain had undeniably become a multi-racial society. Here two of her subjects study the form from the Royal Enclosure at Ascot.

The Notting Hill carnival annually produces an explosion of uninhibited fun. Although sometimes marred by violence, convivial scenes such as this have become a symbol of inter-racial harmony.

in the key areas of housing and employment. Religion too proved to be a source of conflict as well as co-operation, with Muslims demanding more recognition of their religion in education and in law.

At the start of the 1990s there was little sign that ethnic groups had become fully integrated in British society. One authority on the subject, the Pakistan-born Dilip Hiro, described the relationship between ethnic groups and white people as 'social, or cultural pluralism'. By this he meant that the ethnic minorities and the white majority are equal as citizens, but keep themselves separate in such things as marriage, friendships, beliefs and diet. He finished his account by asking:

Source 5

Dilip Hiro, *Black British, White British* (2nd edition), 1991.

The basic question to ask is: are we to remain prisoners of the past, insisting on an ... image of a Briton as a person who is white, Christian, clean-shaven, wearing a suit or skirt?, Or should we start conceiving a pluralistic image of being a Briton, possibly black or brown, Hindu or Muslim, wearing a turban, a kanga or sari?

Questions

1 Read Source 1 again. What does it tell you about the difficulties that ethnic minorities had in integrating with white people?

2 According to Source 2 why were Greek Cypriots in London unwilling to accept 'assimilation' (integration) into society?

3 Look at Source 4 and read the captions carefully.
   a What point about race relations is made in the captions?
   b How do the photographs support that point of view?
   c How could Source 3 be used to disagree with that point of view?
   d Judging by what you have read in Sections 2 and 3, how far do you agree with that point of view? Explain your answer.
   e The author wrote his book as a tribute to the Queen on her 60th birthday. How might this have affected his view of race relations?
   f Why might a black historian such as Dilip Hiro (Source 5) disagree with the view in Source 4?

4 Nationalism in Britain

In three large areas of the United Kingdom people throughout the twentieth century have demanded the right to control their own affairs. Nationalists in Ireland, Scotland and Wales have worked to break free of the government in London so that they can govern themselves. In southern Ireland they succeeded, gaining independence in 1922. Everywhere else nationalists have been less successful, in the 1990s still remaining under the rule of Westminster.

You can find out about Irish nationalists in the focus study on pages 148–170. In this section we will look at nationalists in Wales – at what they hoped to achieve and at how they went about it.

Why Welsh nationalism?

Welsh national identity

At the start of this century Wales was an unusual part of the United Kingdom. For a start, nearly half a million people spoke only Welsh. In north-west and west Wales, half the population did not speak English.

In all parts of Wales, religion was a vital part of everyday life. Half a million people went regularly to chapel, as non-conformist churches such as the Presbyterian and the Baptist churches were known. Chapel-goers observed strict standards of behaviour, for example abstaining from alcohol and never working on Sundays. A religious revival which swept Wales in 1905 boosted the number of chapel-goers to 549,000.

The culture of the Welsh also made them a distinctive people. More than for most other people in the United Kingdom, singing, poetry and music-making was an important and regular part of ordinary people's lives.

Language, religion and culture were the three most important features of Welsh national identity, but not the only ones. In Source 2 a British social historian describes several other unusual features of Welsh society.

Source 1

The *Gorsedd*, a group of bards and druids, pose for the camera in front of Caernarfon Castle in 1894.

Source 2

John Stevenson, *British Society 1914–1945*, 1984.

In 1901 nine out of ten people in rural Cardigan had been born within the county or just over its border. Here ... the language of common speech, Welsh, classified a family's position by the size of its holding and the number of animals it could maintain – '*Lle buwch*' (a cow place), '*Ile ceffyl*' (a one-horse place) and '*Ille doubar*' (a place of two pairs) .... Cottagers performed labour service at haymaking to service their cows and obtain the right to plant potatoes in farm fields by '*dyled gwaith*' (work debt) or '*dyled tato*' (potato debt) performed at harvest time.

Threats to Welsh identity

All these things that gave the Welsh their identity came under threat soon after the start of the century. As communications with the rest of the United Kingdom improved, more people took to speaking English and the number of Welsh-speakers fell. The religious revival of 1905 did not last and by 1910 the non-conformist churches were reporting sharp falls in their membership. To counter the decline of Welsh language and religion a group of thinkers formed a Welsh Nationalist Party in 1925.

Plaid Genedlaethol Cymru, as the new party was called (later shortened to *Plaid Cymru*), was at first a middle class organisation. Consisting mostly of Welsh-speaking teachers, lecturers, chapel ministers and professional people, it had no more than 2,000 members by 1939. Their over-riding aim was to halt the decline of the Welsh language. The leader, Saunders Lewis, explained why this was so important:

Source 3

From an article by Saunders Lewis, leader of *Plaid Cymru*, in *Y Faner*, the party newspaper, in 1923.

Language is the fruit of society, is essential to civilisation, and is the treasury of all the experiences and memories of a nation. It keeps the visions, and desires and dreams of the nation and treasures them in literature. It holds the memory of the nation, its knowledge of its beginnings, of its youth, its suffering, its problems and its victories – all that constitutes the history of a nation.

The rise of Plaid Cymru

Plaid Cymru remained a tiny party for many years, rarely winning more than 1,000 votes in general elections. Most people, especially those in industrial and mining areas, voted for the Labour Party. In the 1950s, however, Plaid Cymru broadened its aims. It started to involve itself in political as well as language issues.

One issue which gained it great publicity was the unlikely subject of water supplies. In the 1950s several English city councils bought land in Welsh valleys which they planned to make into reservoirs by building dams across them. Plaid Cymru did all it could to stop the valleys being drowned. Its strongest protests were against a dam that Liverpool Corporation wanted to build across the Tryweryn valley in north-west Wales. There was no authority in Wales which could stop Liverpool from drowning a Welsh village. Gwynfor Evans, Plaid Cymru's leader from 1945 to 1981, explained why he found this unacceptable:

Source 4

From *Land of My Fathers*, the autobiography of Gwynfor Evans, 1976.

Englynwyr folk poets.

Penillion Literally 'old stanzas', a form of verse used in singing.

I loved the wonderful vigour of the society in the Tryweryn valley where there was a fine company of englynwyr* and harpists. Like Thomas Pennant in the eighteenth century I too heard penillion* singing that continued for hours in farmhouses. 'They would continue singing without intermission and never repeat the same stanza; for that would occasion the loss of honour of being held first of the song.'

The protest failed, the dam was built and the valley was flooded to make a reservoir, but campaigns like this gave Plaid Cymru great publicity. This, combined with a fall in support for the Labour Party in the late 1960s, allowed it to increase its votes to 175,000 in the 1970 general election and to win several seats in Parliament.

Direct action groups

Plaid Cymru was only one of several organisations which aimed to protect the identity of the Welsh. The Welsh Language Society, formed in 1962, aimed to halt the spreading use of English in Wales. For the next twenty years it carried out a campaign of direct, but non-violent action to publicise its aims. Its most effective protests were the painting over of English place-names with Welsh names on road signs.

Several nationalist groups used violent methods. The Movement for the Defence of Wales attacked dams and power lines. In 1969 it also tried to

Source 5

A demonstration by the Welsh Language Society near Dolgellau in November 1975.

set off a bomb during the ceremony at which Prince Charles was crowned Prince of Wales. The Free Wales Army, with a badge of the 'White Eagle of Snowdon', made bomb and arson attacks on water pipelines, army bases and government offices. The Sons of Glendower made arson attacks on houses which English people had bought as holiday homes in Wales.

Devolution

Under pressure from both Scottish and Welsh nationalist groups in 1976 the British government drew up plans for a Welsh and a Scottish assembly to help run the affairs of the two nations. In Wales, an elected 80-member assembly would help run education, health and social services, industry and local government (although the Westminster Parliament would have the power to block its decisions).

There was much opposition in Wales to this 'devolution' of power. Many people, especially in South Wales, feared that extreme nationalists would get control of the assembly and that they would force everyone to speak Welsh. In 1979 Welsh and Scottish voters were able to show in a referendum what they thought about devolution. In Wales, only a fifth of voters supported the measure, while in Scotland there was only a small majority in favour. The devolution plans for both Scotland and Wales were dropped.

The vote against devolution was a big setback for Plaid Cymru and it became a less powerful force in Wales in the 1980s. Only on the language issue were the nationalists able to make progress. In 1982, after a campaign of withholding their TV licence fees, nationalists forced the government to allow Wales a new Welsh language TV channel, S4C (Sianel 4 Cymru). Bowing to pressure from the Welsh Language Society, English road signs throughout Wales were replaced with dual language signs. Following the Education Reform Act of 1989, Welsh became a compulsory subject for all pupils in Welsh schools. This means that everyone in the next generation in Wales should have at least a basic command of the language.

Questions

1 Look at Source 3:
   a Imagine that nobody in the United Kingdom can speak English. Give an example of something important 'in the memory of the nation' that might be forgotten.
   b How does your answer to (a) help you to understand Plaid Cymru's attempts to halt the decline of the Welsh language?

2 What does Source 4 tell you about Plaid Cymru's reasons for opposing the building of reservoirs in Welsh valleys?

3 a Suggest why the people in Source 5 so disliked road signs in English.
   b Why do you think they concentrated their campaign on removing or painting over English road signs?

4 Look back to Source 2 on page 141. What similarities are there between Greek Cypriots in London wanting their children to learn Greek, and Welsh nationalists wanting to preserve the Welsh language?

5 Judging by what you have read in this section, have Welsh nationalists made any progress in the twentieth century? Explain your answer carefully.

Review: National identities

1 Investigation: a local study

Pupils in many schools, especially those in large cities, are from a variety of different ethnic backgrounds – European, Asian, Caribbean or African. They may have parents, grandparents, or other family members who can provide information about why they migrated to Britain. If you are in a school like this, you have the opportunity to carry out a local study into patterns of migration in the twentieth century.

a Find out from as many people as you can (classmates, or neighbours, for example) *when* their parents/grandparents/great grandparents etc arrived in Britain, *where* they came from, and reasons *why* they decided to migrate.

b Make a map like the one on page 132 of *A Changing Nation*. For each person in your survey, label the map to show the date, origin and reason for migration, (Copymaster 6 may be used here).

c When your labelled map is complete, use it as the main illustration in a talk, or a tape presentation, or a written account about 'Migration to Britain' in your locality during the twentieth century.

2 Essay

Dilip Hiro, a British historian, summed up the experience of many non-white immigrants after they arrived in Britain as 'White rejection, black withdrawal'.

Using the sources and information in sections 2 and 3, find evidence of:
a 'white rejection' of non-white immigrants,
b the 'withdrawal' of non-white immigrants from the rest of British society.

Use the evidence you have gathered to write an essay in answer to this question:
Is the phrase 'white rejection, black withdrawal' an accurate description of what happened to immigrants to Britain in the twentieth century?

Focus study · Conflict and co-operation in Northern Ireland

Armed soldiers at the scene of a bomb explosion in a Catholic bar in Belfast.

Scenes like that in the picture above are rare in most British towns and cities. In one part of the United Kingdom they are common. For a quarter of a century the people of Northern Ireland have regularly experienced riots, murder, arson, kidnap, and bombing. Nearly 3,000 have been killed and thousands more injured in these Troubles.

This focus study looks in detail at the Troubles of Northern Ireland. Section 1 shows how they have their origins in four hundred years of British history and explains how the present-day division of Ireland between north and south came about in 1922. Sections 2–4 show how several long-standing problems in Northern Ireland led to violent conflict in 1968–69, while sections 5–6 examine why attempts at co-operation have always failed.

1 Ireland becomes a free state

A divided people

The 'troubles' in Northern Ireland are the result of divisions among its people. The population is divided first and foremost along religious lines. Protestants and Catholics mostly live in separate communities and it is rare for them to socialise or to go to school or work together,

This is not all. Deep political, social and economic divisions lie beneath the religious division. The two communities have different political aims. Most Protestants are 'Unionists' who want Northern Ireland to remain part of the United Kingdom. Most Catholics are nationalists who want Northern Ireland to be united with the Republic of Ireland in a single Irish state.

Protestants and Catholics have historical reasons for their differences. Both have powerful traditions and deep loyalties which they can trace back hundreds of years, so history is something else that divides them.

Underpinning these divisions are social and economic inequalities. For hundreds of years Protestants and Catholics could tell each other apart by their standing in society, by the work they did, the homes they lived in and the property they owned.

When the Great War began in 1914, however, hundreds of thousands of Irishmen – Catholics as well as Protestants – joined the British army to fight against Germany. For the time being, most Irishmen fought together in a common cause.

But not all. Around 12,000 Irish Volunteers decided not to join the British army. Most belonged to two extreme groups, the Irish Republican Brotherhood (IRB) and Sinn Féin (pronounced *shin fayn*, meaning Ourselves Alone). Soon after the war began, they decided to rebel against British rule. Their aim was to expel the British from all Ireland. They thought the British government would be too busy fighting Germany to stop them.

The Easter Rising, 1916

The rebellion began on Easter Monday 1916. Led by Patrick Pearse of the IRB and James Connolly, leader of a 'Citizen's Army', around 1,600 Irish Volunteers took control of fourteen key points in the city of Dublin and opened fire on British troops.

The rising failed. After five days of heavy street fighting, killing 300 civilians, 130 British soldiers and 60 rebels, the Volunteers were forced to surrender. As they were taken to prison, angry Dubliners spat and cursed at them for bringing death and destruction to the city.

Public opinion soon swung the other way when the British authorities tried and executed all but one of the sixteen rebel leaders. Disgust at the executions turned anger against the rebels into support for their cause. As a result, Sinn Féin won 73 seats out of the 105 Irish seats in Parliament in the 1918 general election.

Led by Eamon De Valera, the Sinn Féin MPs refused to attend the Parliament in Westminster. Instead they formed their own Parliament in Dublin, the Dáil Eireann (Irish Parliament, pronounced doyle.) They demanded that all of Ireland should be independent from Britain.

The rise of the IRA

On the same day as the Dáil first met in 1919, the Irish Volunteers renewed their armed rebellion against British rule. Calling themselves the Irish Republican Army (IRA), they began a series of attacks on soldiers, policemen and British officials. The British recruited recently demobbed soldiers to fight back. Known as Black and Tans because they wore dark green police belts and hats with their khaki army uniforms, these soldiers used extreme violence to try to crush the IRA. Hundreds of civilians, soldiers and IRA were killed as the two sides fought each other in a war of ambushes, shootings, burning and bombing.

In 1920 the British government tried to halt the violence by reforming the way it ruled Ireland. A Government of Ireland Act divided Ireland into two countries. One was made up of six of the nine counties of Ulster. The other consisted of the other 26 counties in the rest of Ireland. Each country was to have its own parliament, but the Westminster parliament would have the final say on any decisions which they made.

The Protestants in Ulster accepted the Act, but the 26 southern counties rejected it. The republicans there continued their war for a fully independent Ireland. By 1921, however, both sides were tired enough of the fighting to agree to peace talks. In a truce with Sinn Féin, the British government offered to give southern Ireland independence as a dominion of the British Empire, like Australia or Canada. The six Ulster counties would remain part of the United Kingdom.

Eamon De Valera and several other Sinn Féin leaders angrily rejected this offer. They said that Britain would keep some influence over Irish affairs if Ireland was a dominion, and so it was not true independence. The IRA, however, was not strong enough to continue fighting the British and public opinion was turning against the violence. In December 1921, therefore, the two sides signed the Anglo-Irish Treaty, dividing Ireland between Ulster in the north and an Irish Free State in the south.

Source 1

British troops in Dublin in February 1921 hold back a crowd during a round-up of IRA suspects.

What difference did independence make to Ireland?

The Irish Civil War 1922–23

Independence did not bring an end to the violence in Ireland. A cruel civil war began soon after the Free State was created. The Anglo-Irish Treaty divided Sinn Féin and other Republicans. Pro-treaty republicans, led by Michael Collins and Arthur Griffith, were soon fighting anti-treaty republicans led by Eamon De Valera. From summer 1922 to May 1923, anti-Treaty units in the IRA, known as Irregulars, fought soldiers of the new Irish Free State in guerilla raids and ambushes. They struck their hardest blow in August 1922 when they killed Michael Collins in an ambush.

The government of the Free State dealt harshly with the Irregulars. Twelve thousand suspects were imprisoned without trial, and 77 rebels arrested carrying arms were executed by special courts. By May 1923 the Irregulars had been so weakened that De Valera called off the fighting.

De Valera and Fianna Fáil

Although defeated in the civil war, De Valera did not give up his struggle for an independent Ireland. Instead of fighting, he decided that the way to get independence was through the Dáil. Sinn Féin, however, had refused to take up their seats in protest against the 1922 Treaty. In 1926 De Valera therefore split from Sinn Féin and set up a new party, Fianna Fáil (Soldiers of Destiny – pronounced fee-anna foyle). Moderate members of Sinn Féin who wanted to enter the Dáil joined the new party and it gradually built up support. When it won elections in 1932, De Valera became President of the committee that governed the Free State. Over the next five years he cut the Free State's links with Britain and, in 1937, introduced a new constitution. This made Ireland a republic and changed the country's name to Eire, Gaelic for Ireland. De Valera himself became Prime Minister.

Economic difficulties

The civil war, combined with an economic slump and bad weather, kept farm output down and prices low. Unemployment in industry remained high. National income rose very slowly as a result, so the government had to restrict its spending. This meant that little was done to overcome the poverty of many Irish people. In particular nothing was done to clear the slums in Dublin which for many years had been seen as the result of British misrule. Children like those in Source 1 continued to run around bare-footed for many years to come.

The new government did spend some money on improving the economy. For example, it set up an Electricity Supply Board to extend the country's electricity grid. Its building of a large power station on the River Shannon helped bring electricity to many poorer areas in the 1930s.

A stagnant society

Society was slow to change in the Irish Free State. A census in 1926 showed that the population structure had changed little in the past 50 years. Over half the population lived in the country and made a living from farming. Four out of five farmers worked small farms which they had bought in the late nineteenth century and most were content to go on doing so. Every year thousands of Irish men and women emigrated to live overseas, just as they had been doing for the past century. By the late 1920s nearly half of all Irish-born people were living overseas, with the result that the number of people living in Ireland hardly grew.

Irish language

Although society was slow to change, the culture of Ireland received a boost from independence. After centuries in which English was the official language of government and education, Gaelic became the country's official language in 1922, used in the civil service, armed forces, police and law courts. From 1926 all infant classes in schools were taught in Gaelic. In secondary schools it became a compulsory subject in 1934.

A Catholic state

Catholics were badly treated while the British ran Ireland. They were far more likely than Protestants to have bad housing or low-paid jobs, for example. Independence meant that Catholics in the Free State were no longer treated as second-class citizens. The Catholic Church itself gained in influence, and was recognised in the new constitution of 1937 as 'the guardian of the Faith professed by the great majority of citizens'.

Source 2

The 1922 border between Northern Ireland and the Irish Free State cut through many towns and villages. This photograph shows the village of Pettigo, on the border between County Fermanagh in Northern Ireland and County Donegal in Eire. The border is the river running left to right through the middle of the village. The Northern Ireland part of the village, above the river in this picture, was renamed Tullyhommon.

Questions

1 Look at Source 2. Using the information in the text, say how life for people in the Irish half of the village would have changed from that of people in the Northern Ireland part of the village after 1922.

2 **a** Use the information and sources in this section to describe ways in which Ireland (i) changed a lot, (ii) changed little after gaining independence as the Irish Free State in 1922.
   b Which of those changes do you think could be described as changes for the better? Explain your answer.

2   Northern Ireland after partition

You have read that political, economic and social problems stunted the development of the Irish Free State after 1921. Different problems afflicted the six counties of Ulster which, together known as Northern Ireland, remained part of the United Kingdom. While the Irish Free State was governed by Catholics, Protestants quickly gained the upper hand in Northern Ireland. By the 1930s Protestants not only controlled Northern Ireland but they also kept Catholics in an inferior position. This section looks at how they achieved such control.

How did Protestants get more power than Catholics?

Source 1 shows that the population of Ulster was unevenly mixed between Protestants and Catholics. This made it impossible to draw a border neatly between them. In three of the counties that formed Northern Ireland, Catholics outnumbered Protestants. Yet, overall, Protestants formed two thirds of the Northern Ireland population.

In areas where the population was mixed, partition was followed by fighting. In Belfast, between 1920 and 1922, 257 Catholics and 157 Protestants were killed, 23,000 Catholics were forced to leave their homes, many of which were burnt down, and 11,000 were driven from their jobs. Some Catholic families, like the one in Source 2, fled to the Irish Free State. Others went to live in areas in Northern Ireland where there were already large numbers of Catholics – such as the Bogside in Londonderry and the Lower Falls in Belfast.

The partition of Ireland was meant to be a temporary measure. However, elections to the Northern Ireland parliament in 1921 gave a large majority to the Unionist Party. This all-Protestant party wanted Northern Ireland to remain part of the United Kingdom. It fiercely opposed the nationalists in Northern Ireland who hoped to reunite the north and south. The Unionists therefore did all they could to strengthen their political power. They did so by making sure that the nationalists could not vote them out.

Source 1

Northern Ireland in 1920.

Source 2

A Catholic family leaves Belfast to seek safety in the Irish Free State, after violent attacks on Catholics in summer 1922.

Voting and the gerrymander

The voting system for Northern Ireland's Parliament and local councils was proportional representation (see Copymaster 9). PR gave seats in Parliament and on councils according to the number of votes each party received, not the number of votes for each candidate. The aim of PR was to give Catholics a bigger say in the government of Northern Ireland than they could get with the first past the post system.

In the local elections of 1920 nationalists won control of 25 out of 80 councils. This alarmed the Unionists. In 1922 the new Unionist government abolished PR for local elections. It also set up a Commission to reorganise the boundaries of the voting districts – called wards. Catholics, however, refused to take part in the Commission because they wanted to stick with the PR system. Without Catholics to oppose them, the Unionists drew the boundaries of wards in ways that would help Protestant candidates in an election.

This fiddling of boundaries was called gerrymandering. An example of how it worked is shown in Source 3. In Londonderry, where there were twice as many Catholic voters as Protestant voters, you might expect there to be twice as many Catholic councillors as Protestant councillors. However, as Source 3 shows, the boundaries of the wards were drawn so that almost all the Catholics were in one ward which had eight councillors. The boundaries of the other two wards, with twelve councillors, were drawn around the areas where the Protestants lived. As a result, Protestants won a majority of seats on Londonderry Council, and kept it in elections for the next 50 years. Across Northern Ireland as a whole, nationalists won only two of the 80 councils in the 1924 elections.

Source 3

The gerrymandered voting districts, or wards, of the city of Londonderry in 1966.

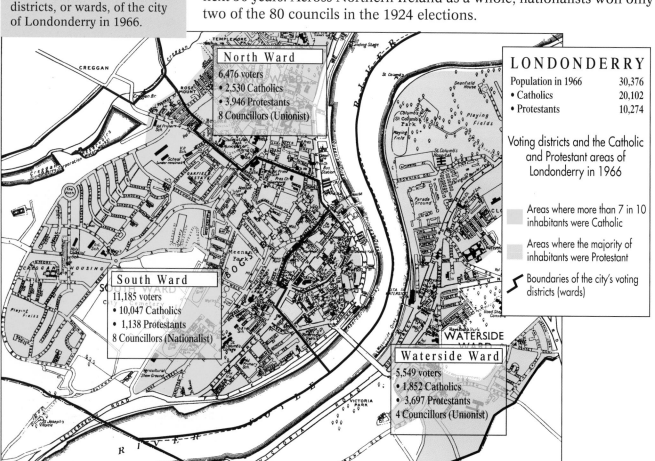

North Ward
6,476 voters
• 2,530 Catholics
• 3,946 Protestants
8 Councillors (Unionist)

South Ward
11,185 voters
• 10,047 Catholics
• 1,138 Protestants
8 Councillors (Nationalist)

Waterside Ward
5,549 voters
• 1,852 Catholics
• 3,697 Protestants
4 Councillors (Unionist)

LONDONDERRY

Population in 1966	30,376
• Catholics	20,102
• Protestants	10,274

Voting districts and the Catholic and Protestant areas of Londonderry in 1966

Areas where more than 7 in 10 inhabitants were Catholic

Areas where the majority of inhabitants were Protestant

Boundaries of the city's voting districts (wards)

Catholics were also put at a disadvantage in elections by two rules about voting. One was that only householders were allowed to vote. As Catholics were often lodgers or sub-tenants of householders, many did not qualify to vote. The other was a rule which gave businessmen extra votes wherever they did business. As there were more Protestant than Catholic businessmen, this helped to strengthen the Protestant vote.

Why did it matter that Protestants controlled nearly every local council? First, local councils were major employers. With responsibilities for such things as housing, education, road repairs, they provided many of the jobs in Northern Ireland. In most places, Protestant councils gave jobs to Protestants in preference to Catholics. Councils also favoured Protestants when it came to the allocation of council houses. By keeping control of both Parliament and local councils, Protestants could therefore not only help fellow Protestants but could also stop Catholics from doing anything about it.

Police and the law

The Unionists' grip on power was strengthened by their control of the police. In the Royal Ulster Constabulary (RUC), there were six Protestant policemen to every one who was Catholic. To back up the RUC was an armed, part-time Special Constabulary of 'A', 'B' and 'C' Specials. The 10,000 B specials were not only mostly Protestant; they were also very violent. They often beat up Catholics when they were brought out to deal with disorders and demonstrations.

The RUC had more power than any other police force in the United Kingdom because a Special Powers Act, passed in 1922, allowed it to do almost anything it liked in an emergency. It could impose curfews, keep people in prison without trial, ban marches and demonstrations, censor the press and search houses without a warrant.

The Special Powers Act was used especially against the IRA which mounted bombing campaigns against the Unionist Government in 1939 and in 1956–62. As we shall see, however, it could also be used to keep Catholics who had nothing to do with the IRA in their place.

Questions

1 Using the information about voting on Copymaster 9, explain why PR would give Catholics more seats in Parliament and councils than they would get with the first past the post system.

2 Look carefully at Source 3.
   a How many adult Catholics and how many adult Protestants lived in Londonderry in 1966?
   b In total, how many Catholic voters and how many Protestant voters were there in Londonderry?
   c Compare the total number of voters with the total adult population of Londonderry. Using the information about voting in this section, suggest why there was a large difference between the two figures.
   d On a copy of the map in Source 3 draw the ward boundaries in a way that you think would give better representation to the Catholics.

3 A divided people

The Unionists could have governed in the interests of all, Catholics as well as Protestants. They did not. With each decade of Unionist rule, the divisions between Catholics and Protestants grew deeper and wider. By the late 1960s the two communities were in a state close to warfare.

How had relations between Protestants and Catholics become so bad? The sources in this section have been chosen to show how the differences between them reached into every area of their lives.

Why were Catholics and Protestants so divided?

Source 1 was written by a Catholic who grew up in Londonderry.

Source 1

Written by a left-wing Catholic journalist, Eamonn McCann, in his history of 'the Troubles', *War and an Irish Town*, 1974.

pantheon A hall or temple containing memorials of dead heroes.

When I was a very small boy we used to sing at passing Protestants:

Proddy, proddy dick
Your ma can't knit
And your da
Won't go to bed
Without a dummy tit....

We came very early to our politics. One learned, quite literally at one's mother's knee, that Christ died for the human race and Patrick Pearse for the Irish section of it.... Pearse ranked high in the teeming pantheon* of Irish martyrdom. There were others. They had all died in the fight to free Ireland from British rule, a fight which had paused in partial victory in 1922.... It was our task to finish the job, to cleanse the remaining traces of foreign rule from the face of Ireland.

Children learned about politics not only in the home, but also as soon as they stepped out of the front door:

Source 2

Max Arthur, *Northern Ireland. Soldiers Talking*, 1987.

When I was a kid, Belfast was divided up into ghettoes. Belfast was actually a lot of little Belfasts. They all had their own names, like Shankill or Tiger Bay. My personal one was Sailorstown, which consisted of about eight streets divided by one street, Nelson Street. All the streets running off one side were Catholic and all the streets running off the other were Protestant, and you'd have found that people would've gone down Nelson Street on one side to walk round the district on the other. They kept to the outskirts, they'd never walk through. I'm sure there were Protestants born on the Protestant side of Nelson Street who had never been through our town .... It was fear that dominated, fear: keep together.

In many of these 'ghettoes' Catholics and Protestants often painted huge pictures on the sides of houses. Sources 3 and 4 show two such murals.

The division between Protestants and Catholics was often unequal, especially in the work they did. With most large employers in Northern Ireland being Protestant, jobs often went to Protestants in preference to Catholics. A weekly Northern Irish magazine reported in 1971 that:

Source 3

A mural on the side of a building in Belfast says Saoirse, Gaelic for 'Freedom'.

Source 4

This mural painted on the end of a terrace of houses in Belfast shows King William of Orange after the Battle of the Boyne.

Source 5

Kathleen Boehringer, *Fortnight Magazine*, 14 May 1971.

... this is a partial list of only the most talked-about cases:

Harland and Wolff: out of 9,000 manual workers, there were an estimated 500 Roman Catholics employed ....;

Mackies: out of 8,500 employees, some 120 Catholics (a startling 1 in 73 or 1.4 per cent);

Sirocco: of 400 employees, no Catholics;

Ormeau Bakery: of some 300 employees, until recently no Catholics (rumour has it that four Catholic roundsmen have been employed to service appropriate areas);

Hugh J. Scott: no Catholics;

Shorts: at the Christmas pay-out, in a section of 450 employees of whom fourteen were Catholics, ten Catholics were paid off.

Source 6 illustrates one way in which it was possible for employers to discriminate against Catholics. It explains why the Linfield football club in Belfast is all-Protestant, even though Catholics play football just as well as Protestants.

Source 6

Paul Foot, *Ireland: Why Britain Must Get Out*, 1989.

scout A member of a football club who watches amateur football matches hoping to find talented new players for the club.

Billy Sinclair, a former player-manager of Linfield ... told me in 1984: 'If you're a Linfield scout* and you see a lad who's good, the second or third question is 'What school did you go to, son?' and if it's Saint something, then all of a sudden the boy isn't good enough. He kicks with the wrong foot.'

Source 7

An Orange Day parade, led by a flute and drum band, marches through a town in Northern Ireland in 1988.

The divisions between Protestants and Catholics are most noticeable when they hold parades to commemorate important events in their history. Many Catholics, for example, take part in parades on the anniversary of the Easter Rising of 1916. Source 7 shows Protestants on 12 July 1988 marching through Belfast on the anniversary of the Battle of the Boyne.

Questions

1 **a** Look at Source 1. Who was Patrick Pearse? Why might he be considered a 'martyr'?
   b Judging by Source 1, what part did history play in forming the way young Catholics and Protestants thought about each other?

2 Look at Sources 3 and 4.
   a Which mural is Catholic and which is Protestant? How can you tell?
   b How were murals like these likely to affect the way Protestants and Catholics thought about each other?

3 Read Source 2.
   a What is a ghetto?
   b Using the information on page 153, briefly describe how Catholic and Protestant 'ghettoes' came into being in 1920–22.
   c How does this help explain the soldier's comment that 'it was fear that dominated'?
   d How would growing up in a 'ghetto' make it likely that Protestants and Catholics would come into conflict with each other?

4 How are Protestant-Catholic relations likely to be affected by having all-Protestant or all-Catholic football teams? Explain your answer.

4   1969: the Troubles start

On 12 August 1969 thousands of Protestants marched through Londonderry in their annual Apprentice Boys' Parade. As they marched, stone-throwing began between Catholic and Protestant groups. This was soon followed by the throwing of petrol bombs. Before long, Catholics had barricaded themselves into the Bogside area of the city and named it 'Free Derry'. Three days later, with police unable to enter the area, the British government sent armed troops to Londonderry to restore order.

This was the start of what people in Northern Ireland call 'the Troubles'. In the Troubles, which continue today, towns and cities have been torn apart by riots and bomb explosions. Thousands of people have been murdered and maimed in shootings, bombings and beatings. Yet Catholics and Protestants had been divided in many ways for many years before then. What made 1969 the year when the Troubles began? Why did open conflict between them not start earlier or later?

Why did 'the Troubles' begin in 1969?

To start answering that question we need to go back to 1963, when Northern Ireland acquired a new Prime Minister, Captain Terence O'Neill.

O'Neill – a liberal Unionist

Like the previous Prime Ministers of Northern Ireland, O'Neill was a Protestant and a Unionist. Unlike them, he had liberal views. He aimed to modernise the society and economy of Northern Ireland and he wanted to improve relations between Protestants and Catholics.

O'Neill began with a programme to modernise the economy. New towns were built. Cities were linked by new motorways. Foreign companies were encouraged to build new factories. A new university opened at Coleraine.

O'Neill broke with the past in several ways, first by making links with

Source 1

The 'Battle of the Bogside'. Catholics in the Bogside area of Londonderry throw stones at police on 13 August 1969. Behind the stone throwers a barricade is being built to keep police out.

the Irish Republic. He went to Dublin for talks with the Irish Prime Minister aimed at improving cross-border trade. He also made links with the Catholics of Northern Ireland. By visiting Catholic schools, and by talking with priests and nuns, he showed his support for the ecumenical movement that was growing in many countries in the 1960s – a movement that tried to bring together the different Christian churches.

Protestant fears

Many Protestants were alarmed by O'Neill's reforms. Extreme Unionists feared he was encouraging Catholics to demand equality with Protestants and that this would threaten their control of Northern Ireland.

The most outspoken of these 'loyalists' was Rev. Ian Paisley, a gospel campaigner and street speaker who bitterly opposed the ecumenical movement. In 1959 he had formed a group called Ulster Protestant Action to defend Protestant interests. Paisley and the UPA stepped up their activities after O'Neill became Prime Minister. They held mass rallies. They launched a newspaper, The Protestant Telegraph, to pour out anti-Catholic propaganda. In 1966 they organised anti-government protest marches which turned into riots. Some of Paisley's supporters also formed an armed terrorist group, the Ulster Volunteer Force, which made shooting and petrol-bomb attacks on Catholic homes and pubs.

Catholic expectations

Since the end of the Second World War, many Catholics' expectations of life had been rising. The start of the Welfare State and the extension of schooling in the 1940s had improved the conditions and opportunities of many Catholics. By the 1960s Catholics were less willing than previous generations to put up with discrimination against them in housing and work.

In 1964 middle-class Catholics formed a group called Campaign for Social Justice. Their aim was to draw attention to the injustices Catholics suffered in local government, housing, and work. More extreme and usually working-class Catholics formed Republican Clubs to campaign for reform.

If O'Neill's reforms went too far for most Protestants, they didn't go far enough for many Catholics. Most of the new factories and motorways were built in the eastern part of Northern Ireland where Protestants were in the majority. The new university was built in Protestant Coleraine rather than Catholic Londonderry. And O'Neill made no attempt to deal with the main Catholic grievances – the fact that they did not have the same civil rights as the Protestants.

Civil Rights

Civil rights are the freedoms and rights which citizens in a democratic society are entitled to. These include the right to vote, the rights of free speech and free association, freedom of belief, and the right to be free of discrimination in social life and at work.

Following the Second World War, growing numbers of people around the world became aware that their civil rights were limited or even non-existent. This was especially true in the United States where millions of black Americans were barred from voting and were segregated from white

Americans. By the early 1960s a powerful Civil Rights Movement was organising a nationwide campaign against these abuses. The campaign of peaceful protests, such as demonstrations and sit-ins, achieved some of its aims when Congress passed Civil Rights Acts in 1964 and 1965. These outlawed racial discrimination in jobs, education, voting and housing.

The success of the American Civil Rights Movement showed people in Northern Ireland that protest marches were an effective way of gaining publicity and putting pressure on the authorities. In 1967 the Campaign for Social Justice and the Republican Clubs joined forces to form a Northern Ireland Civil Rights Association (NICRA.) Their aims were:

Source 2

Aims of the Northern Ireland Civil Rights Association.

1 equal voting rights
2 an end to the gerrymandered voting districts
3 laws against discrimination by local governments
4 fair allocation of council houses
5 the scrapping of the Special Powers Act
6 the disbanding of the B Specials.

NICRA organised peaceful protests like those which had been successful in the United States. In August 1968, for example, 2,400 of them marched to Dungannon to protest against the housing policy of the town council there. Singing 'We shall Overcome' as they went, the marchers got wide press and television coverage.

Marching has a special importance in Northern Ireland that it did not have in the United States. One of the ways in which both Protestants and Catholics celebrate important dates in their history is by marching. The government was well aware that such marches could lead to fighting between them. When civil rights supporters arranged a march through a Protestant area of Londonderry on 5 October 1968, the government banned it. When the marchers ignored the ban and started marching, police attacked them with batons and water cannons, injuring 77 of them.

Such events outraged some civil rights supporters and made them think that more direct action was needed. Students in Belfast took the lead and formed a new, left-wing civil rights group called People's Democracy. They were inspired not only by the United States Civil Rights Movement, but also by a student protest movement that swept across Europe in 1968.

1968: year of student protest

1968 was a year of near-revolution in several countries. In the United States hundreds of thousands of young people joined massive peace marches to protest against the Vietnam War. In France, student protest against the university authorities led to a week-long battle with police in Paris, and to a general strike which nearly brought down the government. In Germany and Britain, as well as France and the United States, students organised 'sit-ins', marches and demonstrations against a whole range of issues.

The Troubles of 1969

In January 1969 People's Democracy staged a march from Belfast to Londonderry. When they reached a little place called Burntollet they were ambushed, stoned and beaten by a Protestant mob. When the marchers reached Londonderry, where cheering Catholics welcomed them, police

Source 3

Students in Paris in May 1968 throw stones at police.

went into the Bogside and smashed houses and abused residents. Riots followed when the residents built barricades to defend themselves from the police.

The growing violence ruined O'Neill's government. Elections early in 1969 showed that support for liberals like himself was falling while support for extremists was growing. On one extreme, Ian Paisley gained a massive number of votes in the February election. On the other, Bernadette Devlin, leader of People's Democracy, was elected to Parliament in a by-election soon after. Following further police riots and bomb attacks by a Protestant group, O'Neill resigned as Prime Minister in April 1969.

His successor was equally unsuccessful in restoring order. Following the annual Apprentice Boys march by Protestants in Londonderry in August 1969, police and Catholics fought a battle for control of the Bogside (Source 1). In the 'Battle of the Bogside', Bogsiders set up barricades, defended them with petrol bombs, and declared the area to be 'Free Derry' under a republican flag. Shortly after, riots also broke out in Belfast, killing seven people and devastating some Catholic areas.

With Northern Ireland on the verge of sliding into civil war, the British government decided it could no longer trust the RUC to deal with the situation. On 14 August 1969 it sent British army troops onto the streets of Belfast and Derry to end the growing 'Troubles' there.

Questions

1 **a** Briefly describe the reforms made by Terence O'Neill.
   b What did (i) Protestants, and (ii) Catholics think about the reforms?
   c Why might it be said that O'Neill's reforms had bad as well as good effects on Northern Ireland?

2 What similarities were there between the aims of the American Civil Rights Movement and the Northern Ireland Civil Rights Association?

3 The events shown in Source 3 happened far away from Northern Ireland. What connection might there have been between this event and the start of the Troubles in 1969?

5 Men of violence

Source 1

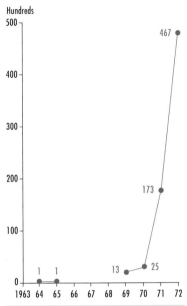

Deaths by political violence in Northern Ireland, 1963–1972.

Look at Source 1. In 1963 not a single murder took place in Northern Ireland. Ten years later the figure had rocketed to 467.

The Troubles brought appalling violence to Northern Ireland. From their start in 1969 to the end of 1975 there were more than 22,000 shootings and 4,500 bomb explosions. Around one in a hundred of the population were killed or wounded in these incidents. People also experienced upheaval and insecurity during these early years of the Troubles. From 1969–1973 around 10,000 Belfast families – 10 per cent of the city's population – were forced to leave their homes because people of another religion threatened them with arson or shooting if they stayed.

When they report such incidents, television and newspaper reporters often describe them as 'sectarian violence'. By 'sectarian' they mean religious violence between Catholics and Protestants. There have been very few weeks since 1969 when the press has not carried stories about sectarian murders committed by 'the men of violence'.

Is this accurate? Was the dramatic increase in violence at the start of 'the Troubles' purely the result of religious differences?

Why was there so much violence in Northern Ireland between 1969–1972?

At first the Catholic population of Northern Ireland welcomed the British soldiers who arrived there in August 1969. For several months Catholics regarded the soldiers as protectors against the RUC. Housewives brought them tea and buns as they patrolled the streets.

These months also seemed to promise the righting of some long-standing wrongs. Under pressure from the government in London, Northern Ireland's government announced a package of reforms. This included an overhaul of the voting system and the scrapping of the B Specials.

In the background, however, extreme nationalist groups were making sure that these moves toward reform would fail and were arming themselves for a war with the British army.

The Irish Republican Army (IRA)

The IRA had fought in the Irish Civil War in 1922–23 (see page 151) and had made armed attacks in Northern Ireland in 1939 and 1956–62 (page 155). After its defeat in 1962 the IRA had developed into a political rather than a military organisation. It put its efforts into a political campaign for a united Ireland and sold many of its weapons.

When the Troubles began in 1969 the IRA was therefore unprepared. It had neither the people nor the weapons to fight the RUC in Derry and Belfast. When it did nothing to help the Catholics there it lost much support. People painted walls with graffiti like 'IRA – I Ran Away'.

This split the IRA into two 'wings'. One was the 'official' wing which wanted to continue the political campaign. The other was a 'provisional' wing which wanted to get weapons to defend the Catholic districts against loyalists and against the police. The two wings clashed and in 1971 fought each other for control of the Catholic areas in West Belfast. Feuding between them continued throughout the 1970s.

The Provisional IRA began its campaign in 1970 by collecting weapons and training volunteers. The army knew that the IRA was arming itself and made weapon searches in Catholic areas. Sometimes in these searches the soldiers broke down doors and damaged people's homes. This naturally angered the Catholics and turned them against the army. The army also lost support in 1970 when it gave soldiers riot shields, visored helmets and batons, and formed them into 'snatch squads' to arrest rioters (Source 2). The IRA fuelled people's anger with anti-army propaganda. Within months of arriving in Northern Ireland the army was seen by Catholics not as protectors but as oppressors.

Source 2

A photograph taken by photo-journalist Donald McCullin shows soldiers in Londonderry in 1970.

The army captured many IRA weapons during house-to-house searches, so the IRA changed its tactics. In April 1970 it began using bombs against government targets such as police stations and post offices. In the summer they also started attacking army and RUC patrols with nail bombs made of cardboard, nails and gelignite.

Loyalist military groups

The IRA campaign enraged the Protestants. In retaliation, Protestants formed so-called 'loyalist' paramilitary groups. The loyalist Ulster Volunteer Force, formed by some of Ian Paisley's supporters (see page 160), attacked the Catholic Short Strand area of Belfast in June 1970. This led to the first gunfight between loyalists and the IRA. In an all-night battle between the two groups, four Protestants and one Catholic were killed in gunfire. In 1971, after the IRA bombing campaign had started, loyalists also formed new military groups. In August 1971 they joined together to form the Ulster Defence Association (UDA).

Source 3

This photograph, taken early in 1972, shows armed IRA men checking the occupants of cars entering and leaving a 'no-go' area of Londonderry.

Internment

As the violence grew steadily worse, the government decided on tough action. Shortly before dawn on 9 August 1971, British soldiers burst into homes all over Northern Ireland and arrested 342 people on a list drawn up by the RUC. All but two were Catholics. After rough questioning 226 were 'interned'. This means they were imprisoned without trial. Their prison was a camp at Long Kesh consisting of high security buildings called H-blocks. The other 116 who were released after questioning told the press about their arrests. Some had stories of being beaten up, others of being thrown blindfold from helicopters they thought were high in the air, or of being made to run barefoot over broken glass and barbed wire.

Internment did not stop the violence. For a start, no loyalists were arrested, nor were many members of the Provisional IRA, for most managed to escape the dawn raids. Many men of violence therefore remained free. Moreover, outraged Catholics took to the streets to protest against internment, and 22 people were killed in riots over the next four days. The arrests seemed to Catholics to prove that the Army was in Northern Ireland to protect Protestant rule. The IRA responded with a blitz of shootings and bomb attacks which killed 127 more people by the end of the year.

Bloody Sunday

The violence in Northern Ireland reached a new height on Sunday 30 January 1972. Although marches had been banned by the government after internment, the Civil Rights Association planned a march through Londonderry to protest against internment. The march was therefore, technically, illegal but the CRA went ahead with it regardless.

As the unarmed marchers approached barriers which the army put across the road to stop them leaving the Bogside, stones were thrown and insults shouted at the soldiers manning the barriers. Snatch squads of paratroopers went into the crowd to make arrests. In doing so they opened fire on the crowd. Thirteen unarmed civilians died and another thirteen were wounded in a massacre which Catholics immediately called 'Bloody Sunday'.

Bloody Sunday triggered off further violence in both Ireland and the British mainland. Rioting, hijackings and barricade-building turned large areas of Belfast and Londonderry into 'no-go' areas for the army. Across the border, 30,000 rioters burned down the British Embassy in Dublin.

With Northern Ireland heading towards a civil war of bombing and shooting between the IRA, loyalists, army and police, the British government lost patience with the Northern Irish government and decided to take control of the province away from it. Northern Ireland was now to be governed by 'direct rule' from Westminster.

Questions

1 How could an IRA member in 1970, who wanted to turn public opinion against the British army use Source 2 to help do so?

2 How can you tell from Source 3 that the Provisional IRA had considerable power in Londonderry in 1972?

3 Look at Source 1, then use the information in this section to answer these questions:
   a How can the rise in deaths by political violence between 1969–1972 be explained by religious factors?
   b What other factors need to be considered when explaining the rise in deaths?
   c Are any of these factors more important than others? Explain your answer.

6 Sharing power

William Whitelaw and power sharing

William Whitelaw, one of the most senior ministers in the government, was given the job of running Northern Ireland by direct rule. In March 1973 he came up with a bold new plan for the future of Northern Ireland.

At the heart of the plan was the idea of 'power sharing'. Northern Ireland would be run by a new kind of government, made up of ministers from each side of the religious divide. For the first time in Northern Ireland's history, Catholics and Protestants would share power equally.

However, first there would be elections for a new parliament. Voting would be by proportional representation. This would decide each party's share in power. When the elections were held in June 1973 nearly all the Catholic votes went to the Social Democratic Labour Party, or SDLP. However, the Protestant vote was split. Moderate unionists who favoured power-sharing got fewer votes than extreme unionists who opposed it.

The Sunningdale Agreement

Leaders from the pro-power sharing parties travelled to England at the end of 1973 for a conference with Irish and British politicians at Sunningdale in Berkshire. The outcome was the Sunningdale Agreement:

- Southern Ireland recognised Northern Ireland as part of the United Kingdom – something it had never done before.

- a Council of Ireland would be set up to discuss matters of common concern between North and South.

- a power-sharing Executive was set up as the new government of Northern Ireland. Led by Brian Faulkner, leader of the Unionist Party, with Gerry Fitt, the SDLP leader, as deputy, it consisted of six Protestants and five Catholics.

This was a big step forward. One of the leaders said that a 'new dawn' was breaking in Northern Ireland. On the way to Sunningdale, Gerry Fitt sang a Protestant ballad, *The Sash*, to the other delegates. Faulkner replied with the Southern Irish song *Galway Bay*. They weren't the only ones to feel so hopeful. In Britain politicians of every party backed the power-sharing plan. In Ireland bishops as well as politicians gave their full support.

Yet five months later power-sharing was dead. In May 1974 the British government reimposed Direct Rule from Westminster. What had gone wrong? Why did power sharing last for so short a time when there was so much support for it?

Why did power sharing fail?

The first problem the power-sharers faced was to persuade their supporters to accept the Sunningdale Agreement. Source 1, by a Catholic journalist, shows the scale of the problem:

Source 1

Eamonn McCann, *War in an Irish Town*, 1974.

> The line in the Bogside from local SDLP chiefs was that the Agreement should be supported because it helped towards the work of ending Northern Ireland and that there was therefore no need for the IRA any longer.
>
> Meanwhile Protestants were being urged by Mr Faulkner to believe that the Council of Ireland would be a mere talking shop, that ... Catholics ... were accepting the Northern State – and that for this reason the Agreement would end IRA violence and should therefore be supported.

Soon after the Executive took power, unexpected events on the British mainland created further problems. A miners' strike in Britain caused severe power cuts and the introduction of a three-day week for most workers. The Prime Minister, Edward Heath, called a general election to test support for his government. Northern Ireland therefore went to the polls along with the rest of Britain. However, this was a national election, so candidates won seats in Parliament by the FPP (first past the post) system, not by PR (proportional representation). In this election, eleven out of the twelve Northern Irish seats went to Unionists who opposed power sharing.

The election produced another upset. Edward Heath's Conservative government lost power to a Labour government. Northern Ireland therefore had a new, Labour Secretary of State, Merlyn Rees.

Despite the problems, the politicians in the Executive quickly got to know and respect each other, and they worked well together. Yet new difficulties began when they asked the Assembly to vote its approval of the

Sunningdale Agreement. A group of Protestant trade unions, the Ulster Workers' Council, said they would go on strike if the vote went ahead. Brian Faulkner and the Executive did not give in to this threat. The Assembly went ahead and voted to support the Sunningdale agreement, upon which the Ulster Workers' Council announced a general strike.

General strike

The strike began on 14 May. Within days, power stations began to close down and there were long electricity blackouts. Gas supplies shut down in some areas. Food ran short and there was no petrol. The organisers of the strike claimed that, by staying away from work, ordinary people were showing how much they disliked the Sunningdale Agreement. But others had a different explanation for the success of the strike. Lady Faulkner, the Chief Executive's wife, later wrote that:

Source 2

Quoted in Philip Whitehead, *The Writing On the Wall*, 1985.

I was actually at the end of a telephone during that strike, and for the first few days the telephone line was constantly occupied by people ringing up from housing estates, places in the country, to say, look, we can't get into our work, there are people with sticks and staves and masks at the end of our road, and what is the government going to do about it?

However, the strike leaders denied such accusations. One of them said:

Source 3

Harry Murray, one of the strike leaders, speaking on Radio 4 Northern Ireland, 24 May 1974.

We never attempted to intimidate anybody going into work – definitely not .... These people are honest, industrious .... It's a constitutional stoppage and we have the backing of I would say 450,000 people.

That view seems to be supported by the fact that there are very few photographs of strikers forcing people to stop work. Source 4 is one of the few that exists.

Source 4

This is the only known photograph of a lorry being hijacked during the 1974 general strike. It shows armed men threatening the crew of a bakers' lorry in East Belfast on 16 May 1974. The youths in masks and balaclavas had stopped the lorry by standing in the road.

Protestant feelings ran high during the strike. When Merlyn Rees returned one evening to his hotel in Belfast, a week after the strike began, he got this reception:

Source 5

From *Northern Ireland. A Personal Perspective*, the memoirs of Merlyn Rees. He was Secretary of State for Northern Ireland (i.e. the British government minister in charge of NI) from 1974 to 1976.

As we walked through the lounge full of middle-class late-night drinkers, the cry of 'traitors' came in unison .... It was a spontaneous response of anger: we, the Brits, were the outsiders, always ready to sell good loyalists down that mythical river into the Catholic South.

After two weeks of general strike, Northern Ireland was at a complete standstill, and the Executive had been unable to get it moving again. On 28 May they resigned and the British government went back to Direct Rule over the province. Delighted Protestants danced in the streets when they heard the news:

Source 6

Protestant women in Belfast celebrate the collapse of the power-sharing Executive on 28 May 1974.

Questions

1 Look at Source 1.
   a Why would the SDLP find it difficult to persuade Catholics in the Bogside that they did not need the IRA any longer?
   b Suggest why Faulkner told Protestants that the Council of Ireland would be a 'mere talking shop'.
   c How might Protestants have reacted if they could have heard what Catholics in the Bogside were being told about the Sunningdale Agreement? What might Catholics have said if they had heard what Faulkner was telling Protestants?

2 The elections for the new Northern Ireland Assembly gave a majority of seats to people who supported power-sharing. The elections for Parliament only seven months later gave a majority to those who opposed power-sharing. How can this be explained?

3 Look at Source 6.
   a What was the 'Executive' mentioned in the newspaper headline?
   b What caused it to 'collapse' on 28 May 1974?
   c Suggest why the people in the picture looked so happy about this event.

Review: Conflict and co-operation in Northern Ireland

The cartoon below is an interpretation of the Troubles in Northern Ireland. Study it carefully, then answer these questions:

1a Look at the wall on the left. What do you think the graffiti 'Rem 1690' and 'Ulster says no' is supposed to mean?

 b On the wall on the right, what do you think the graffiti '1916', the 'Provos' and 'H blocks' is meant to mean?

2a What is unusual about the stairs the people are climbing?

 b Why do you think the cartoonist drew the stairs in this way?

3   Look at the characters on the stairs.

 a What kind of person do you think each character is meant to represent?

 b Which character does the cartoonist seem to blame for the Troubles?

 c Judging by what you have read in this book, is the cartoonist right to blame this person?

 d Who else on the stairs could also be blamed for the Troubles? Why?

4   The cartoonist is Northern Irish. How might this affect his interpretation of the Troubles?

5a Some people might say the cartoon is a fair interpretation, some that it is unfair. What kind of people might think it unfair?

 b Why would it be difficult to make an interpretation of the Troubles that everybody accepted as fair?

This cartoon was drawn in 1991 by a Northern Irish political cartoonist, Martyn Turner. It was used to illustrate the front cover of a book called *Troubled times*, about the Troubles in Northern Ireland from 1970 to 1991.

Communication and culture

JOSH BROOMAN and MALCOLM CHANDLER

General Editor: Josh Brooman

Contents

A changing world of communications

1 Mass communications 1: radio 174

2 Mass communications 2: television 178

3 Recorded music 182

4 The growth of leisure 187

Coursework assignments · Changing culture and communications

1 What did people do before television? 192

2 The best of everything? The beginnings of television 194

3 What about the children? 196

4 The birth of the teenager 198

5 Were the Sixties Swinging? 200

6 The revolting Seventies 202

7 Summer holidays between 1900 and the 1950s 204

8 Why were holiday camps so popular? 206

LONGMAN

Longman Group UK Limited
Longman House, Burnt Mill, Harlow, Essex
CM20 2JE, England and Associated Companies throughout the World.

First published 1994

ISBN 0582 251591

Set in Concorde and Tecton

Printed in Great Britain
by Butler and Tanner Ltd, Frome and London

The Publishers' policy is to use paper manufactured from sustainable forests.

Design and production by Hart McLeod

Cover photograph *Hiking* by J.M. Tucker. Photograph Laing Art Gallery, Newcastle upon Tyne (Tyne and Wear Museums).

Acknowledgements

The written sources in this book are taken from many different kinds of published material. Some were originally written in old-fashioned or unusual language. This has not been altered, but in most cases, unusual or difficult words are explained in the margin. In many of the sources words have been left out. A cut in the middle of a sentence is shown like this ...; and at the end of a sentence like this ....

We are grateful to the following for permission to reproduce photographs:

Butlin's Museum, 207; Camera Press, 186; reproduced by permission of EMI Music Archives, 182; GEC-Marconi, 174; Hulton-Deutsch Collection, 178, 184 top left, 185, 192, 196, 200 right; 202, 204, 206 top and middle; John Frost Historical Newspaper Service, 175; Laing Art Gallery, Newcastle upon Tyne (Tyne and Wear Museums), 189 top; Roger Mayne (photographer), 191; National Railway Museum, York, 188; Peter Newark's Historical Photographs, 206 bottom; Popperfoto, 183; Punch, 201; from the *Radio Times*, 7 June 1946, courtesy the BBC, 179; RCA BMG Records 1981, 203; courtesy Sue Read, 189 bottom; Retna/Sam Wix, 173; Thomas Cook Holidays, 190; Topham Picture Source, 184 right, 193; from the cover of the *TV Times*, 7 October 1955, 181.

A changing world of communications

The 'Live Aid' concert at Wembley Stadium on 13 July 1985. The television pictures of the concert, shown on giant screens in front of and at each side of the stage, were transmitted by satellite to every country in the world.

If you wanted to communicate with very large numbers of people a hundred years ago, there was only one way to do it: in print. Journalists, governments, novelists, missionaries, and anyone else who needed to communicate with a mass audience, could do so only through the printed word – books, newspapers, magazines, for example.

Look at the picture above. It shows the 'Live Aid' concert in 1985, staged simultaneously in London and Philadelphia to raise money for famine relief in Africa. An estimated 1.5 billion people watched the television broadcast of the concert – roughly a third of the world's entire population.

The ability to communicate with such massive audiences has been one of the greatest changes of the twentieth century. It has brought with it other great changes in the way we think and behave. This book looks at the growth of mass communications in the past hundred years, and investigates some of the ways in which our national culture has changed as a result.

1 Mass communications 1: radio

Many people spend a large part of their leisure time watching television or listening to the radio. These two forms of mass communication have had a profound impact on twentieth century life. In the next two sections of the book we investigate the early development and growth of radio and television, and their impact on people's lives.

Wireless communication

The ground work for mass communications in the twentieth century was laid in the nineteenth century by two inventions which allowed people to communicate by wire: the electric telegraph and the telephone.

As the telegraph and telephone came into widespread use, inventors searched for a way to transmit sound without wires. The Scottish scientist, James Maxwell, paved the way in 1865 when he proved the existence of an unseen form of radiation, electromagnetism. Twenty years later the German scientist Hertz made a machine that produced radio waves and a receiver which could detect them from a distance.

The most practical of these early experimenters was an Italian-Irish inventor called Marconi. Marconi came to Britain in 1896 after failing to interest the Italian government in his experiments. He brought with him a secret black box containing a transmitter and a receiver which rang a bell when it picked up radio waves from the transmitter. Over the next five years he vastly increased the distance over which radio waves could be received. In 1899 he sent radio signals across the Channel and in 1901 he transmitted a message across the Atlantic Ocean.

These early wireless messages were in morse code, not voice. Marconi saw the wireless as a form of point-to-point communication, like telegraph or telephone but without wires. He used it at first to communicate with ships at sea, and set up a company to make equipment and to run a chain of coastal wireless stations. However, unlike telegraph or telephone, radio waves do not travel only from one point to another. They are scattered, or 'broadcast' in every direction. Anyone with a receiver can pick them up. It was not long before radio makers realised that radio could be used for 'broadcasting' messages for information or entertainment. On Christmas Eve 1906 an American scientist, Reginald Fassenden, made the first ever broadcast of words and music.

Source 1

A poster of 1902 advertising a demonstration of Marconi's 'wireless telegraph'.

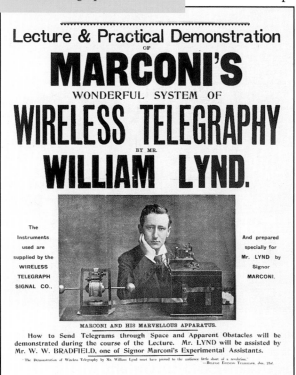

Lecture & Practical Demonstration
OF
MARCONI'S
WONDERFUL SYSTEM OF
WIRELESS TELEGRAPHY
BY MR.
WILLIAM LYND.

The Instruments used are supplied by the WIRELESS TELEGRAPH SIGNAL CO.,

And prepared specially for Mr. LYND by Signor MARCONI.

MARCONI AND HIS MARVELLOUS APPARATUS.

How to Send Telegrams through Space and Apparent Obstacles will be demonstrated during the course of the Lecture. Mr. LYND will be assisted by Mr. W. W. BRADFIELD, one of Signor Marconi's Experimental Assistants.

"The Demonstration of Wireless Telegraphy by Mr. William Lynd must have proved to the audience little short of a revelation."
—BELFAST EVENING TELEGRAPH, Jan. 21st.

The start of regular broadcasting

The First World War boosted the development of the wireless. The Admiralty, for example, used radio to send messages to its warships all over the world. The demand for wireless sets not only increased the profits of the Marconi Company which made them, but also led to the development of more powerful sets. Soon after the war the Marconi company made the first speech 'broadcasts' in Britain. In 1922 it started the first regular broadcasting service from station 2LO in London. It was quickly followed by rival radio stations in Manchester and Birmingham.

Regular radio broadcasting had first started in the United States a year earlier, in 1921. It was immediately popular. New radio stations mushroomed. By May 1922 there were 219 radio stations 'on the air'. However, there weren't enough wavelengths for so many stations, and it was often difficult to hear any of them properly. To avoid this happening in Britain, Marconi and the other new radio firms joined together in 1922 to form the British Broadcasting Company (BBC).

The manager of the new BBC was a Scottish engineer, John Reith. He had strong views about the kind of programme that the BBC should transmit. He wrote in 1924 that:

Source 2

From *Broadcast Over Britain*, a book which John Reith wrote in 1924 outlining his views about the purpose of the BBC.

I think it will be admitted by all, that to have exploited (used) so great a scientific invention for the purpose and pursuit of 'entertainment' alone would have been a prostitution of its powers and an insult to the character and intelligence of the people.

Source 3 shows what was probably a typical family of listeners in the early 1920s, and Source 4 gives us an idea of what they listened to while Reith was in charge of the BBC.

Source 3

The front cover of *Radio Times*, 21 December 1923. The radio to which the family are listening is on the plant stand on the right of the picture. The bent horn is the radio's loudspeaker.

THE CHRISTMAS NUMBER
RADIO TIMES
"JUST A SONG AT TWILIGHT"
6D

Source 4

BBC radio programmes for Sunday, 23 May 1926.

3.30-4.40	A popular orchestral concert from the wireless orchestra conducted by Herman Finck, including Masque *The Merchant of Venice* (Sullivan); selections from *A Midsummer Night's Dream* (Mendelssohn); Suite, *Choppiano* (arranged by Finck); Roy Henderson, baritone, singing *Largo al Factotum* (Rossini) and other songs ...
4.40-5.30	Orchestral works by Herman Finck, including *March of the Giants*; Entract, '*Idle Dreams*; Pot Pourri, *Finckiana*; Dance Suite, *Vive la Dance* etc.
5.30-6.00	Shakespeare's heroines, No 4. Three scenes from the *Merchant of Venice* with Cathleen Nesbit as Portia.
6.00-6.30	Close Down.
6.30-7.45	Service from Carlisle Cathedral with address by the Bishop of Carlisle.
8.00-8.10	Bow Bells rung by the Ancient Society of College Youths relayed from St Mary-le-Bow.
8.10-8.55	Wesley Memorial Service.
8.55-9.00	The Week's Good Cause: the John Groom Crippleage and Flower Girl's Mission.
9.00-9.15	Weather forecast and news.
9.15-10.30	Albert Sandler, violinist, and the Grand Hotel, Eastbourne, orchestra with Kate Winter, soprano, in a concert of popular classics ...
10.30	Close Down.

As in the United States, radio was immediately popular in Britain. Within a few years more than 2 million people were listening regularly to radio programmes. By 1939 there were very few homes in Britain which did not have a radio set. In that year, the Post Office sold 8.9 million radio licences.

The popularity of radio

What made radio so popular? One answer can be found in Source 5. It comes from an investigation by two researchers into the impact of radio on everyday life. The researchers made their investigation in a working-class area of Bristol where they were told what things were like before everyone had a radio:

Source 5

From a survey in 1939 of the effects of radio on everyday life, *Broadcasting in Everyday Life*, by Hilda Jennings and Winifred Gill.

The street and public house offered the main scope for recreation outside the home. On Sunday afternoons and fine summer evenings the whole family would stand at the street door or sit on chairs on the pavement. When tension in a street ran high, quarrels easily arose and quickly spread. Witnesses told the survey worker that 'There was a row every night in some streets'. The rougher children 'ran the streets'. Rival street gangs raided each other or even pursued victims into their own homes.

The researchers found that, before they had radios, families spent their time talking about the ups and downs of family life, about the affairs of their neighbours, weddings, births and funerals in the area, and about arguments in the street. By 1939, they wrote:

Source 6

Hilda Jennings and Winifred Gill, *Broadcasting in Everyday Life*, 1939.

Broadcasting has supplied not only a new way of spending leisure by family 'listening-in' but a vastly wider range of conversation. This was agreed on all sides. One listener gives a picture of his home. 'You get the family sat in the house of a night and there's a talk on the wireless. Someone doesn't agree and pulls it to pieces. Then they all has a go and gets outside of it. I've known them argue for hours.

In the 1920s wireless sets used crystals to pick up radio signals. In the 1930s radio companies found ways of mass-producing a more efficient device, the thermionic valve. Crystal sets gave way to valve radios which could pick up a wider range of signals, or frequencies. Although the BBC (reorganised as the British Broadcasting Corporation in 1927) was still the only British radio station in the 1930s, listeners increasingly 'tuned in' to stations across the Channel such as Radio Luxemburg and Radio Normandy which provided lighter programmes than the BBC.

During the Second World War the BBC expanded its output of radio programmes, broadcasting in 47 languages to occupied countries all over the world. It also started a second radio channel, the Forces Programme, which broadcast light music and comedy programmes. At the end of the war this became the Light Programme (later Radio 2), separate from the original Home Service (later Radio 4). There was also a new Third Programme (later Radio 3) for serious music and talks.

Radio listening continued to grow in the 1950s when a new kind of radio became widely available. In 1948 American scientists invented a device which could replace bulky radio valves. The transistor was much smaller and cheaper to produce than a valve, and it did not generate heat. Cheap, portable transistor radios became common during the 1950s.

In the 1960s the BBC's monopoly on radio was challenged by 'pirate' radio stations such as Radio Caroline broadcasting from ships moored a little over three miles from the coast, outside British waters. The pirate broadcasts of pop music, with advertisements, were so popular that the BBC was eventually forced to start its own pop channel, Radio One, in 1967. In the same year the BBC also opened several local radio stations. Shortly after, in the 1970s, independent commercial radio stations such as Capital Radio in London began to open. By 1990 there were around 80 independent local radio stations in the United Kingdom.

Questions

1. **a** Compare Source 4 with one day's output from a present day radio station. What similarities and differences are there between the two?
   b Radio was very popular in the 1920s. Why might this seem surprising in view of Source 4?

2. **a** Look at Source 3. What kind of family would you say is shown in this picture: working class, middle class, upper class?
   b Now read Sources 5 and 6 again. How are the families described in these sources different from the family in Source 3?
   c Despite the differences between the families, how does radio seem to have had similar effects on them?

3. Using the sources and information in this section, explain why radio became so popular in the twentieth century.

2   Mass communications 2: television

Shortly after the BBC began regular radio broadcasts, an inventor called John Logie Baird began experiments into what he called 'seeing by wireless'. In 1924, after two years of experiments, he succeeded in his aim. He sent a picture of a cross through the air from one side of a room to another. In 1925 he made the first television picture of a human being.

Elizabeth Wood, a schoolgirl, saw some of these early pictures in a demonstration which Baird gave in Selfridges department store in 1925:

Source 1

From an interview with Elizabeth Wood, in a television documentary made in 1985 about the early days of television.

It was a little disappointing really, because of black lines wiggling across and it jumped up and down …. And then we all clapped rather politely because we were all rather frightened of television. I think the trouble was that we believed that, if they could make this film, they could see into our houses. We could see them, they could see us.

Source 2

John Logie Baird (1888–1946) in front of the televisor in 1926. He is holding Stukey Bill, a dummy he used in his early experiments because nobody was willing to sit for hours in the bright light needed to make a television picture.

Baird's early pictures had only thirty lines. Television pictures today have 625. Baird's pictures were therefore very blurred. He spent the next few years trying to produce clearer pictures. In 1932, however, the EMI-Marconi company developed a new method of making pictures with a cathode ray tube. With 180 lines, EMI's pictures were much clearer than Baird's.

Baird versus EMI-Marconi

By this time the BBC was making plans to broadcast television as well as radio programmes. Only the BBC was allowed to transmit radio or television signals in Britain. There was therefore a lot of money to be made by the company whose television system the BBC decided to use. Baird and EMI competed with each other to produce clearer pictures in the hope that the BBC would adopt their equipment.

When the BBC began television broadcasting in 1936 it experimented with both systems, using the Baird system one week and the EMI-Marconi system the next. Baird by now had 240 lines and EMI had 405 lines. It soon became clear that the Baird system was of poorer quality and less reliable than EMI. In 1937 the BBC stopped using it.

BBC television

By 1939 the BBC studios at Alexandra Palace in London were broadcasting daily programmes to around 80,000 television sets in London. But broadcasting was suddenly halted on 1 September 1939, the day the Second World War began. It was feared that German aircraft could use TV signals from the transmitting aerial at Alexandra Palace to guide them to their targets. There was no television in Britain for the next seven years.

Alexandra Palace began broadcasting again in 1946. Source 3 gives us an idea of the kind of programmes viewers could watch.

Source 3

A page from the *Radio Times* showing television programmes for 9–11 June 1946. Television broadcasting had started two days earlier after its seven year break during the Second World War.

Source 4

Number of television licences issued in Britain, 1947-1959.

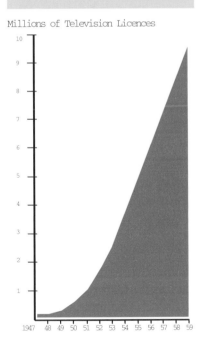

Millions of Television Licences

Until 1950 television could be seen only by a few hundred thousand people in the London area. Two thirds of the British people had never seen a television, let alone owned one. Ten years later almost half the adult population was watching television for an average four hours every night of the week. What brought about this sudden change?

Why did TV watching increase so much in the Fifties?

Widespread television watching became possible in the 1950s when the BBC built new transmitters to carry programmes to all parts of the country.

Until 1950 there was only one transmitter, at Alexandra Palace in London. In 1950 a second transmitter opened at Sutton Coldfield in the Midlands, and the number of television owners quickly rose to 600,000. In 1951 a third transmitter opened at Holme Moss, bringing television to Manchester. When transmitters at Wenvoe (South Wales) and Kirk O'Shotts (Scotland) opened, 80 per cent of the population was within reach of television pictures. By 1959, as Source 4 shows, there were nearly ten million television sets in the country.

This boom in television ownership was helped by a new form of credit called hire purchase (HP). People could buy expensive items such as televisions by making a small payment and then paying the rest in instalments over the next few years. Source 5 suggests why many people did so.

Source 5

Man, aged 60+, describing his early memories of televison viewing to Tim O'Sullivan, a media studies lecturer, in *Television Memories and Cultures of Viewing, 1950–65*.

You could tell from the aerials who had and who hadn't got sets. I remember that we were one of the first three in the road to get one. If you had a car and a TV set, you'd really arrived.

The biggest boost to television watching in the 1950s was the coronation of Queen Elizabeth in 1953. Over a million new sets were sold in the weeks leading up the Coronation. Mrs Gerrish, then aged eleven years, recalled:

Source 6

Mrs P.J. Gerrish, who answered a radio appeal for people to send in their reminiscences of growing up in the Fifties. Quoted in Chris Tarrant, *Ready Steady Go*, 1990.

Eleven Plus An exam taken at the end of primary school in the Fifties and Sixties. As well as testing attainment, it was also used to decide what kind of secondary school you went to: grammar, secondary modern or technical school.

My Dad said we'd have one if I passed the Eleven Plus*: 'It will help you at grammar school'. But the Cup Final was on the weekend before the results of the exam were announced so we got one anyway (so much for helping at grammar school). It was 1953 and the Coronation was due on 2 June, so we were suddenly very popular.

We only had a small bungalow, and the set was in a small dining room. In one corner went the table, and all the chairs were marshalled into position. Some people even brought their own. Old friends, neighbours and even the bachelor curate all squeezed in, and put their lunch offerings on the table in the corner.

Nearly 8 million people watched the Coronation in their own homes and 10.4 million watched in the homes of friends. A further 1.5 million crowded into cinemas, pubs and halls to watch.

The Coronation was not the first or last time when television seemed to draw the British people together. Television helped to create a calendar of nationally important events. Sporting events such as the Oxford–Cambridge boat race, the Grand National, the Cup Final, cricket test matches, tennis at Wimbledon became events of national interest watched by a nationwide audience. Television also provided a national audience for events such as Remembrance Day (11 November) and the Queen's Christmas Day message. Television in the early 1950s was very old-fashioned by today's standards. Presenters wore bow ties and evening dress. During the weekly play, the week's major event, there was a ten minute interval in which the screen went blank and a bell was rung to tell viewers when the interval was over.

Source 7

One of the first issues of the *TV Times*, the guide to ITV programmes which started in 1955. *The Adventures of Robin Hood*, which it featured, was the most popular children's programme of the 1950s.

The only paper giving **NEW TV** programmes in full   No. 3   4ᵈ

TV TIMES

OFFICIAL PROGRAMMES   SUNDAY **OCT 9** — SATURDAY **OCT 15**

	Page			Page
Viewing Guide and Play Bill	3	COVER PICTURE	Sportscreen	14
Looking Around	4-5	RICHARD GREENE (above), whose flashing smile and dark good looks are known to millions of cinemagoers, plays the part of Robin in "The Adventures of Robin Hood" —the serial which appears every Sunday at 5.30.	Fashions with an Irish lilt	15
Jack Hylton—Master Showman	9		The stories of the Hallé	17
Meet the Visionettes	10-11		A Goon's-eye view	19
The Pajama Game	12		When the camera goes visiting	20-21
Should Parliament be Televised? by W. J. Brown	13		Charm in the Morning	22
			The Young View	23
		See story—pages 6-7.	Double-Crossword	30

And all the Programmes—Pages 24 to 37

The screen also went blank between six and seven every evening, when children's programmes were over. This was called the 'toddlers' truce' when small children could be put to bed.

This began to change when a Television Act of 1954 set up an Independent Television Authority which chose commercial television companies to broadcast in each region of the country. Independent television started broadcasting in September 1955.

ITV not only gave viewers different programmes (Source 7), but also forced the BBC to compete with it for a share of the audience. One example of this concerned the 'toddlers' truce'. When ITV started, it observed the 'toddler's truce' and stopped broadcasting between six and seven each evening. But going off the air for an hour each day reduced the profits of the independent companies. They put pressure on the government to end the truce. When the government agreed to this, the BBC followed ITV's lead and started broadcasting between six and seven. The first day it did so was Saturday 16 February 1957. A five-minute news bulletin at six o'clock was followed by a programme aimed at young people, 'Six-five Special'. This was to become one of the BBC's most popular programmes for many years.

Questions

1. If televisions had not needed roof aerials in the 1950s, would as many sets have been sold? Explain your answer after reading Source 5.

2. Read Source 6 carefully. How can it be used to help explain why people wanted to buy television sets in the early 1950s?

3. Look at Source 7 and suggest why the *TV Times* gave so much publicity to the Adventures of Robin Hood, a children's programme.

4. Using the sources and text in this section, explain why the figures in Source 4 rose so sharply.

3   Recorded music

A method of reproducing music and speech already existed when radio was invented. An American, Thomas Edison, had invented a 'phonograph' in 1877. This recorded the air pressure of sound waves by scratching a groove into a sheet of tin foil wrapped around a turning cylinder. Similar machines were developed over the next twenty years, using first wax cylinders and then flat discs made of shellac to carry the groove. Known as a gramophone, this machine quickly became a popular form of entertainment. One of the attractions of the gramophone can be seen in Source 1, the trademark of the Gramophone Company, which later became EMI (Electrical and Musical Industries).

Source 1

In 1899 the British artist Francis Barraud painted a dog called Nipper listening to the voice of his dead master on a phonograph. The Gramophone Company bought the painting and persuaded Barraud to paint in a gramophone. This became the company's trademark. It still appears today on every disc or tape produced by EMI.

These early records were made by recording sound waves direct onto a master disc. The sound quality was therefore very poor. The invention of a new kind of electric valve in 1906 made it possible to record sound waves electrically. By the 1920s electrical recording was being used to make shellac discs turning at 78 revolutions per minute (rpm). These brittle records were easily broken and had a short playing time. In 1948 the Columbia record company brought out an 'unbreakable' plastic disc turning at only 33rpm, the 'Long Playing record', or LP, which could play for half an hour each side. In 1958 the LP was further improved with the introduction of stereo sound.

Since the introduction of the LP the quality of recorded music has steadily improved. Reel-to-reel tape recorders, introduced in Germany in 1936, became easier to use with the development of tape cartridges and cassettes at the end of the 1960s. The personal stereo, developed in the 1970s, allowed taped music to be played outside the home. In the late 1980s the compact disc's superior sound quality, using digital recording, led to the decline of the LP, despite being more than double the price.

Until the mid twentieth century, people who wanted to listen to music were more likely to turn on the radio than put on a record. Radio was cheaper and records broke easily. From the 1950s, however, more and more people started buying records. Young people especially spent pocket money or wage packets buying 'singles' to play at home, or else feeding juke boxes in pubs and coffee bars.

Over the next 30 years, recorded music became a central part of young people's culture. A 14-year-old school pupil wrote in 1993 that:

Source 2

From *The happiest days of my life?*, an article by an anonymous 14-year-old at a London comprehensive school, in *The Guardian*, 24 May 1993.

> By the time they are my age – fourteen – most normal kids have formed into groups which are almost totally music-orientated .... I expect that different schools in different parts of the country use different slang. New groups and slang are emerging all the time .... At our school the main groups are Ravers, Metallers, Fashion Victims and, of course, Trevs and Sharons ....

How did this come about? Why have strong connections developed between music and young people's culture? What else, apart from music, has led to the growth of such groups? The rest of the sources in this section help to answer that question by showing how some of the main youth groups developed in the Fifties, Sixties and Seventies.

Source 3

Teddy Boys listen to a record on the juke box in a coffee bar in 1955.

Music, youth and culture

Source 3 shows one of the earliest youth groups associated with music. Listening to a record on a juke box are four Teddy Boys.

Teddy Boys emerged as a group in south London in 1954. They had long hair, greased and swept back, and they wore long Edwardian jackets and thick crepe-soled shoes. The music they listened to was mostly American rock'n'roll, by performers such as Bill Haley, Elvis Presley, or Little Richard.

Music was not the only influence on Teddy Boys. They met usually in coffee bars where they drank espresso coffee. This reflected the fact that 15,000 Italians migrated to Britain between 1945 and 1951, many of them opening cafés or working in the catering trade, for example, Charles Forte and the Berni brothers. Many others worked as hairdressers. Through cafés, fashions and hairstyles, an Italian dimension was added to the American culture of the Teddy Boys.

The Teddy Boy style evolved in the late 1950s and early 1960s into a culture centred around motor bikes. British motor bike manufacturers, such as Triumph or Norton Villiers, were then world leaders in the production of high performance machines. Bikers like those in Source 4 kept the hair styles of teddy boys but dressed in jeans and leather jackets. (There was no law at that time requiring them to wear crash helmets.) Like the Teds they listened and danced to rock'n'roll music and were thus known as Rockers.

In 1963 a new youth group emerged to rival the rockers. Mods (Source 5) drove Italian scooters (Lambretta or Vespa) rather than motorbikes, their hair was carefully cut, their clothes expensive and tailored. Girls' styles seemed especially modern, with mini-skirts being far shorter than any previous fashion of skirt. Instead of rock'n'roll they listened to music inspired by black singers and groups: rhythm and blues, soul and Tamla from the United States, and ska from Jamaica.

Mods spent a great deal of money on clothes, records, hair and chrome accessories for their scooters. This reflected an important economic change that had started in the 1950s. Between 1955 and 1960 average weekly earnings in Britain rose 34 per cent, while average prices rose fifteen per cent. This trend continued in the Sixties. By 1969 earnings had risen 130 per cent, but prices had risen 63 per cent. With wages rising at twice the rate of prices, wage-earners had more and more to spend on consumer goods.

Mods and Rockers disliked and mocked each other's style and tastes. Fights between them often broke out in the streets or in pubs. The worst violence took place in 1964 when hundreds of Mods and Rockers fought each other in Bank Holiday battles on the beaches of Margate, Clacton and Brighton. Source 5 shows a group of Mods arriving in Clacton on one of these weekends of violence.

Source 4

Bikers in the early Sixties.

Source 5

Mods, on Lambretta and Vespa scooters, wearing parkas and pork-pie hats, arrive in Clacton on a bitingly cold bank holiday in May, 1964.

Teddy Boys, Rockers and Mods were mostly male and working class. Young women and middle-class teenagers in the 1950s were more likely to have been 'beatniks', listening to skiffle and jazz music. Beatniks rejected established society, especially what they called 'materialism' – the desire for such things as cars, expensive clothes and other consumer goods. Many belonged to the Campaign for Nuclear Disarmament (CND) to protest against the building of nuclear weapons by the Superpowers.

Beatniks died out by the end of the Fifties, but a similar group emerged in the middle of the Sixties. Hippies too rejected established society and aimed to live an 'alternative' life style. They advocated world peace and protested against the Vietnam War in the Far East. Many used drugs, especially cannabis and LSD, to heighten their awareness, and the experience of being 'high' on drugs was reflected in 'psychedelic' clothing and music (Source 6).

Source 6

Hippies, like these three young men on Epsom Downs on Derby Day, shocked many people, especially the elderly with their appearance, drug-taking and political views.

Many young working-class people scorned hippies as idle and unaware of reality. Towards the end of the 1960s a new subculture emerged in London and the Midlands. Like the Mods before them, Skinheads listened to Jamaican reggae and ska music, but modelled their behaviour on Jamaican 'rude boy' style. With shaved heads, boots, trousers held up at half mast by braces, skinheads were aggressive and often unpleasant. In contrast to the peaceful, international outlook of hippies, skinheads actively looked for 'bother' and took pride in their British nationality. Hippies, Asians and gay people were all equally likely to be beaten up by skinhead 'crews' patrolling the locality where they lived.

Source 7

A group of skinheads, probably belonging to the right-wing National Front, show off their tattoos.

Questions

1 This section describes six youth subcultures and shows how they developed. Their development can be displayed in a chart like Source 8. It shows how one group led to another, and how they related to each other. At the bottom of the chart are two of the subcultures of 1993 mentioned in Source 2.

Source 8

Youth groups from the 1950s to the 1990s.

1950s	Teddy Boys		Beatniks
1960s	Rockers	Mods ↓ Skinheads	Hippies
1970s			
1980s			
1990s	Metallers	Ravers	

By talking to people you know in their twenties and thirties, try to find out which were the main subcultures in the 1970s and 1980s. Put them in order on a copy of the chart above and add to it any information about them that you can collect.

2 Using the sources and information in this section, say what was involved in the development of youth subcultures apart from music.

4   The growth of leisure

People today spend much more time and money on a greater variety of leisure activities than at the start of the century. Entertainment and recreation have become major industries.

The main reason why people today spend more time on leisure is simple. They spend less time at work than people a century ago. At the start of the century a six-day working week of 55 hours was common for manual workers. After 1920 the length of the 'normal' working week dropped steadily, falling to 47 hours by 1945, 44 hours in 1950 and 40 hours by 1970.

A second reason for the growth of leisure is that people have more money to spend on it. Average earnings have steadily increased throughout the century. Moreover, the prices of many things have not risen as fast as earnings. In many cases they have dropped. People in work with regular earnings therefore have more to spend on non-essential goods.

The development of transport has also influenced the growth of leisure. In cities early in the century, people increasingly used trams, buses and bikes to go not only to work but also to cinemas, sports events, pubs and other places of leisure. Trains and motor coaches allowed them to travel longer distances for leisure purposes. A rise in car ownership after the Second World War allowed faster and more flexible leisure journeys.

As the time and money for leisure grew, along with the ability to travel, leisure became a major industry. Three main suppliers of leisure services emerged. There were commercial suppliers such as travel agents, cinema chains or television companies. There were voluntary groups such as sports clubs and hobby groups. Lastly, local government increasingly provided facilities such as libraries, parks and playing fields.

The rest of this section looks at these developments through a case study of one of the most popular forms of leisure: the holiday.

The rise of the holiday

At the start of this century holidays for most workers were single days off work. As a Durham miner recalled:

Source 1

A Durham coal-miner interviewed in the 1980s by Stuart Archer and Nigel Shepley, in *Witnessing History. Looking at Oral Evidence*, 1988.

In the mines you got Whitsuntide, Easter, Christmas, all the recognised holidays. But no pay. You had to save up to guard against these periods coming on. There was never any going off anywhere.

In many places there were also local festivals and holidays that involved a day off work. This is reflected in Source 2, a children's song heard in Oldham in the 1930s, but dating back to at least the nineteenth century.

Source 2

A song recorded in Oldham by Mass Observation, a research group set up in 1937 to record observations of everyday life in Britain.

Pancake Tuesday is a very happy day.
If you don't give us a holiday we'll aw run away
Eating tawfy, cracking nuts,
Stuffing pancakes deawn awr guts.

In some parts of the country, extended holidays were also traditional. In Lancashire cotton towns, for example, the mills all shut down for 'wakes' week at the end of June, giving employees a week away from work.

Towards the end of the nineteenth century more and more employers gave their employees paid holidays, often as a result of pressure from trade unions. In 1897, for example, the Amalgamated Society of Railway Servants persuaded the railway companies to give their workers a week's paid holiday after five years' service. In 1911 the Trades Union Congress started campaigning for paid holidays for all workers.

By the early 1920s around a million manual workers had holiday pay agreements. The number rose to four million during the 1930s. In 1938 Parliament passed a Holidays with Pay Act, giving a week's paid holiday a year to workers who had not already won this right. By 1945 10 million workers were taking up to two weeks holiday a year.

With more employers giving their workers paid holidays, and with the value of wages steadily increasing, more and more workers were able to go away for a holiday. The most common form of holiday was the day trip. Workers had been going on day trips since the mid-nineteenth century, when the railway companies started running excursion trains from the industrial cities to seaside resorts. This continued to be a popular form of escape, as Source 3 shows.

Source 3

Miners and their families pour off an excursion train at Blackpool in 1919.

In the Twenties and Thirties, advances in road transport opened new destinations and new kinds of holiday to holidaymakers. Road transport had developed rapidly since the start of the century. In 1903 speed limits rose from two mph to twenty mph, and in 1930 from twenty to thirty mph. As speeds rose the prices of cars dropped. The Austin 7, a small family car, cost £225 when it appeared in 1922. By the early 1930s its price was down to £118. This allowed more and more people to buy cars. Car ownership rose from 32,000 in 1901 to 109,000 in 1919, a million in 1930 and 2 million in 1939. Most of these cars were used for outings and holidays.

For those who could not afford a car, a new pedal cycle cost around five pounds in the 1930s, or 48p a month on hire purchase. Whether they drove, cycled or walked, people increasingly took holidays or had outings in the countryside. What was it about the countryside that drew so many people to it? One reason can be guessed at from Source 4. It is a letter which a Lancashire woman wrote to her local newspaper in about 1937.

Source 4

One of 220 letters sent to a local paper in Lancashire in response to a competition on 'How I would like to spend my holidays' in the late 1930s. Quoted in Gary Cross, *Worktowners in Blackpool*, 1990.

I would like nothing better than a week in the Welsh mountains, not the seaside with its boisterous crowds, fun fairs and noisy hawkers. I hear enough noise at work. I can imagine the spot I would choose, a farmstead in a deep green valley, with a view of mountains on every side, and there would be a lake near for boating and swimming. And oh, I would love to eat my mid-day meal off a white table-cloth, preferably in the garden and I would like to have milk in my tea. It sounds silly but if you could see me having my mid-day meal in the mill, you'd realise. Sat on the floor. Tea with no milk, in a thick pint pot, there would be cotton fibres settling on my food, and the mice would be peeping out of their holes waiting for the crumbs ....

Source 5

Hiking, first exhibited in 1936 by J.M. Tucker, shows one of the most popular leisure activities of the 1930s.

Where did people who hardly ever went to the countryside get that sort of image from? One way may have been from paintings that were reproduced in magazines and on chocolate boxes. The Twenties and Thirties saw the development in art and literature of a romantic view of the English countryside. The painting in Source 5 is a good example of this view.

The tourist industry

As the number of people going on holiday rose between the wars, holiday-related businesses boomed. In seaside resorts especially, people were able to make money by providing holidaymakers with accommodation, food and entertainment. Hotels and boarding houses, fish and chip shops and ice-cream stands, fairgrounds, dancehalls and souvenir shops all expanded into what came to be known as the 'tourist industry'.

The large profits to be made out of tourism led to the growth of specialised holiday companies catering for a mass market. Between the wars, this took the form of the holiday camp, offering 'all-in' holidays in which accommodation, meals and entertainment were laid on in a self-contained holiday complex. The most famous holiday camps were run by Billy Butlin, who opened his first camp in Skegness in 1936. Source 6 gives an idea of what a Butlin's holiday involved.

Source 6

Part of the advertising brochure for Butlin's Holiday Camp at Skegness in 1938.

Source 7

Page from a holiday brochure advertising summer holidays on the continent in 1994.

Holiday camps were an example of what came to be known in the 1960s as 'package holidays' in which travel, accommodation and meals were all arranged by a tour company. By 1970 the package tour was the most common form of holiday, and most of these were in southern Spain. The main reason for this development was the availability of large jet aircraft.

Air travel on scheduled flights is expensive because the price of a ticket is based on the fact that many seats are often unsold. If planes always flew with every seat sold, prices could come down because the running costs could be spread over more passengers. This is what tour operators realised in the 1960s. With many thousands of holidaymakers all headed to a few resorts in Spain, tour operators hired aircraft in the knowledge that they could sell every seat. The same applied to accommodation. By agreeing to fill a large number of hotel rooms for a whole season, tour operators were able to persuade hotel owners to slash their prices.

Between 1965 and 1970 ten very large tour operators came to dominate the market for package holidays abroad. They dealt with such large numbers of people that they were able to price their holidays – flight, hotel and meals – at a figure hardly more than the lowest scheduled air fare. As a result foreign holidays doubled from 4 million in 1961 to 8 million in 1976.

Questions

1. What do Sources 1 and 2 reveal about holidays in the early part of the century?

2. Look at Source 3. What does this photograph tell you about the connections between leisure and transport?

3. Look at Source 5.
   a What does the artist make you feel or think about the countryside?
   b How does Source 4 help us to understand why many people wanted to spend leisure time in country scenes like Source 5?

4. Source 6 is an advertisement for a package holiday.
   a Explain the meaning of the term 'package holiday'.
   b How can this advertisement be used to explain why package holidays became so popular in the 1930s and after?
   c What similarities and differences are there between the package holidays shown in Sources 6 and 7? How can the differences be explained?

Coursework Assignments •
Changing culture and communications

A group of Teddy Boys in London, 1956.

The assignments which make up the rest of this book are all intended to assess your skill in the use of historical sources – that is, your ability to get evidence from historical sources and to form judgements about their reliability and value. There are eight assignments altogether; each one is linked to a section in part one (pages 173 - 190) which acts as an introduction. Five of the assignments are 'closed'. This means that you are presented with a range of sources and then a series of questions. The answers to the questions are based solely on the sources and on your own knowledge. No further resources are needed.

The remaining three assignments are in the form of investigations. Here you are given one general question to answer and a range of sources for evidence. However, if these assignments are tackled, further research is recommended, by asking people about their memories and experiences. The best answers to this type of assignment will not only make use of the sources provided, but will back these up with your own findings.

Be careful, however. Research must be carried out properly and findings must be recorded and presented accurately. Remember that people's memories can easily fade, and the past can often seem much better than it really was.

Whichever style of assignment is tackled it is essential that you treat the sources as evidence and not merely as information. Who produced the source, what form it takes, why it was produced and when, must all be taken into account if the source is to be evaluated effectively and used as evidence.

1   What did people do before television?

Television can arouse very mixed emotions. For some people it has led to great improvements in entertainment and education. For others it has meant an end to conversation and family life. So what was life like before television became widely available in the early 1950s? How did people amuse themselves? Were things really better?

Source 1

Two people born in the 1930s remembering life in the late 1940s. They were talking the 1980s.

I can recall great big picnic parties. We used to go off on our bikes. About seven or eight families would get together and ride off to the North Downs for a picnic and rounders and cricket.

One enjoyed very simple things then. I can remember going out bluebelling on my bicycle. Carpets of bluebells. We used to bring flowers home and put them into vases. The roads were much emptier. It was much safer on your bicycle.

Source 2

A man born in 1920 remembers life between the wars. He was talking to a friend in the 1980s.

Children were expected to amuse themselves. There were very few family outings, as large families were common and bus fares even at a penny or twopence each could not be afforded. A walk to the nearest park or perhaps a stream, with baby in the pram, two toddlers and several older children, was a treat when an overworked mother could spare the time. A few sandwiches – banana or fishpaste – and a bottle of cold tea made a real feast.

We played marbles, tip-cat, flicking cigarette cards, hide and seek, hopscotch, all in the due seasons. Most children could not afford wooden hoops when that season came around but an old bicycle wheel with a tyre still on it made a good substitute. In better-off families quite big girls – eleven or twelve – would play with dolls' prams.

Most of our games depended on imagination. A shop would be set up in a garden with a plank over a brick for scales. Stones were potatoes and dockleaves were cabbages. The boys would play cricket but they seldom had a proper bat or wickets – just what a handy Dad could make.

Source 3

Children playing cricket in the street in 1935.

Source 4

A memory of games in the 1930s, written in the 1980s.

In the winter only the rougher children played in the road – indoors there was nearly always a small coal fire and a large table to sit around for Ludo, Snakes and Ladders, Happy Families, Snap or card games. We swapped comics among friends, such as *The Magnet*, *Girl's School Friend*, *The Rainbow*, *Bubbles*, *The Gem* and *Hotspur*.

Source 5

A memory of childhood in the 1930s, from an interview in the 1980s.

We went to bed much earlier than children do today, at about half past seven or eight o'clock even when we were ten or eleven. We were allowed to read for a while, but it was considered 'bad' for you if you didn't go to bed. There was unquestioning obedience not only in the schools but in the home too. You never thought of arguing, or of saying, 'I don't want to go to bed'. On schooldays it was come home, have something to eat, do your homework and then to bed. There was never time for anything else.

Source 6

From Charles Booth, *Life and Labour of the People of London*, 1902.

A policeman said, 'Every evening crowds of them come back from their work and loaf about in the streets; they join in whatever is going on, and … there are no places of amusement for them to go to.'

Source 7

From Nancy Sharman, *Nothing to steal*, 1977.

Uncle Joe bought a wireless from Currys for some money down and then an instalment of sixpence a week. Our excitement was truly electric! Mum had a pink glow in her cheeks and we children were getting under Uncle's feet. He unwrapped the shiny black and white set, and hushed us up while he read the instructions. You could have heard the proverbial pin drop. One end of the sideboard was cleared and the wireless was placed on it as reverently as if it had been the Crown Jewels. There was a great length of wire called an aerial … Uncle connected it up. 'Hey Presto'. Music came out …. We were indeed entering the electric age.

Source 8

A group of children fishing in a local river in 1954.

Assignment

To complete this assignment effectively you need to read Section 1 (pages 2–5) for background knowledge. It will also help to do some further research by asking people about their memories of life before television. Then you need to look carefully at the sources. They are not in any order. You need to sort them out chronologically and to take account of the type of source and why it was produced. Then you should try to answer the question 'What did people do before television?' When you write your answer refer to each source directly and explain how useful it is.

2 The best of everything? The beginnings of television

Television broadcasting did not begin seriously in Britain until after the Second World War. The first managing director of the BBC, John Reith, had said in the 1920s, 'The policy of the BBC … is to bring the best of everything into the greatest number of homes.'

This assignment allows you to decide whether or not John Reith's policy was kept to. For background knowledge you should read Section 2 (pages 178 - 181).

Source 1

From the *Radio Times*, 11 May 1950.

10–12a.m. Demonstration film
3p.m. "Your wardrobe", a fashion programme
3.30p.m. "Lake of Lucerne", a travel film
3.45–4.00p.m. "Andy Pandy", a programme for the very young
8.00p.m. "Country Visit": Television Sheep Dog Trials
8.30p.m. "October Horizon", a play by Lydia Ragosin
10–10.15p.m. News (sound only)

Source 2

From S. Harris, *Finding out about Life in Britain in the 1950s*, 1985.

In 1949 two-thirds of the people of Britain had never seen a television working and only 350,000 households owned one. By 1958, on an average Sunday evening, half the population of the country were engaged in watching the 'tele'. In 1950 the *Radio Times* television programmes took up the last pages of a 40-page issue. By 1959 they took up pages 8–19 of a 48-page issue.

Source 4

An advertisement in a national newspaper in 1958.

Source 3

An advertisement from the *Radio Times* in 1950.

Source 5

J.B. Priestley, a well-known writer and broadcaster, writing in 1962.

Most of us are quite content to stare at programmes we would never leave the house and go 50 yards to see. We watch and listen in an idle dream …. We could smile and yawn at scenes of torture and murder. Very little appearing on that tiny screen in the living room appears quite real …. Really good television, I believe, will begin when we have to pay for something on the night, to see it. We shall give it a different kind of attention and demand value for money.

Source 6

A man born in 1948 describes the impact of the satirical programme *That was the week that was* when it began in 1962. He was talking to a friend in the 1980s.

I was barely 14 years old when TW3 began, but my parents allowed me to stay up and watch it ….

Two sketches have stayed in my mind. One was a commentary in which the Queen and the Royal Family travelled down the Thames in the Royal Barge which began to sink. Phrases from the 'commentator' like 'The Queen, smiling bravely, is now swimming for her life while Lord Snowdon takes a colour photograph' brought a gasp of amazement from the audience. The other very controversial item I remember was a *Consumer guide to Religions*. This was presented in the same way as *Which?* magazine compares different vacuum cleaners or fridges – what they do for you, whether they give good value for money and so on. Many viewers telephoned the BBC to complain.

Source 7

A man born in 1950 describes the impact of *The Forsyte Saga*, a drama series shown on the BBC in 1967.

People organised their whole week around the next episode …. Several of my friends never went out the night on which it was shown, never invited anyone in, never even answered the phone while it was on. Part of the success of the series lay in the fact that the actors who played the children looked like the actors playing their parents. The long, peaceful scene in which the senior member of the family, Old Jolyon, drifts off to sleep and gently dies in a chair in his garden on a summer day is one of the most moving scenes I have ever seen on television.

Source 8

The most popular British television programmes in 1977.

Morecambe and Wise Christmas Show (BBC1) (Christmas Day)	28.7 million
Mike Yarwood Christmas Show (BBC1) (Christmas Day)	26.1 million
Bruce Forsyth and the Generation Game (BBC1) (Christmas Day)	24.6 million
Miss World (BBC1) (17 November)	24.5 million
You Only Live Twice (film) (ITV) (17 November)	24.5 million
The Silver Jubilee Royal Variety Gala (ITV) (4 December)	24.5 million
The Royal Windsor Big Top (BBC1) (29 May)	22.8 million
The Queen's Speech (Christmas Day)	22.7 million
Jesus of Nazareth (ITV) (10 April)	22.3 million
Silver Jubilee Fires of Friendship (BBC1) (6 June)	22.0 million

Assignment questions

1. What can you learn from Source 1 about television in the early 1950s?

2. In what ways does the evidence of Source 2 add to the evidence of Source 1?

3. Do Sources 3 and 4 prove that television improved in the 1950s? Explain your answer.

4. In what ways do Sources 3 and 4 support the evidence of Sources 1 and 2?

5. Sources 5 and 6 give different impressions of television in the early 1960s. How do you explain the differences?

6. How useful are Sources 7 and 8 in explaining why television became so popular?

7. Use the evidence of the sources and your own knowledge to explain whether John Reith's policy has been carried out.

3 What about the children?

One of the great arguments about television has been about the effects that it has had on children. Has it been good or bad? This assignment allows you to try to answer this question. You should read Section 2 (pages 6–9) for background knowledge.

Source 1

A woman born in 1949 talking in the 1980s about the effects of television upon children.

I think the television must have been the biggest change in the lives of children this century. Before that, they must have spent so much more of their time out exploring, especially in the summer. I remember how it changed our lives – it gave us a wonderful sense of entertainment, but I also think it meant we discovered less for ourselves than previous generations of children did.

Source 2

BBC television programmes for children, from the *Radio Times*, 5 June 1959.

11.20–11.45a.m. For the Schools: Science and Life
2.05p.m. For the Schools: *A Tale of Two Cities* by Charles Dickens
2.35–2.50p.m. Watch with Mother: Andy Pandy
5.00–5.30p.m. A Summer in Sicily, a film tour of the ancient splendours of Sicily
5.30–6.00p.m. *Heidi* by Joanna Spyri, episode 4

Source 3 From the *Radio Times*, 11 July 1950.

For two years now letters have been pouring into the box at Alexandra Palace from mothers of the very young. 'Please' they say, 'Please put on something suitable for children of three' …. But what to give them?

To meet at least some of their demands, a new friend is coming to meet them. Andy Pandy will make his bow on Tuesday at 3.45, again on Thursday and on Tuesday and Thursday of the following week. Although Andy Pandy's arms and legs are attached to strings, he is something more than a puppet ….

The four programmes will be regarded as experimental, and television will welcome any comments from mothers.

Source 4 Children watching television in 1957.

Source 5

A photograph of the 1970 Blue Peter appeal to raise money for holidays for underprivileged children.

Source 6

From Nance Lui Fyson, *Growing up in Britain in the 1970s*, 1986.

Source 7

Two children interviewed in the early 1970s.

Girl aged 15 I don't watch much telly ... because I'm hardly ever in the house ... unless I'm at the youth club and something good's on, you know, I watch it then, like *Top of the Pops*.
Boy aged 13 I like TV when there's nothing else to do .... There are few programmes that I watch every week.

Source 8

Results of an opinion poll into how young people spent their time in 1979.

By the 1970s, 96 per cent of all homes in Britain had at least one television. Children aged 5–15 were watching more than anyone else, and more than their age group had watched in the 1960s. The average by 1978 was about 24 hours viewing a week by children, girls watching somewhat less than boys.

Young people were also much more likely to be watching a colour television in the Seventies than in the Sixties. The number of colour television licences was only 75,000 in 1968 but rose dramatically to nearly 12,000,000 by 1978.

Men %		Women %	
Pub	52	Dancing	54
Pop music	50	Going out with partner	53
Playing sports	48	Parties	50
Going out with partner	47	Friends	50
Friends	43	Pop music	47
Parties	43	Shopping	38
Dancing	38	Pub	38
Attending sports	35	Reading	35
TV	30	TV	35
Cinema	27	Walks	34
Reading	25	Radio	31
Radio	22	Playing sports	28
Walks	20	Cinema	26
Theatre/Concerts	16	Theatre/Concerts	19
Cards	13	Attending sports	18
Classical music	11	Cards	11
Shopping	6	Classical music	10
Church	4	Church	6

Assignment questions

1. What can you learn from Source 1 about the effects of television upon children? Explain your answer.

2. Does Source 2 support the views put forward in Source 1?

3. In what ways does Source 3 add to your knowledge of the early years of children's television?

4. How useful are Sources 4 and 5 as evidence of how children's television changed between the 1950s and 1970?

5. Sources 6 and 7 are both about television in the 1970s. How do you explain the differences between them?

6. Does Source 8 support the evidence of Sources 6 and 7? Explain your answer.

7. Use the sources and your own knowledge to explain the effects that television has had upon children.

4   The birth of the teenager

'Teenager' is a relatively new word. If you had used it only fifty years ago, it would not have been understood. So why did it develop and what did it mean? For background knowledge you should read Section 3 (pages 182–186).

Source 1

A woman born in 1940 describes life in the 1950s. She was talking in the 1980s.

treadle A sewing machine powered by pressing a lever up and down with your foot.

When I first started work [1956] I bought a sewing machine – a second-hand treadle*. It cost £2. Every week I'd buy material to make a dress for the weekend. Material cost about 2/6 [12¹/₂p] a yard. They had very full skirts – dirndls they were called. Underneath you wore net and nylon petticoats stiffened with sugar and water. Some had bones in them and you had to be very careful how you sat down! It was much easier to make dresses then – dress-makers were always busy.

Source 2

Average weekly wages 1950–1960.

1950	1952	1954	1956	1958	1960
£7.28	£8.65	£9.88	£11.76	£12.65	£14.10

Source 3

Consumer spending (in 1958 prices) 1948–1960.

	1948	1955	1960
Motor cars and cycles	£71 million	£354 million	£600 million
Radios, TVs, electrical goods	£152 million	£345 million	£463 million
Recreation	£169 million	£265 million	£352 million

Source 4

Colin MacInnes, *England, Half English*, 1961.

Today, youth has money, and teenagers have become a power. In their struggle to impose their wills upon the adult world, young men and women have always been blessed with energy, but never, until now, with wealth. After handing over to Mum a pound or two, they are left with more spending money than most of their elders, crushed by adult obligations. They are a social group whose tastes are studied with respect – particularly by the entertainment industry.

Source 5

Peter Lane, *A History of Postwar Britain*, 1971.

In 1958 Mary Quant was one of the first to design clothes, shoes, make-up, hair-styles for the under-20s, for whom London's Carnaby Street became a mecca.

New words like 'fab' and 'gear' were used in shops (like Lord John's) where 'dolly' assistants wanted to serve the affluent young. The clothes were simple and, above all, they were relatively cheap. In the 1940s, Dior and others had catered for the very rich, and the less well-to-do had imitated these fashions. In the late 1950s designers catered for the 'classless' society of young people. The Dior revolutionary New Look had begun at the top of the income/age scale and had then spread downwards: the Quant/Carnaby Street Revolution began with the young and spread upwards to older women, many of whom complained that they found it impossible to find a shop to provide them with the clothes they needed – everyone seemed to be catering for the young.

Source 6

Part of an article in *The Times*, 12 May 1956.

solvent Having plenty of ready cash.

We have in these Teddy children, a highly solvent*, semi-articulate working-class youth with a strong sense of corporate identity ... it has its own simple but tremendously vigorous culture.

Source 7

From *The Daily Dispatch*, 15 October 1954.

All Slain(e) by their Frankie .... Laine came to Belle Vue Manchester last night. He sang to 14,000 teenagers .... Girls banging each other's heads as Laine sang .... Youths screaming above the screams of the girls ....

He sang the hit tune, 'My Friend', which has a religious theme. Again came the screams until Laine impressed on his fans that they should remain silent during such a song ....

The adulation of this man bewilders me. I felt as if I had become mixed up with a crowd of idol worshippers at the shrine of a voice they love and fear.

Source 8

From C.A.R. Hills, *Growing up in Britain in the 1950s*, 1983.

Soon there were legions of young pop singers, all singing a new rhythmical, raw music appealing to the teenage market: singers like Marty Wilde, Billy Fury, Adam Faith, Johnny Gentle, Vince Eager, all of them usually with middle-aged backing groups interjecting noises like 'waah', 'bup-bup', or 'boom-boom'. The songs they sang would seem simple by modern standards, with little variation and words like:

I love you with my heart
and I hope we will never part.

Assignment questions

1 What can you learn about teenage fashions from Source 1?

2 In what ways do Sources 2 and 3 agree about life in the 1950s?

3 Sources 1, 2 and 3 are all about life in the 1950s. How useful are they are evidence about life then?

4 Does Source 4 support the evidence of Sources 1, 2 and 3? Explain your answer.

5 How valuable are Sources 5 and 6 as evidence about the impact of youth culture?

6 How can Sources 4, 5, 6 and 7 be used to help explain why adults sometimes found teenagers difficult to understand?

7 Teenage culture emerged for the first time in the 1950s. How useful are these sources in helping you to understand why this happened?

5 Were the Sixties Swinging?

For many people the Sixties were a golden age. In the 1950s Rock and Roll had made enemies, but 'Beatlemania' swept all before it and youth culture became acceptable. Everything seemed to be directed at the young. New fashions, new music, new art and new film made Britain seem modern, youthful and exciting. The American magazine *Time* described the new Britain in a twelve-page cover story in 1966, on 'London – the Swinging City'. Ever since, many people have described the Sixties as 'swinging' – a time when the young were making the pace and when society seemed to be changing not only rapidly but also for the better. Is this an accurate description? What, according to the sources in this section, was 'swinging' about the Sixties?

Source 1

Paul McCartney talking in 1984 about Beatle concerts.

There'd be a lot of screaming, rather than like nowadays, people are a little more reserved. It was never as crazy as they used to say it was. If you'd see a bunch of kids coming towards you, you could stop them. They'd only want your autograph; and you could chat.

The thing about fans was I used to do the same thing myself. I felt like I understood what they were on about. Some people who didn't understand what they were on about thought they were coming to get them and ran. So Johnny Ray and people like that would run and they'd rip his jacket off.

Source 2

A woman born in 1948 talking in the 1980s.

As a nearly teenager in 1960, I was awkwardly weighed down with stockings and suspender-belts, vests and tummy-flattening girdles. The 1960s brought Freedom!

Clothes were simple to wear and simple to make. The shift dress (only two pattern pieces) could be run up on a sewing machine in a couple of hours. Skinny-rib polo-neck jumpers and A-line mini-skirts were separated by belts of metal rings round waists which fell symmetrically halfway between neckline and hemline.

I longed for the ideal shape for Sixties' clothes – a beanpole with matchstick legs – but I knew I really had curves in the wrong places. In many ways the long skirts which became an alternative to the mini in the late Sixties were a welcome relief.

Source 3

From the *TV Times*, 1965.

The Weekend Starts Here
KEITH FORDYCE
·WITH·
CATHY McGOWAN
invites you to meet a galaxy of gue
stars, including
THE FOURMOST
THE ANIMALS
THE MOJOS
KING SIZE TAYLOR
THE PARAMOUNTS
SANDIE SHAW
PROGRAMME EDITOR
FRANCIS HITCHING
ASSISTANT VICKI WICKHAM
DIRECTED BY PAT LUMSDEN
Rediffusion Network Production

Source 4

Two young men model fashions for a London department store in 1967.

Source 5

Frances Wheen, *The Sixties*, 1982.

A mod called Denzil, interviewed in the *Sunday Times* magazine in 1964 described an 'average' week. On Monday night he would go dancing at the Mecca, the Hammersmith Palais, the Purley Orchid or the Streatham Locarno. On Tuesday night he would be at the Scene Club in Soho. Wednesday was Marquee night, while Thursday was set aside for hair-washing. On Friday he would be back at the Scene Club. Saturday afternoon was spent shopping for clothes and records; after that he would go out dancing and would rarely return before nine o'clock on Sunday morning. On Sunday evenings he would go to the Flamingo – or he might get an early night.

Source 6

A cartoon from *Punch*, 4 December 1963.

"I can't come out tonight, Doris— I'm washing my hair."

Source 7

A man born in 1948 remembers going to a Beatles concert.

Suddenly there were John, Paul, George and Ringo dressed in grey Beatle jackets – Ringo's drums bearing the familiar lettering of *The Beatles*. All the girls started screaming. A few fainted; others tried to climb onto the seats or stood in the gangways doing the Twist. Afterwards, they had to turn fire hoses on the crowd outside to stop them storming the stage door.

Source 8

From *The Daily Mail*, 25 May 1964.

Mrs Mary Whitehouse, a schoolteacher, has launched a national campaign to help writers who find it difficult to induce BBC TV to screen their work. She said yesterday 'Authors who speak out strongly for the established Christian faith and write plays which inspire a sense of purpose and hope find it extraordinarily difficult to get their work accepted.'

Mrs Whitehouse, 53, is founder of the Women of Britain Clean up TV Campaign. She added 'It became necessary because of the built-in censorship which the BBC exerts against much which is good and clean in our national culture.'

Source 9

Numbers of students in full-time education in Britain.

1961	200,000
1969	390,000

Source 10

From *The Daily Mail*, 9 September 1968

cassock An ankle-length black gown worn by clergymen and clergywomen.

Minister's wife Marjorie Janney, 29, wore a micro dress to church yesterday. It was twelve inches above the knee. And she heard her husband in the pulpit hit out at narrow-minded people who scorn 'mod' gear.

Glamorous Mrs Janney said 'They didn't like my mini-skirts'. Then they were only six inches above the knee.

Mr Janney was preaching at the eleventh anniversary of the church he helped to build. 'I have thrown my cassock* away – often I don't even wear a clerical collar.' And his wife joked – 'I'm going to use his cassock for a maxi-skirt this winter.'

Assignment

To complete this assignment effectively you will first need to read Section 3 (pages 10–14) for background knowledge. It will also help to do further research by asking people about their memories of the Sixties. Secondly you need to look carefully at the sources. They are not in any order. You need to sort them out chronologically and to take account of the type of source and when and why it was produced. Then try to answer the question 'Were the Sixties Swinging?' When you write your answer, refer to each source directly and explain how useful it is.

6 The revolting Seventies

The 1960s had shown that the young had come of age. In 1970, for the first time, 18-year-olds were allowed to vote. The Seventies, however, were to prove very different. Why did things change so quickly? You should read Section 3 (pages 10–14) for background knowledge.

Source 1

From *The Guardian*, 27 August 1986, written by Sally Ann Lomas who was born in 1960.

I grew up believing that to be a teenager was everything you could wish for in opportunity and fun …. In 1974 I was ready to hit the world …. But something odd was going wrong. The youth clubs, the theatre clubs, the dance halls and coffee bars were closing …. Pocket money didn't seem to stretch very far, dads rebelled against ever-present demands for more, their pockets suddenly empty. Saturday jobs were scarce. And yet, the television told us, the radio did too, that to be young was 'it' …. There was this strange perplexing gap between the image and the experience.

Source 2

Colin Cross, *The New British*, *The Observer*, 1973.

Between 1961 and 1971, real income per head rose by 29 per cent. Half of all British households now have cars, two-thirds have refrigerators and nine out of ten have television sets. Most of the supporters of Edward Heath and Harold Wilson have never had it so good.

But by the standards of the other modern industrial countries, we are being left behind. By 1966, our national income per head was less than that of the Americans, Canadians, Swiss and Danes; it had also been overtaken by every country in the EEC except Italy.

Source 3

From *The Guardian*, 12 March 1970.

'We went to hear the Blue Man and the Red Man and we couldn't make out what the Blue Man was on about. We think he fancied himself.' That is how three of Britain's first teenage voters came to decide to vote against Mr Tom King, Conservative candidate for this election.

Source 4

An account of a government plan to tackle unemployment, written in 1977.

Places would go only to those young people who had been unemployed for at least six weeks, and priority would also be given to those who were the least qualified with the poorest employment prospects …. All young people on courses under the programme would be paid an allowance of £18 a week, including £2 for travelling expenses ….

Source 5

A photograph taken on 19 May 1977 at the Rainbow, a venue in London, during a concert given by the Jam and the Clash.

Source 6

Part of a speech made by the Home Secretary, Reginald Maudling, in the House of Commons in June 1970.

We are dealing with a symptom of a deeply troubled society. The full rigour of the law is essential. But repression alone is not enough. We must identify the reasons and causes of this phenomenon. In a time like this when life should be so full of opportunities, challenge and possibility, what is the emptiness that draws so many young people towards the use of drugs?

Source 7

From *The Listener*, 30 June 1977.

The punks are busy ranting, spitting and vomiting their way to the top .... The adrenalin-fuelled 'new-wave' sound, a relentless high speed mix of almost clockwork drumming, robotic guitar chords and screamed vocals, represents a revolt against the over-sophisticated excesses of 'studio rock': punk rock was meant to be as live as a high voltage socket, unrehearsed, if necessary badly mixed, but vibrant with the unrestrained energy and violence of the street.

Source 8

The cover of the album *Aladdin Sane* by David Bowie, released in 1973.

Source 9

A woman born in 1952 remembers the Monty Python comedy television programmes of the early 1970s.

The programmes were very different from any other comedy shows that I had seen. The sketches could be described as silly, absurd or brilliant, depending on your point of view. For example, often the cast wouldn't finish a sketch with a conventional punchline. Instead someone would come on and stop the sketch because 'it was too silly' or a policeman would appear and arrest the cast. One of their most famous sketches was 'The Ministry of Silly Walks' performed by John Cleese and Michael Palin. It was about a man trying to obtain a government grant for his silly walk. John Cleese's silly walk is still one of the funniest things that I have ever seen on TV.

Assignment questions

1. What can you learn from Source 1 about growing up in the 1970s?

2. In what ways does the evidence of Source 2 help to explain the picture given in Source 1?

3. How valuable is Source 3 as evidence of the attitudes of 18-year-old voters to politics in 1970?

4. Does the evidence of Sources 3 and 4 support Sources 1 and 2? Explain your answer.

5. How valuable are Sources 5, 6 and 7 as evidence about the behaviour of young people in the 1970s?

6. How useful are Sources 8 and 9 as evidence about the entertainment industry in the 1970s?

7. In the 1970s teenage culture often became extreme. How useful are these sources in helping you to understand why this happened?

7 Summer holidays between 1900 and the 1950s

Between 1900 and 1950 more and more British people went on summer holidays. This assignment lets you try to find out why this happened. For background knowledge you should read Section 4 (pages 16–18). Then read the sources and answer the questions.

Source 1

The daughter of a doctor, talking in the 1970s to the author of a book about Kent, describes her holidays at the beginning of the century.

Why Margate? Because it wasn't all that distant from London and my father had an idea that the air was very pure. He liked good, cold, brisk air and he liked fishing. Also because it wasn't a very difficult journey. We would come by train, and there used to be great excitement when we got to Whitstable .... The other thing was to come down by boat. That was very exciting. The Royal Sovereign all the way down from Tower Bridge to Margate Pier.

Source 2

Part of a newspaper report describing the extension of the pier at Lytham St Anne's in 1904.

For this enormous outlay the company – and St Anne's – gets a most valuable addition to its attractions, and a cluster of oversea building which is second to NONE on the coast ... storm and rain will be of no consequence: visitors, instead of remaining indoors when the melancholy drip of rain robs them of their holiday, will be able to get shelter where they will be capitally entertained .... The pier and pavilion will be brilliantly lighted by Sugg's high-pressure system ... all the chairs and benches ... have tip-up seats. No fewer than 1000 persons can be seated .... Shops have already been let .... There are public lavatories for both sexes .... NO EXPENSE HAS BEEN SPARED.

Source 3

A description of Blackpool published in a magazine in the 1930s.

vim An old-fashioned word for energy and enthusiasm.

Blackpool, extending for about seven miles along a bracing, windswept sea-front, is known the world over for its gaiety; but all its lively, boisterous good spirits are built upon a solid foundation, for the place is a hundred per cent health resort .... Here the very air brings vim*, and the making of amusement is a business, so there is always something to do! There seems room for everyone, even in a place to which the railway company brings in a single day as many as 100,000 people.

To pass muster at Blackpool, everything has to be of the very best, and this particularly applies to the indoor amusements at the Tower, Winter Gardens, Palace, Grand Theatre, Opera House and cinemas. There are three piers, and the daily programme is unequalled anywhere ....

Source 4

A photograph of Southend beach taken in the 1930s.

Source 5

Part of a speech made in the House of Commons on 27 November 1937.

This Bill will make it obligatory on the part of employers to give to every person an annual holiday of eight consecutive days with pay. The present conditions are somewhat deplorable in certain trades and industries … practically 72 per cent of working people are without an annual holiday with pay. In thousands of cases, especially in homes where there are three or four little children, it is not a question of providing for a holiday at the seaside, because even if holidays were granted they are in such circumstances that they could not get away to the seaside for a day ….

Source 6

Part of a survey conducted by the British Tourist Board in 1948.

Percentage of the British population:
that spent holidays away from home   50
that had occasional day trips   9
that did not go away from home   41

Source 7

A woman born in 1943 remembers holidays in the 1940s and the 1950s. She was talking to a friend in the 1980s.

I don't remember it as being important. Not like today – no one asked where you'd been when you went back to school. Once every three years we went to relatives. My uncle moved to Brighton when I was eleven, which was very kind of him as I'd never seen the sea until we went to stay with him. Other years, when we didn't go away, we used to go on day trips on a Midland Red coach from Warwick, where I lived. We'd go to places like Wicksteed Park near Northampton where they had swings and slides, Bourton-on-the-Water, Weston-super-Mare or Rhyl. Staying anywhere, except with relatives, was something we just couldn't afford.

Source 8

A man born in 1941 remembers his childhood holidays. He was talking in the 1980s.

Towards the end of the 1940s we went by train to a place near Cromer and had a week in a caravan by the sea, but in the early 50s we got a car and after that we toured and did bed and breakfast. I remember we went to Devon.

Assignment questions

1 What can you learn from Source 1 about holidays in the early twentieth century?

2 In what ways does Source 2 support the evidence of Source 1?

3 Sources 1 and 2 are both about seaside resorts in the 1900s. How useful are they as evidence about holidays at that time?

4 How useful are Sources 3 and 4 as evidence of what holidays were like in the 1930s?

5 Source 5 gives a different view of holidays in the 1930s to that given in Sources 3 and 4. How do you explain the differences?

6 Sources 6, 7 and 8 all refer to holidaymaking in the years immediately after the Second World War. How reliable are they as evidence that holidays were becoming more common in Britain after 1945?

7 Why did seaside holidays become more common between 1900 and the 1950s? Use the evidence of the sources, Section 4 and your own knowledge to help you answer the question.

8   Why were holiday camps so popular?

In 1936 Billy Butlin opened his first holiday camp (see pages 16–18). Holiday camps soon became very popular and still exist today. In fact they are so much part of British life in the twentieth century that a television series *Hi-de-Hi* was written about a fictional holiday camp called Maplins.

Holiday camps inspired very different reactions amongst people in Britain. For some they were almost unthinkable, for others they were the ideal holiday. Many thousands of people returned year after year to the big camps at Bognor, Minehead and Skegness. Why did holiday camps have such an impact? What was it about them that made them such an important part of so many peoples lives?

Source 1

Holidaymakers in a Butlin's Holiday Camp in 1953.

Source 2

A woman describes going to a holiday camp for the first time. She was talking in 1983.

Just before the war we tried out a holiday camp. We had a little chalet and I remember Dad being put out because he said he couldn't get out of bed without putting his feet out of the window! It was very tight! But we children thought it was marvellous – there was a swimming pool, and games which you could join in or not, as you wanted, such as quoits, tennis or miniature golf. In the evenings they had dances, with the good old-time dancing with fox-trots and waltzes. They had cinema shows, but I don't remember us children doing a lot in the evenings, since we went off to bed at eight o'clock. They had competitions – they held a photographic competition and I had a little box Brownie camera with which I took a picture of some ducks on the water and won a prize! There was also a beauty contest for men. My father and his brother went into the parade dressed up in their wives' swimsuits!

Source 3

A holiday camp knobbly knees competition the 1950s.

On arrival each camper was allocated a House (like school) and during your stay you would be expected to participate in all the entertainment programmes to try to win points for your house. Houses usually took the names of Royalty – Gloucester, Kent, Windsor, Connaught etc, and rosettes were worn to denote which House you supported. Good humoured banter was much in evidence. Prizes were given to winners of competitions and often during evening meal times the progress of your house was announced to loud cheers and groans.

During mealtimes (there was no self-catering) a huge wheel would be spun to see which table won a bottle of champagne. In the 1950s this was the height of opulence.

Entertainment was programmed throughout the day: Swimming Galas, House Football Matches, Treasure Hunts, Dances, Fancy Dress, Knobbly Knee competitions etc. Campers threw themselves into all these activities with gusto, everything was free to enter and people were determined to enjoy themselves.

Perhaps the memories of war were still fresh and peace had created a period of released tension.

WET Holidays

It rains on the Continent too! What could be more miserable than a wet holiday in a strange country?

Butlin's guarantee a good holiday in any weather

OUR GUESTS SAY

when it's WET it's FINE at Butlin's

the best BRITISH holiday

most people write for details t Butlin's, 439 Oxford Street, Londo: but BUTLIN'S BRITAIN will find u:

Source 4

An advertisement from the *News of the World*, 8 June 1958.

Source 5

A description of a Butlin's Holiday Camp in 1953, from Sarah Harris, *Finding out about Life in Britain in the 1950s*, 1985.

Source 6   A newspaper advertisement from February 1953.

YOU MAKE NEW FRIENDS at Butlin's

WHERE YOU WILL MEET THE KIND OF PEOPLE YOU'D LIKE TO MEET

On your Butlin holiday you are sure to enjoy yourself among the finest array of entertainments, amusements and amenities obtainable anywhere — and all included in the All-in Tariff. In your sleeping chalet at the edge of the sea and in your dining hall you are surrounded with service. At Butlin's you do no more for yourself than you would expect to do at any first-class hotel. Come to Butlin's this year and enjoy a *real* holiday.

FREE BROCHURE : *Send postcard to*
BUTLIN'S LTD. (Dept. H.B.), 439 OXFORD STREET, LONDON, W.1

Source 7   From an article in *Picture Post*, 13 July 1946, describing a Butlin's Holiday Camp.

My friends K3 and K4 were having everything provided for them. This code number represented a typical family, who were being checked through at the camp reception office which everybody refers to in army slang as 'Admin'. They collected a number for their chalet, a number for their dining-room position, a number for their luggage and a name for the house they were going to belong to during their stay.

The members of a house eat together, play together and compete against other units in such competitions as the knobbliest knees, the camp 'lovely' and the mass keep fit exercises. The house captain, a member of the Butlin staff, is chosen for his jollity and talent as a mixer. At frequent intervals he rallies his house over the camp radio with such call as 'Hi-di-Hi'. The house responds 'Ho-di-Ho'. Mr Butlin denied a newspaper report that if a camper refuses to respond he is penalised.

A smile on everybody's face is the Butlin motto, and they walk through the camp smiling, even when there's gravel in their shoes and they have heard that one about the elephant for the tenth time that day.

Assignment

To complete this assignment effectively you will first of all need to read Section 4 (pages 187 - 190) for background knowledge. It will also help to do some research by asking people about their memories of holidays in the 1920s and 1930s. Secondly, you need to look carefully at the sources. They are not in any order. You need to sort them out into chronological order and to take account of the type of source and when and why it was produced.

Thirdly, you can do some more research by asking people why they went to holiday camps and what they thought of them. If you do research you must keep a careful record of what you find out and present your findings accurately. Then you should try to answer the question 'Why were holiday camps so popular?' When you write your answer refer to each source directly and explain what you have learnt from it and how useful it is.

INDEX

accidents, compensation 7
air travel 190
Alexandra Palace studios 179–80
Amalgamated Society of Railway Servants 188
anti-semitism, Facist movement 78
art 189
Asquith, Herbert 52
assembly line workers 17–18, **19–20**
assimilation, ethnic groups 141
Attlee, Clement 54, 116
Australia, voting rights 56
autocracy, structure 49

Baird, John Logie **178**
Bank of England, Depression 73
Bank Holiday riots **184**
Beatles 200, 201
Beatniks 185
Bevan, Aneurin 119, 120–3, **127**
Beveridge Plan 114–16, 120–1
Beveridge, William **115**
bicycles 188
Black and Tans 150
Blackpool, holidays 204
boat race, Oxford-Cambridge 180
Boer War 95
Booth, William **90**, 91
Bowie, David 203
Brighton
    Bank Holiday riots 184
    holidays 205
British Broadcasting Company (BBC) 175, 177, 178
British Medical Association (BMA) 123
British Tourist Board 205
British Union of Facists (BUF) 55, 78, **80–2**
Brittain, Vera 35
Brüning, Heinrich 74–5, 79
Butlin, Billy 189, 206
Butlin's holiday camps **189**, **206**, 207

Cabinet, role 48
Cable Street, Battle of 80, 82
Campaign for Nuclear Disarmament (CND) 185
cannabis 185
Capital Radio 177
Caribbean 133
cars
    assembly workers 18, **19**, 20
    ownership 187, 188
cassette tapes 182
casual labour dockers **14–15**, 16
cathode ray tubes 178
Catholics
    IRA development 163–5
    Irish Free State 152
    Northern Ireland 149, 153–62
census figures 27, 40, 105
children
    discipline 193
    infant mortality rates **105**
    leisure activities 192–3
    television **196**, 197
    welfare 98–9, 103, 106, 114
Churchill, Winston 95, **97**, 116
cinemas 187
civil rights movements 160–1
civil servants 38, 42, 48
Clacton, Bank Holiday riots **184**
clothes, teenagers 198–201
coffee bars 183
Collins, Michael 151
Columbia record company 182
commercial television 181

Commission for Racial Equality 140
Commonwealth **133–5**, 139–40
Commonwealth Immigrants Act 140
communications
    leisure 187–90
    radio 174–7, 183
    recorded music 182–6
    television 178–81, 194–7, 201, 203
Communist Party 55, 71, 80, 86
compact discs 182
computers 10, 12, **20**, 21
Connolly, James 149
conscription 31, 102
Conservative Party 49, 52, **53**, 55
cotton industry 21, **22–3**, 24, 41
councils, role 47
countryside **189**
cricket 180, **192**
crystal radios 177
Cup Final 180
Cyprus 132, 133

Davison, Emily 66
day trips **188**
De Valera, Eamon 149, 150, 151
Defence of the Realm Act 102
democracy, structure 47
dentists 112, 119
Depression see Great Depression
Devlin, Bernadette 162
devolution 146
diets
    comparison 92–3
    improvement 107
    Second World War 114
digital recording techniques 182
discipline, children 193
discs, shellac 182
dockers 6–7, 13, **14–16**, 17
doctors 111, 119–23
dole money
    Depression 68, 69, 73
    Jarrow Crusade 77
    limitations 113
domestic servants
    post-First World War 37
    statistics 6
    working conditions 28–9, **30**, 33
drugs 185
drunkenness **57**, 59, 102

Easter Rising 149
economy, definition 67
Edison, Thomas 182
education multicultural 141–2
Education Reform Act 146
elderly, welfare reforms 99
elections
    first past the post system **55**
    proportional representation 56
    structure 47–9, **52**
Electrical and Musical Industries (EMI) 178, **182**
Eleven Plus examination 180
Eligibility of Women Act 63
Elizabeth II, coronation 180
employment see also work
    Northern Ireland 156–7
    racial discrimination 137, 140
English language 131
entertainment industries 187–90
Equal Franchise Act 63
Equal Pay Act 65
ethnic groups 131
evacuees, Second World War 114

Facism
    Germany 75, 78–9, **81**, **83–5**
    UK 55, 78, **80–2**
factory workers
    conditions 18, **19**, 20, 28
    munitions **31**, 32, **33**, 34, 43
Faith, Adam 199
Family Allowances Act 117
farming
    conditions 17
    imports **11**
    Land Army 34–5, 36
    machinery **10**, 11, **12**
Fassenden, Reginald 174
Faulkner, Brian 167, 168
Fawcett, Millicent 62
first past the post (FPTP) system **55**
First World War
    coalition government 54
    cotton industry 22–3
    Ireland 149
    voting rights 60–1
    wireless development 174
    women workers 26, **31–6**
Fitt, Gerry 167
Fleming, Alexander 107
football **131**, 157–8, 180
force-feeding, suffragettes 60, **61**
Forces Programme 177
Ford, Henry **18**, 19–20
foremen
    dock work 14
    job security 8
    women workers 32
Forte, Charles 183
France, student protests 161, **162**

Gaelic language 152
Gandhi, Mohandas **23**, 24
Germany
    Depression 74, **75**
    Nazi government **83–5**
    Weimar Republic 49–50, **51**
gerrymandering **154**
Gold Standard 74
government
    international comparison **48–51**
    responsibilities 109
Government of Ireland Act 150
gramophones 182
Grand National 180
Great Depression
    cotton industry 24
    dockers **15**
    unemployment **67–86**, 104
Great War see First World War
Green Party 55
Greer, Germaine 65
Griffiths, James 118, **127**

Haley, Bill 183
Hannington, Wal 85–6
Hardie, Kier 53
harvesting **12**
haymaking **10**
health and safety 7, 32
health visitors 106
Heath, Edward 167, 202
Hindenburg, Paul 79
Hippies **185**
hire purchase (HP) 180
Hiro, Dilip 143, 147
Hitler, Adolf 75, 79–80, 83–5
holidays 187–90, 204–7
Holidays with Pay Act 188

Holme Moss, BBC studios 180
Home Service 177
Hong Kong **132**, 133
House of Commons
    Jarrow Crusade 76
    reform 100
    structure 47, 48
House of Lords
    reform 100
    structure 48
housewives, working conditions 8, **9**, 25, 28
housing
    comparison 93, **94**, **108**
    discrimination 137–8, 140, 143
hunger-strikes, suffragettes 60, 61

immigration **133–5**
Immigration Act 140
Independent Television Authority (ITV) **181**
India 24, **132**, 133, 134
industry Depression **70–2**
internment N. Ireland 165
Irish Free State 150–1, **152**
Irish Republican Army (IRA) **150**, 163, **165**, 166

Jamaica, music 184, 185
Japan heavy industries 21, 23–4
Jarrow Crusade 76, **77**
jazz music 185
Jews 132

Kenya 134–5
Kirk O'Shotts, BBC studios 180

Labour Party 49, 52–4, **55**
    formation 96
    government reforms 117–23
Laine, Frankie 199
Lancashire cotton industry 21, **22–3**, 24, 187, 189
Land Army 34–5, 36
laws, Parliament 48
leisure
    communications 187–90
    pre-television 192–3
    television 194–5
Lewis, Saunders 144
Liberal Democratic Party 49, **55**
Liberal Party
    decline 52
    government reforms 98–101
Light Programme 177
literature 189
Live Aid concert **173**
Lloyd George, David 39, **60**, **97**
    people's budget 99, 101
    social reform 96, 103, 128
London Swinging Sixties 200–1
London, Jack 7, 91, 92
London Transport 133
long playing records (LPs) 182
Lytton, Constance **60**

Macdonald, Ramsay 73
machinery, farming **10**
machinery see also technology
magazines 42
Malaysia **132**, 133
Marconi, Guglielmo 174, 178
Margate, Bank Holiday riots 184
Markiewitcz, Georgine **63**
marriage
    post-First World War 38, 42–3
    pre-First World War 27–8, 59
Married Women's Property Act **64**
mass communications 173–90
materialism 185